www.wadsworth.com

www.wadsworth.com is the World Wide Web site for Thomson Wadsworth and is your direct source to dozens of online resources.

At www.wadsworth.com you can find out about supplements, demonstration software, and student resources. You can also send email to many of our authors and preview new publications and exciting new technologies.

www.wadsworth.com
Changing the way the world learns®

FROM THE WADSWORTH SERIES IN THEATRE

Anderson/Anderson, *Costume Design,* Second Edition

Barranger, *Theatre: A Way of Seeing,* Fifth Edition

Barton, *Acting: Onstage and Off,* Third Edition

Brockett/Ball, *The Essential Theatre,* Eighth Edition

Brockett/Ball, *Plays for the Theatre,* Eighth Edition

Dean/Carra, *Fundamentals of Play Directing,* Fifth Edition

Essig, *Lighting and the Design Idea,* Second Edition

Huberman/Pope/Ludwig, *The Theatrical Imagination,* Second Edition

Hudson, *How to Write about Theatre and Drama*

Jonas/Proehl/Lupo, *Dramaturgy in American Theatre: A Source Book*

Madden, *A Pocketful of Plays: Vintage Drama*

McGaw/Clark/Stilson, *Acting is Believing,* Eighth Edition

Olivieri, *Shakespere without Fear: A User-Friendly Guide to Acting Shakespeare*

O'Neill, *The Actor's Checklist: Creating the Complete Character,* Second Edition

Parker/Wolf/Block, *Scene Design and Stage Lighting,* Eighth Edition

Schneider, *The Art and Craft of Stage Management*

Shapiro, *An Actor Performs*

Shapiro, *The Director's Companion*

Worthen, *The Harcourt Anthology of Drama,* Brief Edition

Worthen, *The Wadsworth Anthology of Drama,* Fourth Edition

LIGHTING AND THE DESIGN IDEA

SECOND EDITION

LINDA ESSIG
Arizona State University

THOMSON

WADSWORTH

Australia • Canada • Mexico • Singapore • Spain • United Kingdom • United States

THOMSON

WADSWORTH

Publisher: Holly J. Allen
Assistant Editor: Shona Burke
Editorial Assistant: Laryssa Polika
Senior Technology Project Manager: Jeanette Wiseman
Senior Marketing Manager: Kimberly Russell
Marketing Assistant: Andrew Keay
Advertising Project Manager: Shemika Britt
Project Manager, Editorial Production: Mary Noel
Art Director: Robert Hugel
Print/Media Buyer: Emma Claydon
Permissions Editor: Kiely Sexton

Production Service: Hockett Editorial Service
Text Designer: Gopa & Ted2, Inc.
Photo Researcher: Linda Sykes
Copy Editor: Sara Wilson
Illustrator: Lotus Art
Cover Designer: Yvo Riezebos
Cover Image: © 2001. Photo by Chris Parry, Axiom
Light. The Hollowlands. South Coast Repertory, Costa
Mesa, CA.
Compositor: Stratford Publishing Services
Printer: Webcom

For more information about our products, contact us at:
Thomson Learning Academic Resource Center
1-800-423-0563

For permission to use material from this text or product, submit a request online at
http://www.thomsonrights.com.
Any additional questions about permissions can be submitted by email to **thomsonrights@thomson.com.**

Library of Congress Control Number: 2003117032

ISBN 0-534-63924-0

Thomson Wadsworth
10 Davis Drive
Belmont, CA 94002-3098
USA

Asia
Thomson Learning
5 Shenton Way #01-01
UIC Building
Singapore 068808

Australia/New Zealand
Thomson Learning
102 Dodds Street
Southbank, Victoria 3006
Australia

Canada
Nelson
1120 Birchmount Road
Toronto, Ontario M1K 5G4
Canada

Europe/Middle East/Africa
Thomson Learning
High Holborn House
50/51 Bedford Row
London WC1R 4LR
United Kingdom

CONTENTS

PREFACE

LIGHTING AND THE *Design Idea* focuses on what I have found to be the most important topics to impart to beginning lighting design students: an understanding of light and its role in live performance, and the process by which that understanding of light is applied to the piece being performed, be it drama, comedy, opera, dance, or live entertainment.

Good lighting design is based on the notion of specificity. That is, all of the choices a designer makes about color, direction, quality, shape, distribution, intensity, movement, and change of light should be specific to an individual production of an individual work. Because technology makes it possible to control light to an ever-greater degree of resolution, it is more important than ever to make sure that design decisions have a firm grounding not only in technique, but also in conceptual approach. This book links technique to concept throughout.

Unlike other texts, this book treats lighting as a design element rather than a technical element. As I do in my classes, I endeavor in this book to guide the student through the artistic processes by which lighting design choices are made. The technological tools upon which the lighting art depends are covered here in detail, but only after the reader has had time and space to consider the role of light itself in the expression of production ideas.

NEW TO THIS EDITION

In the first edition of this book, lighting design process was both the content and the structure of the book. That format continues here, but that content has been significantly expanded. Specifically, this revision provides the following new, updated, and expanded coverage:

▶ Chapter 1 now addresses both the historical context within which lighting design developed as an individual discipline and a contemporary process of lighting design that emphasizes collaboration between the lighting designer and director and other designers. Discussion of collaboration has been foregrounded throughout the design process explained in the subsequent chapters.

▶ The new Chapter 2, "Light and Vision," provides coverage of light sources, both natural and artificial. This chapter presents an overview of many of the sources available to the lighting designer—including LEDs—and their potential for use on the stage.

▶ Chapter 3 on the functions and properties of light has been expanded and clarified. For example, functions of light such as the definition of three-dimensional space and revelation of three-dimensional form have been explained and articulated separately in order to make clear to the student the potential advantages of exploiting either or both of these functions. Similarly, the properties of shape and distribution are discretely explained so that the student can begin to understand different patterns of distribution (point, linear, planar) as tools for achieving the overall shape of light on the stage.

▶ The section on script analysis found in Chapter 5 has been expanded and refined. It includes more text examples, especially with regard to assessing a play's language and form.

▶ Completely new coverage of computer visualization, automated lights and computer-aided drafting, and their places in design process can be found in Chapters 7, 10, and 12, respectively.

▶ Chapter 11 on control systems has been updated and reorganized. It has also been placed later in the book so that the topic relates to design process in a more sensible, understandable, and practical way.

▶ Numerous new production photos and paperwork examples are found throughout the book. These are drawn from commercial and not-for-profit professional theatres, ballet, and opera companies, as well as academic theatres. They depict a diverse range of great works of dramatic literature from William Shakespeare to Suzan-Lori Parks. By using examples from both academic and professional theatre, lighting design students will be able to make the theoretical leap from their own hands-on experiences to what goes into making a Broadway-scale production.

ORGANIZATION

The first four chapters are designed to give the student a comprehension of light and its properties and the way light and lighting design can function on the stage.

The second quarter of the book (Chapters 5 through 7) focuses on design process from conceptualization through design development.

The chapters that make up the third quarter of the book (Chapters 8 through 12) deal with those parts of the design process that happen in the lighting designer's studio: choosing color, placing lights in the theatre, choosing precise instrumentation, and completing the lighting paperwork of light plot, section, and hookup.

The last chapters cover the implementation of the lighting design in the theatre.

ACKNOWLEDGMENTS

When I began writing the first edition of *Lighting and the Design Idea*, I had been teaching for only five years. I acknowledged in the preface to that edition many of the directors who helped me clarify the design process I use both as the structure of the book and in my work as a professional lighting designer. With another ten years of teaching under my belt, I must now thank my students for helping to clarify my pedagogical methods. Clear, direct explanation and production examples drawn from diverse sources have enabled me to share my enthusiasm for and love of theatrical lighting not only with theatre majors interested in lighting but also with the general-interest student majoring in everything from art to zoology. This book can be used with students of different backgrounds and experience. I have used it successfully with both novice students and more advanced students.

Lighting designers Ken Billington, Don Holder, Mark Stanley, Allen Lee Hughes, and others provided many of the pictorial examples in the book and I thank them profusely for the use of their lighting paperwork and production photographs. Dan Gallagher provided the wonderful academic theatre example of *The Physicists* used throughout the book. Brandon Thrasher provided invaluable assistance in organizing and keeping records of the art program.

I have received a lot of constructive feedback from my colleagues since the first edition, and want to thank those people here: John Culbert, Curt Ostermann, Sabrina Hamilton, Neil Peter Jampolis, Jane Reisman, Judy Staicer, the late Curtis Senie, Craig Wolf, Joshua Williamson, and many others to whom I apologize for leaving you off this list. My editor Holly Allen solicited reviews from professors teaching from the book as well. Their reviews provided significant guidance to me as I developed the plan for revision. They include: Paul Brunner, Oklahoma State University; Matthew D. Jordan, Western Washington University; and Jonathan M. Middents, University of Houston.

Revising this book has been a very intensive experience. I thank my family, and especially my husband and favorite electrician, Ethan Aberg, for their support and understanding while I gave my word processor so much of my attention.

1

STAGE LIGHTING: CONTEXT AND PROCESS

LIGHT is the radiant energy that enables us to see the world. It enables us to see the stage and the performers on that stage in a specifically directed way. Light does more than merely illuminate or enable visibility. By manipulating the properties of light and the elements of composition, by understanding the human visual process and the effects that light has on it, the lighting designer creates a unique lighting environment—a visual context—for each production, be it drama, musical theatre, opera, dance, or other live entertainment (see Figure 1.1).

CONTEXT

Throughout the history of theatre, as advances were made in lighting and stage technologies, corresponding advances were made in the role of lighting as a *design* element, which, in turn, led to further the development of new technologies. Lighting design theory goes back at least to the Renaissance when visionaries such as Niccolo Sabbatini put reflectors behind candles in the wings. But the practice

FIGURE 1.1
Lighting designer
Allen Lee Hughes
created this simple
but striking com-
position for *Six
Characters in Search
of an Author.*
Directed by Liviu
Culei; set design by
Liviu Culei; cos-
tume design by
Smaranda
Branescu.

of lighting design as we know it is a fairly recent development, going back only to the beginning of the twentieth century.

As the functions and technologies of lighting design have changed, so have the processes of lighting design. More and more, both in North America and Europe, directors and design teams are using visual elements to express their production ideas. To do so effectively, they collaborate to develop the images that eventually appear on the stage. Between the collaborative junctures of conception and realization, the lighting designer employs his or her talent and technique to develop a design that will best meet the artistic vision of the creative team.

THE DEVELOPMENT OF LIGHTING DESIGN AS A DISCIPLINE

The art of scene design has been part of theatre since theatrical performance moved indoors in the sixteenth century. Lighting design has only been recognized as a separate and valued discipline since the middle of the twentieth century. One of the precursors to this development and one of the first theatre practitioners to make use of the powerful effect of specifically designed lighting was the actor/manager Sir Henry Irving, who ran London's Lyceum Theatre from 1878–1902. Irving was the first to completely darken the audience area. He also experimented with color effects such as washes of colored light for emotional effect. During his time, color changing could have been accomplished by a semaphore-style color changing light, as shown in Figure 1.2.

Two theorists and designers, Adolphe Appia and Edward Gordon Craig were even more important to the evolution of modern stage lighting. Appia strongly objected to the idea that three-dimensional people should act in front of two-dimensional scenery. Instead, he advocated three-dimensional scenery that could be lit three dimensionally by "form-giving light." Appia's sketch for a "rhythmic scene" in Figure 1.3 is a good example of his ability to render three-dimensional stage space with light. Appia, in his *Music and the Art of the Theatre* comparing lighting to spatial arrangement, wrote, "lighting, apart from its obvious function of simple illumination, is the more expressive. This is so because it is subject to a minimum of conventions, is unobtrusive, and therefore freely communicates external life in its most expressive form."[1]

The mother of contemporary theatrical lighting design is, without a doubt, Jean Rosenthal. However, even she referred to Stanley McCandless as "The granddaddy of us all."[2] McCandless was trained as an architect, but was teaching stage lighting when Rosenthal found herself in one of his classes. McCandless

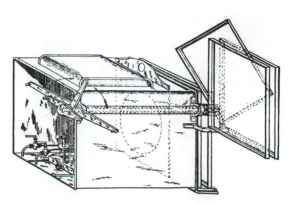

FIGURE 1.2
"Automated" lighting, in the form of this mechanically controlled, semaphore-style color changer, was in use at the end of the nineteenth century. (From Rees, Terence. *Theatre Lighting in the Age of Gas.* London: The Society for Theatre Research, 1978, p. 63, plate 40.)

FIGURE 1.3
A sketch by
Adolphe Appia
for one of his
three-dimensional
Rhythmic Scenes.

first published his *Syllabus of Stage Lighting* in 1931, and his incredibly influential book, *A Method of Lighting the Stage* followed a year later. In this book, McCandless organized lighting around four lighting functions and four controllable properties of light. He was the first to organize electric stage lighting in any methodological way and it was this very act of organization that inspired Rosenthal and so many others.

Jean Rosenthal was hired by The Work Progress Administration's Federal Theatre Project in the 1930s when fellow lighting designer Abe Feder was unable to take on the task. She went on to become choreographer Martha Graham's lighting designer and designed the original productions of many of the most important shows of the middle part of the twentieth century, including *Hello Dolly* depicted in Figure 1.4. Rosenthal was one of the very first people to receive program credit as "Lighting designed by."[3]

FIGURE 1.4
Among the many Broadway shows for which Jean Rosenthal designed lighting is the original production of *Hello Dolly*. Directed by Gower Champion; set design by Oliver Smith; costume design by Freddy Wittop.

LIGHTING DESIGN PROCESS

Jean Rosenthal wrote, "Lighting design, the imposing of quality on the scarcely visible air through which objects and people are seen, begins with *thinking* about it."[4] In the simplest possible explanation, lighting design process breaks down into four distinct steps:

1. Read/assimilate/understand the material being designed
2. Decide what it should look like
3. Figure out how to make it look that way
4. Make it look that way on stage, in the theatre

The second and fourth items on this list are done collaboratively with the other members of the creative team. These members include the director (or choreographer in the case of dance), set designer, costume designer, lighting designer (of course), sound designer, and potentially also the playwright, composer, music director, projection designer, or other project-specific personnel.

Ideally, the collaborative process also includes the assimilation and understanding of the piece, as well as discussions among all the members of the team. With ideas flowing freely, the team, led by the director, develops the driving concepts for the production. Sometimes, the lighting designer is brought into the process after these concepts have already been developed. This does not mean that the lighting designer is no longer able to play a key creative role, but rather that the lighting designer must integrate his or her own vision with the director's to best serve the needs of the specific production.

The lighting designer collaborates with the other visual designers on several levels: conceptual, graphic, and technical. First, the designers must conceptualize

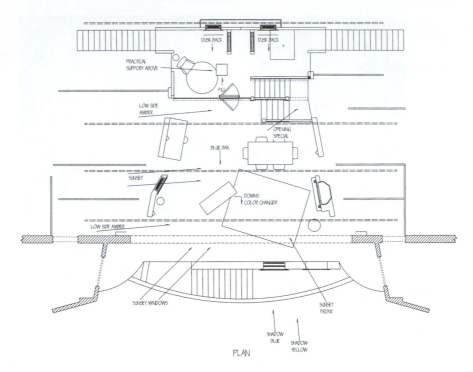

PLAN

FIGURE 1.5
This schematic diagram for Skylight Opera Theatre's production of *Ain't Misbehavin'* indicates potential directions and colors of light with arrows labeled with the compositional purpose for that lighting idea. Directed by Sheri Williams Pannell; set design by Megan Wilkerson; costume design by Melanie Schuessler; lighting design by the author. Drawings from this production are used as examples throughout the text.

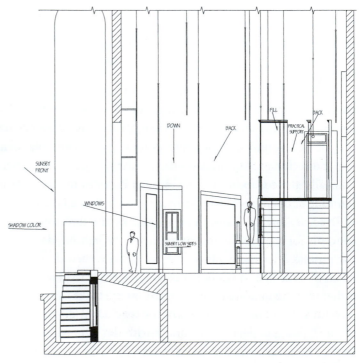

SECTION

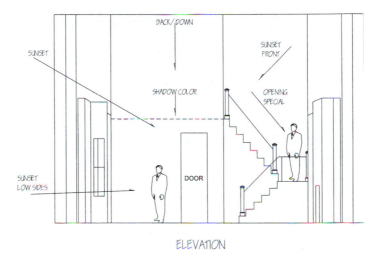

ELEVATION

FIGURE 1.5
(continued)

the visual elements of a production so that they are working toward the implementation of shared ideas. Subsequently, the lighting designer must work closely with director and the set and costume designers to establish visual hierarchy and compositional focus (see Chapter 4). And, the lighting and set designers work together throughout the process on technical issues involving the placement and masking of lighting positions and lighting equipment in and around the set.

The design process can be circuitous: ideas overlap, new ideas are introduced midway through, and budget cuts may necessitate revisions. In this text, however, the design process is presented in a more linear fashion. After laying a foundation with the principles of light and vision (Chapters 2 and 3), and composition (Chapter 4), the text uses lighting design process as its structure, beginning with reading/assimilating/understanding the material being designed. Design is about making choices, and those choices should start with ideas about the play, opera, musical, dance, or performance being designed. Following initial close readings (Chapter 5), the designer researches the script, the playwright, and the visual, emotional, and dramatic requirements of the play to formulate design ideas (Chapter 6).

The collaborative team meets to generate the production ideas that will become the actualized set, costume, and lighting designs. In other words, the team decides what it might look like. Crucial at these early meetings are discussions of the style of the production and the manner in which the various design elements will function in the overall mise-en-scène (directing scheme).

With some conceptual grounding coming out of these early meetings, the lighting designer can begin the design development phase of the process (Chapter 7). Based on these ideas and his or her own connection to the material, the lighting designer decides what various moments of the play will look like and how those moments relate to one another over the course of the performance event. The preliminary design ideas can be communicated to the director and the rest of the creative team, and often the producer or production company, through a variety of means that may include a storyboard of images for each scene, color sketches of key moments, visual research materials that help express the lighting intent, computer-generated renderings, or simply a discussion of lighting possibilities and intentions.

When the team is in agreement about what direction the lighting should take, the designer starts to figure out specifically how to make it look that way. The first step in this process is to develop schematic diagrams of the lighting, such as the one shown in Figure 1.5, that indicate the direction, color, (Chapter 8) and purpose of each light in a composition. These diagrams are then used to develop the light plot, which indicates exactly where each light will hang in the theatre (Chapter 9) to achieve the direction and purpose indicated on the schematic diagrams. A light plot, such as the one pictured in Figure 1.6, indicates specific lighting instrument type (Chapter 10) and placement and, along with the channel hookup (Chapter 11), is the drawing from which the production electrician will execute the design (Chapter 12).

The design process, however, does not end with the creation of the light plot. The real excitement of lighting design begins in the theatre (Chapter 13), and prior to that, while watching rehearsals in the rehearsal hall or theatre. The lighting designer watches rehearsals to become familiar with both the blocking (movement and placement of performers on the stage) and the pacing of the show. The lighting designer also watches rehearsals to confirm that the production being rehearsed is consistent with the one that had been discussed in the earlier design meetings. Ultimately, what is happening with the performers on stage *is* the show, and the lighting designer must be willing to adapt the design as required, to meet the needs of performance.

Attending rehearsal also enables the designer to develop a cuing scheme. Once the lights are hung and focused (aimed) in the theatre, the designer builds and refines the lighting looks or "cues" (Chapter 14) throughout the technical rehearsal period and previews prior to the opening performance. The lighting design continues to evolve during this period, which may be as short as two days, or, for a large commercial musical, as long as several weeks.

Throughout this process, the lighting designer manipulates light and its various properties to create images on the stage that implement the intended visual environment. As will be discussed in subsequent chapters, the concept that propels the decision-making processes of a production may be driven by simple notions or complex networks of thoughts, but always by *ideas*.

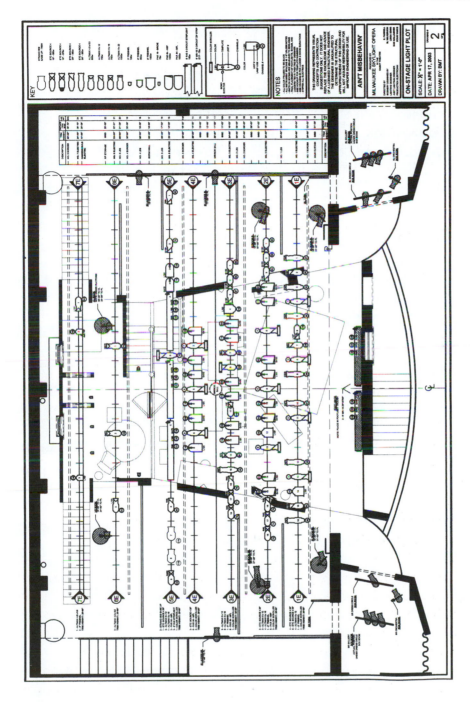

FIGURE 1.6
The light plot for
Ain't Misbehavin'.

KEY TERMS

APPIA, ADOLPHE	MASKING
BLOCKING	McCANDLESS, STANLEY
CHANNEL HOOKUP	MISE-EN-SCÈNE
CHOREOGRAPHER	MUSIC DIRECTOR
COMPOSITION	PROJECTION DESIGNER
CRAIG, EDWARD GORDON	ROSENTHAL, JEAN
CUE	SABBATINI, NICOLO
DIRECTOR	SCHEMATIC DIAGRAMS
FEDER, ABE	STORYBOARD
IRVING, SIR HENRY	STYLE
LIGHT	WASH
LIGHT PLOT	WINGS
LIGHTING DESIGNER	

NOTES

1. Appia, Adolphe *Music and the Art of the Theatre,* Corrigan and Dirks trans. University of Miami Press, 1962, p. 22.

2. See Rosenthal, Jean and Lael Wertenbaker, *The Magic of Light,* for more on Rosenthal's early career and the development of lighting design in the 1930s.

3. Rosenthal's papers, including plots and cuing sheets for many of these productions, currently reside in the Wisconsin State Historical Society archives.

4. Rosenthal, p. 3.

2
LIGHT AND VISION

SCIENTISTS and illuminating engineers define light as "radiant energy capable of exciting the retina to provide a visual sensation."[1] In other words, light is energy that we see. To be able to manipulate light to create stage environments that implement ideas about performance, one must first have some understanding of light, light sources, and the visual/perceptual systems that interpret that energy as sight.

SOURCES OF LIGHT

Most of the light on earth can be traced back to solar radiation. Even the energy that is used to produce artificial light is derived, albeit indirectly in most cases, from the energy of the sun. Sun energy, when it comes to earth in the form of light (as opposed to heat or other forms of radiated energy) has discreet properties that affect the human experience. Sunlight is a full spectral light, meaning that it renders all object color fairly equally (see Chapter 8). It is, if unimpeded by clouds or smog, strongly directional. That is, sunlight travels in rays that follow a specific path. Sunlight also has a specific color temperature; although considered to be "white" light, it is white light that we perceive to be either cooler or warmer than other types of white light.

Sunlight is, however, altered by the atmosphere. On a clear day, the sunlight is still strong and directional and has a fairly warm color. In this instance, though, the sky acts as a secondary light source, diffuse and cooler in color (see Color Plate 1). Sunlight reflected off of exterior and interior surfaces is also a factor in the way we perceive light on a sunny day. As an exercise in observation and "seeing light," take a friend outside on a sunny day and notice his or her face. The side lighted by the sun is probably bright and clear, but the shadow cast by that sunlight is illuminated as well. The shadows are "filled in" by the *skylight* and the externally reflected light. Even in a natural light situation, there are three light "sources," the direct sunlight, the skylight, and the reflected light, which may be extensive, as on a snowy day, or negligible, depending on location.

On a cloudy or overcast day, the sun's radiation is completely diffused by the atmosphere. The sky acts as one large sheet of light, emitting light in multiple directions. Shadows, if present at all, are indistinct, as seen in Figure 2.1. Skylight is therefore said to be a sheet source.

In the theatre, to harness light to dramatic advantage, one uses an artificial light source in a luminaire (light fixture). Artificial sources, like natural sources,

FIGURE 2.1
Cloud cover diffuses sunlight, making the sky into a sheet source.

ROB & SAS Photography/CORBIS

have unique color and distribution properties. In the United States, incandescent (or halogen incandescent) light sources are the most prevalent for theatrical use. All incandescent sources consist of a very thin coil of wire that, due to the resistance of the wire, heats up and glows when electricity passes through it. Because the wire can be coiled quite tightly, incandescent light can approach a point source in its distribution. A point source is omnidirectional, with light being emitted in all directions, as illustrated in Figure 2.2. A point source is also the most efficient light distribution for optical control. This means that light from an incandescent source, because it is small and can be specifically located, can be controlled by lenses and reflectors to create very defined shapes of light, including the conical light distribution from the most common stage spotlights.

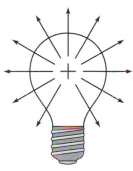

FIGURE 2.2
A point source emits light in all directions.

In terms of color, incandescent light sources tend to appear "warmer" (more yellow/orange) than sunlight. Different types of incandescent lights may burn at slightly different colors within the incandescent range. Even a candle, though quite orange in color, may be considered an incandescent light because the wick is heated to incandescence.

Figure 2.3 describes the halogen cycle. In a halogen incandescent light, an inert gas is introduced inside the bulb to increase lamp life and enable the lamp to burn hotter and for a longer period of time than otherwise would be possible for a lamp with such a tightly wound filament. Halogen incandescent lamps are used in the most common fixed-focus theatrical luminaires in the United States. Color Plate 2 depicts a stage lighted with halogen incandescent sources colored by theatrical gel media to create an impression of afternoon sunlight.

Another type of point source illumination can be achieved by the family of high intensity discharge (HID) light sources. HID sources of various types are found in the theatre in most automated (moving) lights, follow spots, and many high-brightness projectors. In Europe, HID sources are used more extensively in luminaires for general stage illumination. HID sources, with the exception of sodium vapor lamps, tend to emit an extremely bright and cool light as illustrated in a floodlight application in Color Plate 4. Their brightness, efficacy, and potentially small size make them ideal for spotlights as well.

In an HID lamp, an arc of electricity is produced across a gap between two electrodes within a quartz envelope. This quartz envelope is usually enclosed within a large glass bulb. The arc is supported by an inert gas. The exact makeup of the gas gives an HID lamp its own unique color characteristics. A simple way to understand HID lamps is that they are like lightning in a bottle.

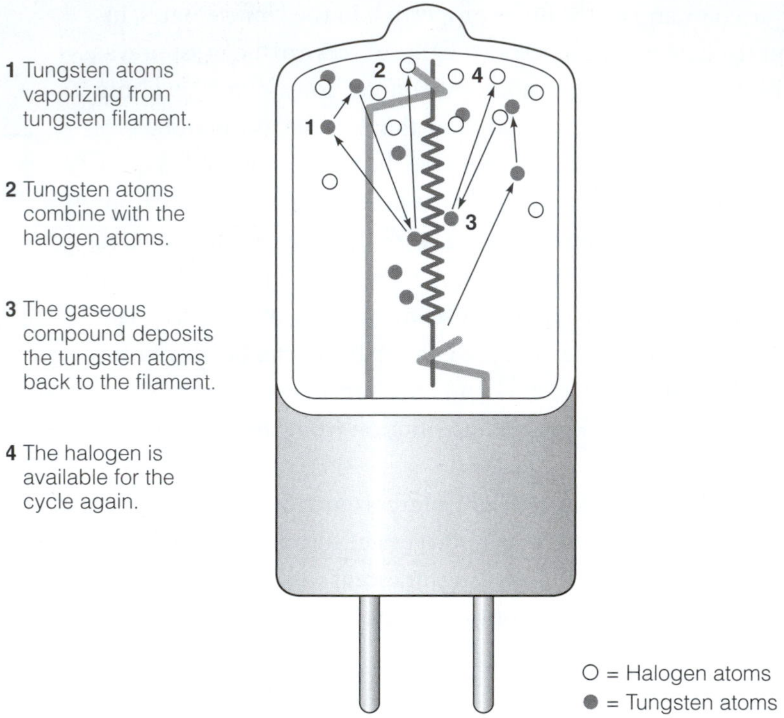

1 Tungsten atoms
vaporizing from
tungsten filament.

2 Tungsten atoms
combine with the
halogen atoms.

3 The gaseous
compound deposits
the tungsten atoms
back to the filament.

4 The halogen is
available for the
cycle again.

○ = Halogen atoms
● = Tungsten atoms

FIGURE 2.3
The halogen cycle.
(Sylvania Osram
Catalogue, p. 33.)

Fluorescent lamps are common in our built interior environments and are used in theatrical fixtures in Europe and sometimes in North America. They are also widely used in luminaires designed for television and film use. In a fluorescent lamp, an arc of electricity is sustained by mercury gas, thus producing ultraviolet radiation. This radiation, in turn, chemically excites the atoms on the phosphor coating of the interior bulb wall, causing the phosphors to fluoresce to produce light. Figure 2.4 illustrates the parts of a fluorescent lamp. Fluorescent lamps are generally tubular and so have a diffuse linear light distribution, as seen in Color Plate 3. A fluorescent tube can be folded in on itself repeatedly to create a "compact fluorescent" lamp, which can be an energy-efficient alternative to traditional household lightbulbs for residential and commercial applications.

The color of the light from a fluorescent lamp results from the mix of minerals in the phosphor coating. Different rare-earth phosphors produce different colors, from warm white similar to an incandescent lamp through daylight lamps that produce a bluish-white color similar to skylight. Because of its diffuse nature, color quality, and tendency to be used as downlights in commercial buildings, fluorescent light is often perceived as "harsh," but can be used on

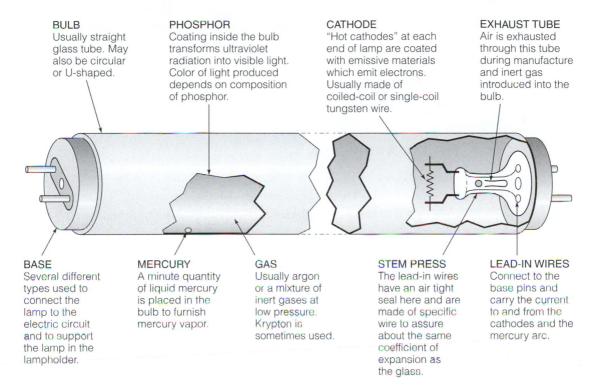

BULB
Usually straight glass tube. May also be circular or U-shaped.

PHOSPHOR
Coating inside the bulb transforms ultraviolet radiation into visible light. Color of light produced depends on composition of phosphor.

CATHODE
"Hot cathodes" at each end of lamp are coated with emissive materials which emit electrons. Usually made of coiled-coil or single-coil tungsten wire.

EXHAUST TUBE
Air is exhausted through this tube during manufacture and inert gas introduced into the bulb.

BASE
Several different types used to connect the lamp to the electric circuit and to support the lamp in the lampholder.

MERCURY
A minute quantity of liquid mercury is placed in the bulb to furnish mercury vapor.

GAS
Usually argon or a mixture of inert gases at low pressure. Krypton is sometimes used.

STEM PRESS
The lead-in wires have an air tight seal here and are made of specific wire to assure about the same coefficient of expansion as the glass.

LEAD-IN WIRES
Connect to the base pins and carry the current to and from the cathodes and the mercury arc.

stage to very interesting effect as in Color Plate 3. In Europe, floodlight fixtures with fluorescent lamps are sometimes used to light backdrops as well.

Another application for fluorescent light sources in performance is for "black light" effects. A black light is a fluorescent lamp that emits ultraviolet radiation that then causes phosphors in scenery, costumes, or makeup to fluoresce, often in startlingly bright colors (see Color Plate 5).

Cold cathode lamps are more commonly known as "neon" lights because neon is popular gas fill for cold cathode lamps. Cold cathode lamps are tubular and filled with a gas such as neon, argon, or krypton combined with other inert gases to produce light. The chemistry of the gases determines the color of the light emitted. For example, neon produces an orange/red light and argon a bluish light. In the theatre, cold cathode lamps are usually used as a scenic element such as lighted signage rather than for the light they emit. Compared to other sources, they do not produce very much light and, because of their linear distribution, cannot be controlled optically the way the point sources can.

In recent years, light emitting diodes, or LEDs, have started to be used in theatrical (as well as architectural) luminaires. LEDs consist of layers of semiconductor material that convert electrical current directly into visible light. LEDs

FIGURE 2.4
The parts of a fluorescent lamp. (Sylvania Osram Catalogue, p. 89.)

are available in red, amber, green, blue, and white. For theatrical use, they are usually used in combination in a floodlight fixture or a strip light for backlighting scenery or for special scenic effects. LEDs do not produce a very large amount of light, but they do produce light very efficiently and have an immeasurably long lamp life.

THE EYE AND VISION

Vision begins when light enters the eye. For the action on stage to be seen, light is emitted by the various light sources discussed previously, delivered to the stage by luminaires, and reflected by the performers and objects on the stage into the audience's eyes. The light enters the eye through a lens and hits the surface at the back of the eye, called the retina. Figure 2.5 shows the parts of the eye. On the retina, special receptor cells called rods and cones send a biochemical signal along the optic nerve to the brain, which interprets those signals as sight.

The rods are located throughout the retina, but are especially concentrated around its edges. These receptor cells are responsible for our black and white and night vision, as well as our peripheral vision. The cones are located in a central area known as the fovea. The cones are responsible for our color vision and our ability to distinguish detail. The physical ability to see is affected by the physiology of an individual's eye, such as the condition of the cornea (the protective layer on top of the lens), the ability of the lens to accommodate to a variety of focal lengths, the color of the cornea and lens, and the overall health of the eye. The intellectual process of perception is more complex, synthesizing the physical act of seeing with the psychological and cultural associations of the visual clues and compositional attributes of the stage picture. There are external factors that affect visual acuity as well.

FIGURE 2.5
This diagram indicates the important parts of the human eye including the lens and the retina where the fovea is located. The fovea is where the cones are concentrated. (From Sobel, Michael, *Light*, p. 35, figure 2.16. Copyright © University of Chicago Press.)

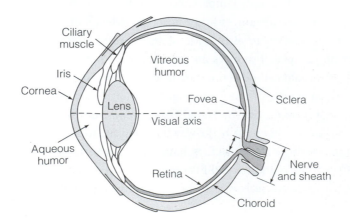

The eye is an amazing mechanism because its optical system of lenses can change depending on the lighting and other physical circumstances. The human eye adapts to light levels by altering the size of the iris. This is analogous to changing the aperture—or F-stop—on a camera lens. In bright light situations, the iris contracts, letting in less light; in low-light situations, the reverse happens. Acknowledging this natural adaptation can help the lighting designer to plan the brightness of a sequence of scenes. The lens of the eye also accommodates to focus on objects at various distances. Ciliary muscles surrounding the lens contract or relax to alter the thickness of the lens. The eye's ability to accommodate is less critical for the lighting designer. The abilities of the eye's cones to see and the brain to interpret color are also changeable. Due to a phenomenon called "retinal fatigue," deep color tends to desaturate if viewed exclusively over a long period of time.

In addition to the psycho-physiological factors that affect seeing, there are five external factors—factors that designers can control—that affect visual acuity, or a human's ability to distinguish detail: contrast, brightness or luminance, size, time, and color. The most important of these factors for the theatrical lighting designer is contrast, as will be seen later in the discussion of compositional tools. Contrast, or difference, is the basic mechanism of seeing. Contrast enables us to distinguish figure from ground. For example, it is easier to read black print on white paper than gray print on colored paper because of the greater contrast between the words (the task) and the background, as Figure 2.6 demonstrates. Contrast ratio refers to the degree of difference, particularly with regard to brightness between two surfaces. For example, a lighting designer may want to maintain a 4:1 contrast ratio between the actor and the background, with the actor being four times brighter than the background.

Brightness, or luminance, is the second external factor affecting visual acuity. Luminance describes the amount of light leaving an area. Quantitatively,

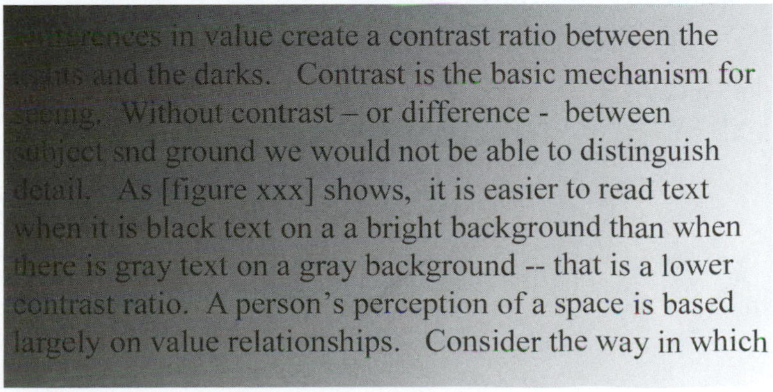

differences in value create a contrast ratio between the lights and the darks. Contrast is the basic mechanism for seeing. Without contrast – or difference - between subject snd ground we would not be able to distinguish detail. As [figure xxx] shows, it is easier to read text when it is black text on a a bright background than when there is gray text on a gray background -- that is a lower contrast ratio. A person's perception of a space is based largely on value relationships. Consider the way in which

FIGURE 2.6
Contrast between text and background is necessary for visual acuity.

Linda Essig

luminance is the result of the amount of light hitting a surface and the ability of that surface to reflect or transmit light. Therefore, a brightly lighted gray surface may have a higher luminance level than a dimly lighted white surface.

Size also affects visual acuity. In discussing the effect of size, we are considering visual size, rather than the actual size of an object. Generally, the "objects" being lit on the stage are human figures of fairly uniform object size. Visual size, however, refers to the size of an object within the entire field of view. Visual size takes into account the distance between the viewer (the audience member) and the stage. Objects of smaller visual size require higher luminance levels—more light and/or higher reflectivity—to be seen. For example, in a large stadium concert in which the performer is quite far away from the audience, the visual size of the performer can be very small. Higher light levels are therefore needed to ensure that the performer is seen adequately. Similarly, intricate details in costumes or scenery must be exaggerated in scale to be visible to the audience in a large theatre or opera house.

Visual acuity is also affected by the amount of time an observer has to view an object. The costume detailing on a character running swiftly across the stage cannot be seen as completely as that on a stationary figure. Choreographer David Parsons exploited the time factor to great effect in his 1982 piece *Caught*. Using a momentary strobe, the leaping dancer is only lighted while in the air and the audience does not have the chance to see the dancer hit the ground. In Figure 2.7 he appears to be walking on air.

Color also affects the audience's ability to see because certain colors are physiologically more reactive or dominant in our visual system. Those colors

FIGURE 2.7
In *Caught*, choreographer David Parsons makes it appear as though the dancer is walking on air by limiting the time the audience has to visually process the action.

© Steven Caras 2000

that are more difficult for our visual system to perceive, such as lavenders, can hinder our ability to distinguish fine detail.

In the most general terms then, large, brightly illuminated, high contrast performers tend to visually predominate the stage composition.

KEY TERMS

BLACK LIGHT	HALOGEN INCANDESCENT
BRIGHTNESS	HIGH INTENSITY DISCHARGE (HID)
CILIARY MUSCLE	INCANDESCENT
COLD CATHODE	IRIS
COLOR	LIGHT EMITTING DIODE (LED)
COMPACT FLUORESCENT	LENSES
CONES	LUMINAIRE
CONTRAST	LUMINANCE
CONTRAST RATIO	OPTIC NERVE
DESATURATE	PHOSPHOR COATING
DIFFUSE	REFLECTORS
DOWNLIGHT	RETINA
ENERGY	RODS
FILAMENT	SKYLIGHT
FLOODLIGHT	SODIUM VAPOR LAMPS
FLUORESCENT	SPOTLIGHTS
FOLLOW SPOTS	ULTRAVIOLET RADIATION
FOVEA	VISUAL ACUITY
GEL MEDIA	VISUAL SIZE

NOTES

1. Rea, Mark (ed.), *The IESNA Lighting Handbook Reference and Application, Ninth Edition.* New York: Illuminating Engineering Society, 2000. p. G19.

3

FUNCTIONS AND PROPERTIES OF LIGHT ON THE STAGE

LIGHT functions in a multitude of ways in performance. When Stanley McCandless first codified modern stage lighting in the 1930s, he defined only four functions of stage light[1]—visibility, form, naturalism, and mood—and put forward four properties of light that could be used to achieve those functions—intensity, color, form, and movement. However, today, live performance is more complex, audiences more sophisticated, and technology so much more advanced than at that time, that McCandless's "method" should be examined only in its historical context. Contemporary lighting can be broken down into many more functions and sub-functions: light provides for visibility, sets the environment or place of the action, presents an image to the audience, establishes the atmosphere of a scene, reveals three-dimensional form, defines three-dimensional space, establishes visual focus, and sets up the style of production. Similarly, luminaires and modern control systems provide greater control over light today, and much more specific articulation of the controllable properties of light is possible—direction, intensity, shape, distribution, color, sharpness (or softness), movement through space, and change.

It is the lighting designer's task to decide which one or more of these functions is most important to achieve at a given moment in the performance and then, through manipulating the controllable properties of light, achieve those functions. By considering each function and each property individually, the lighting designer has a mosaic of smaller tiles to work with to create stage pictures of great resolution and clarity.

FUNCTIONS

Visibility is the most apparent function of stage lighting. Light, as noted earlier, is necessary to stimulate our visual system, enabling us to see. But on the stage, light can do much more than merely illuminate. A single candle on the stage next to an actor may provide visibility, enabling the audience to see that actor, albeit incompletely. In the theatre, we rarely ask "is it enough light?" but rather ask, "is it the right light?" The former question is answered by the physical relationship between the candle, actor, and audience. The latter question is answered only in relation to the intent of the lighting design within the concept of the entire production.

The lighting designer may choose to provide for uniform visibility as in Figure 3.1. Alternatively, visibility may be designed to be more selective of parts of the performer's body or of individual areas of the stage, as Figure 3.2 shows. Here the lighting picks out, or makes visible, just isolated areas of the stage.

Another critical function of stage lighting is to provide the visual clues to the audience that convey information about the environment such as time of day, weather conditions, and even the location in which a scene takes place. By using

FIGURE 3.1
For the touring production of *1776* depicted here, lighting designer Charlie Morrison created a lighting composition that provides uniform visibility on the performers. Directed by Daniel Stewart; set design by Zeke Leonard.

Lighting by Charlie Morrison; photo by Charlie Morrison

John Ambrosone

angle and color of light as well as degree of contrast, the lighting designer can convey the sense of afternoon, as Color Plate 2 illustrates. By projecting patterns of leaves, windows, or bars, the lighting may locate a scene in a forest, interior room, or jail, respectively. Weather conditions may be conveyed through the use of color and softness or sharpness of the light, and so on. By providing visual clues, the lighting reminds the audience members of their own visual experiences, their own sense of place.

The connotations and connections lighting conveys also enable lighting to suggest an image to the audience that may be reminiscent of not just a specific locale or time but a specific visual icon. For example, the lighting depicted in Figure 3.3 was specifically designed to be reminiscent of a well known painting by Joseph Wright of Derby, *An Experiment with an Air Pump,* depicted in Figure 3.4. There is no rule that requires a certain image be used for a specific work. Rather, the specific images the design team chooses to convey to the audience are unique to an individual production of a piece and are based on ideas about the material.

Furthermore, lighting can present a stage picture that triggers an emotional response from the audience. Traditionally referred to as "mood" by McCandless,

FIGURE 3.2
For *Man and Superman,* the lighting creates isolated areas within which the actors are only partially visible. Directed by David Wheller; set design by Christine Jones; costume design by Catherine Zuber; lighting design by John Ambrosone.

FIGURE 3.3
This moment in *Oxygen* was designed to be reminiscent of Joseph Wright of Derby's painting *An Experiment with an Air Pump*. Directed by Norma Saldivar; set design by Brian Proball; costume design by Gail Brassard; lighting design by the author.

FIGURE 3.4
An Experiment with an Air Pump, painting by Joseph Wright of Derby.

the atmosphere created by the lighting compositions may be designed to work in parallel or in contrast to the emotions of the actors. Light cannot "act" the way a human being can, but lighting can act upon an environment and be used to create an atmosphere that can be, for example, mysterious, cheerful, or romantic. It is up to the actors then to play with or against that visual atmosphere to heighten the impact of the overall emotional mood of the scene. If, for example, within a romantically atmospheric setting, characters behave violently toward one another, their violence can seem heightened because it is contextualized within its visual opposite as in *Cuba and His Teddy Bear* shown in Figure 3.5. It is in the intersection of the performer and the atmosphere that the emotional mood—as well as the production style—of the scene is created.

The lighting, in conjunction with the other production elements, establishes the style of a given production. Style, a very difficult term to define, refers here to three related concepts. The style of the lighting can first be considered to be the *manner* by which the environment or *place* of the play is visually represented. For example, time of day and weather conditions can be presented using the actual colors of daylight and angles of light that make the actors look "natural." On the other hand, in designing a night scene for Shakespeare's *Twelfth Night,* the sunlight, moonlight, or stars need not be realistic, but can rather be represented by strings of carnival lights, as in Figure 3.6. Shakespeare's language frees the lighting designer to explore metaphorical visual ideas for time of day, rather than literal ones.

Some initial questions to consider with regard to style are: how tied to psychological reality and visual reality will the lighting be? Will lighting establish a "real" place in a "real" way? How does the visual context relate to the style of the acting?

Style also refers to the overall visual genre of a production. Often, theatrical or visual genres are labeled by cultural "-isms" such as "expressionism," "surrealism," or "romanticism." These labels have visual connotations as well, so if a production adopts a specific visual style it leads to a potentially unified look for a show. Designers and directors may use art and architecture of the same genre to which the play belongs as a jumping-off point for making design decisions. There are also genres of performance that may have theatrical conventions associated with them, so by employing those conventions, the lighting supports the historical genre of a piece. For example, footlights are a lighting convention associated with American melodrama.

Production style is also influenced by the form or shape of the piece. Is it a multi-scene cinematic extravaganza? Or is it a one-scene, one-act play with little, if any, physical change? The shape of the play itself affects the style of the cuing (the light changes) more than any other lighting element. Style is not established

FIGURE 3.5
Cuba and His Teddy Bear. Directed by Bill Hart; set design by Donald Eastman; costume design by Gabriel Berry; lighting design by Anne Militello.

FIGURE 3.6
In the Old Globe Theatre production of *Twelfth Night,* a string of carnival lights rings the sun. Directed by Jack O'Brien; lighting design by Chris Parry.

merely in static images on the stage, but also in the rhythm of the light cues. Light changes that are based in the reality of a setting sun or a light switch being turned on onstage in the course of the action establish a very different production style than, for example, a spotlight snapping on with the downbeat of a musical number. The conventions of the theatrical form, as well as the production's point of view toward both that form and the content of the piece, help guide those cuing choices.

Light reveals three-dimensional form. By creating highlights, shade, and shadow, light makes objects on stage appear either flat or sculpted, two-dimensional or three-dimensional. By altering the amount and quality of light on an object—the face of an actor for instance—the perception of that object changes. Figures 3.7A–C illustrate how light fulfills this function. In the first photograph, a mannequin's head is silhouetted against a lighted ground. Only the two-dimensional profile shape is perceptible. When lighted directly from the front, as in the second photo, the profile shape is still obvious, but the facial details are only vaguely perceptible. By using lights from varying directions and of differing intensities, both the shape and the three-dimensional form of the head are well defined.

The perception of three-dimensional space can also be altered and articulated by light. Painters since the Renaissance have made use of aerial perspective to give a sense of depth to their paintings. Theatrical lighting designers can do the same thing if desired. To achieve aerial perspective, objects in the background are depicted as both hazier and cooler in color than those in the foreground, thus mimicking the effects of atmosphere. For example, in Raphael's well known work *La Belle Jardinière* shown in Color Plate 6, the tremendous vista is realized by the increasing "mistiness" of the mountains as the background recedes. Similarly, lighting the upstage planes of a stage in cooler, more diffuse light can increase the perception of depth.

The space of the stage can be defined in a more literal way by light through the use of exposed lighting instruments. In his design for *Chesapeake,* lighting

FIGURE 3.7A
If lighted only from behind, a head appears in silhouette, with only its two-dimensional shape defined.

FIGURE 3.7B
When lighted straight from the front, the facial features are visible but are not well defined.

FIGURE 3.7C
By lighting a face from multiple angles, both the two-dimensional shape and the three-dimensional forms are articulated.

Linda Essig

FIGURE 3.8
Exposed booms in forced perspective help frame the stage and increase the sense of depth in Chris Dallos's lighting design for *Chesapeake*. Directed by Wendy Dann, set design by Michael Schwelkardt, costume design by Christianne Myers.

Chris Dallos

designer Chris Dallos employed exposed luminaires on booms that seemingly receded in space to visually frame the action and create a sense of depth and perspective in what was otherwise a shallow space (see Figure 3.8).

Another way that light creates depth is through the *establishment of visual focus*. Establishing visual focus not only defines the three dimensionality of the stage, but even more importantly guides the audience's attention. Because the human eye is naturally drawn to areas of high brightness and/or high contrast, the lighting designer can do much to control where the audience looks. Color composition can also be used to achieve visual focus as warmer colors tend to dominate compositionally and cooler colors to recede as noted earlier.

PROPERTIES

To achieve the various functions of light, the lighting designer manipulates and controls light. Eventually, an understanding of the technology of lighting will be necessary to control those properties, but first light itself—and its effect on the stage—must be examined. The lighting designer controls the properties of direction, intensity, shape and distribution, color, softness/hardness, movement through space, and change to create and compose the lighting environment. Lighting designers have a responsibility to ensure that every alteration made in these properties is a visual and conceptual choice and not an arbitrary answer to the need for illumination.

Direction refers to the angle of light hitting an object or performer on the stage. Where does the light come from and where does it go? Direction of light is a function of the position at which the light source is hung and its focus or aiming angle. In controlling the direction of light, the lighting designer also controls the placement, shape, and direction of shadow.

Direction of light provides important visual clues to the audience about time of day and orientation. The relationship between angle of light and shape of shadow is an indicator of time of day drawn from common human experience. Long shadows across a plaza as in Figure 3.9 are an indicator of sunset or early morning. Compact shadows directly below one's body are an indicator of midday light.

Changing angles of the light on stage accomplished through cuing can be an indication not only of the passage of time, but can also help to orient a setting to the cardinal points of the compass. For example, if a play depends on a fairly high degree of reality, such as *Long Day's Journey Into Night,* pictured in Figure 3.10, then the lighting designer may want to set up the orientation of the "sun" in relation to the house (the set) in such a way that the dramatic impact of the passage of time is heightened. If light is coming through a window on the left side of the stage in the early morning, representing or functioning as "sunlight," then as the sun sets later in the play, the light representing sunlight would no longer be coming from the stage left side. Instead, in the middle section of the play, the stage would seemingly be lighted by the indirect light of dusk, creating a potentially moodier atmosphere more appropriate to that part of the play.

Direction of light can even help to establish the style of a production. For example, low sidelight might support a more abstract style, stark uplight an expressionistic style, or an angle of light between 30° and 45° a more realistic style.

Directionality plays a crucial role in the revelation of form on the stage. As noted earlier, the ways in which the audience perceives three-dimensional form

David H. Wells/CORBIS

Figure 3.9
The length of shadows is an important visual clue to the time of day.

Mark Avery

FIGURE 3.10

Lighting can help set up the reality of time and place for a play that relies on a high degree of reality, such as *Long Day's Journey into Night*. Lighting design by Arden Fingerhut.

are dependent on the direction of light hitting that form. Just as the moon, when lighted frontally, looks like a flat white disk, a full moon, so too the human face and body or other stage objects are perceived as flat or dimensional depending on lighting angle. Figures 3.11 through 3.20 show the way some common angles of light model the human face in different ways.

FIGURE 3.11
Figure lighted by downlight (also called toplight).

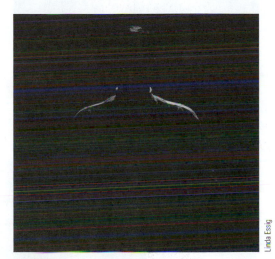

FIGURE 3.12
Figure lighted by backlight.

FIGURE 3.13
Figure lighted by diagonal backlight.

FIGURE 3.14
Figure lighted by high sidelight.

FIGURE 3.15
Figure lighted by mid-high or head-high sidelight.

FIGURE 3.16
Figure lighted by
low sidelight.

▶ 3.11 Downlight, or "toplight," originates from directly above the actor. It defines form in an abstract way and isolates the form in space. Downlight is not good, when used alone, for facial visibility because it casts most facial features in deep shadow. Downlight also has a tendency to de-emphasize the height of a figure or the verticality of a scenic element.

▶ 3.12 Backlight originates from upstage, behind the actor. This angle of light shows the silhouetted shape of the actor and can serve the important function of separating the actor from the background.

FIGURE 3.17
Figure lighted by steep front light.

FIGURE 3.18
Figure lighted by straight front light.

FIGURE 3.19
Figure lighted by low front light.

FIGURE 3.20
Figure lighted by diagonal front light.

▶ 3.13 Diagonal backlight, because it wraps around the side of the figure, shows both shape (outline) and three-dimensional form.

Sidelight emanates from the stage-left or stage-right sides of the figure and can be used to sculpt form in space.

▶ 3.14 High sidelight emanates from 45° or more above and directly to the side of the actor. This angle of light is fairly "natural" and so can be used as a realistically motivated sunlight or moonlight, as well as in more abstract compositions. It is an angle of light that shows both shape and form and provides for some facial visibility on the lighted side.

▶ 3.15 Mid-high sidelight, or "head-high" light, comes from the same height as—or slightly above—the performer's head. This angle tends to abstract the form somewhat and is a very popular angle of light (as is low sidelight) in dance because it sculpts the whole form of the body in space and emphasizes the dancing body as much as the head.

▶ 3.16 Low sidelight emanates from a light below horizontal, close to the floor, and directly to one side of the performer. It is a highly sculptural angle that illuminates the underplanes of the body. This can be used to enhance verticality, especially in composing for dance where performers may be jumping, leaping, and lifting.

▶ Front light, when used alone or in combination with other directions of light, enables the audience to see facial features, but can also be used to fulfill the functions of sculpting form, establishing style and so on.

▶ 3.17 Steep front light emanates from more than 45° above horizontal and in front of the actor. This is a very sculptural angle that also provides visibility. Note, however, the dark shadows under the eyes, nose, and chin.

▶ 3.18 Straight front light provides excellent visibility but tends to flatten out facial features. This angle of light can also flatten the figure against the ground and/or cause shadowing on the background. Nevertheless, if a "sparkle in the eye" is desired, this is the appropriate angle of light.

▶ 3.19 Low front light, or "uplight," from a floor-mounted instrument provides a highly stylized and unnatural arrangement of light and shadow. Low front light can be used to set both atmosphere and style of a production.

▶ 3.20 Diagonal front light traditionally is optimally placed to emanate from 45° above and 45° to one side of the actor. This angle of light is generally perceived to be "natural" and simultaneously provides both modeling and visibility.

Various directions of light are usually used in combination with one another to form lighting compositions. These compositions provide the right balance of visibility and sculpting, foreground/background separation, and atmospheric, environmental, and stylistic effect for a specific production.

Intensity literally refers to the candlepower of a light source, a measurement of the amount of light—luminous flux—emitted in a given direction. On stage, we are more concerned with the perception of intensity, or the "brightness" of the visual composition and its components. The brightness, or amount of light transmitted to the audience, is a result of the amount of light that actually leaves the lighting instruments, the distance between the light and the stage, and the reflectivity of the objects on the stage. The intensity of light, coupled with the careful orchestration of the surface finishes, constitutes the value composition of the stage picture. "Value" here refers not to a monetary or emotional value but rather to the relative positions between the lightest light and the darkest dark.

There are a number of ways to control intensity of light and perceived brightness. One obvious means is by use of a dimmer. Lighting control technology enables the designer to dim a multitude of light sources to various levels of intensity. Altering the amount of electricity to an incandescent lamp, or altering the current to a fluorescent lamp decreases light output. Mechanical dimmers are usually used to dim HID sources. These frequently take the form of a douser—essentially a Venetian blind that closes in front of a light source, as shown in Figure 3.21.

Wybron, Inc., Colorado Springs, CO

FIGURE 3.21
A mechanical douser such as one of these can be used instead of a dimmer with HID light sources.

The source chosen, of course, affects the intensity of light on stage as well. The light output from a 500-watt (500W) incandescent lamp, for example, is significantly less than that of a 2000W lamp. Also, lighting instruments such as floodlights that optically control light to spread it over a large area provide less light at a given point than an instrument with a tighter beam, distributing light over a smaller area, given the same lamp type.

Yet another way to reduce the intensity from a lighting instrument is to place something in front of it that cuts out some of the light without changing the light's color or quality. Such filters are called neutral density filters and, like sunglasses, can reduce the amount of light emitted by a fixed proportion without altering any other properties of the light.

Moving the light closer or farther away alters the amount of light that reaches the stage—illuminance. The incident light, the amount of light that actually hits an object, is inversely proportional to the square of the distance between the light source and object. Mathematically, this effect, known as the "inverse square law" is expressed as incident light = (candlepower/distance²) × cosine angle of incidence, where candlepower is the intensity of the light source measured in candelas. The resulting incident light is measured in lux in a metric system or in footcandles. Figure 3.22 shows the relationship between distance and incident light.

Brightness is relative. One perceives an object or a space as being brightly lighted when seen next to an object that is not as brightly lighted, or in relation to some experiential standard for brightness. Because the human eye adapts automatically to changes in environmental brightness, the audience may need to be visually "reminded" of the standard for brightness or darkness. In other words, audience members cannot sustain the notion of brightness over a long period of time, because their eyes will adapt. To accommodate this natural adaptation, if a long scene—or an entire play—is to be perceived as "bright" from beginning to end, the overall light level may need to be subtly increased over the course of the scene.

FIGURE 3.22
The relationship between distance and incident light (illuminance).

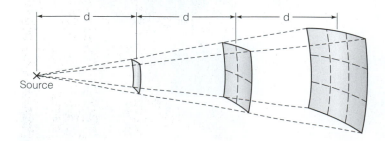

Relative brightness is also important to remember when lighting an episodic show with many short scenes. If the design intent is for the audience to perceive a scene as being particularly bright, one should try to visually contextualize that scene by juxtaposing it with scenes that are less brightly lighted.

Shape of light, like intensity, can be controlled in a number of ways, although these all have to do with the choice and placement of instrumentation. As noted earlier, different light sources have different patterns of distribution, including point sources, linear sources, or sheet sources, each creating a differently shaped light.

Point sources of light can be optically controlled to produce an almost limitless palette of shapes. By passing the light through an optical assembly of reflectors and lenses, the commonly used ellipsoidal reflector spotlight can change light from a conical or round shape to squares, triangles, or any type of projected shape. Shutters can be used to shape the light into triangles or squares as in figure 3.23. By projecting a metal or glass template pattern, also known as a "gobo," any shape can be projected. Projected shapes can be used to give important visual cues to the audience as to the location, atmosphere, or style of a production. For corporate theatre productions, instruments can be used to project logos or even text.

FIGURE 3.23
Lighting designer Allen Lee Hughes uses shutters to frame the character Elizabeth in the Boston Lyric Opera production of *Don Carlos,* directed by Leon Major; set design by John Conklin; costume design by Martha Mann.

Richard Feldman

Automated spotlights usually have the ability to project multiple gobos. They also may have the ability to morph their beam shape or texture using a variety of attributes including moving shutters and beam effects.

Light itself is only visible when it hits something. Therefore, the shape of

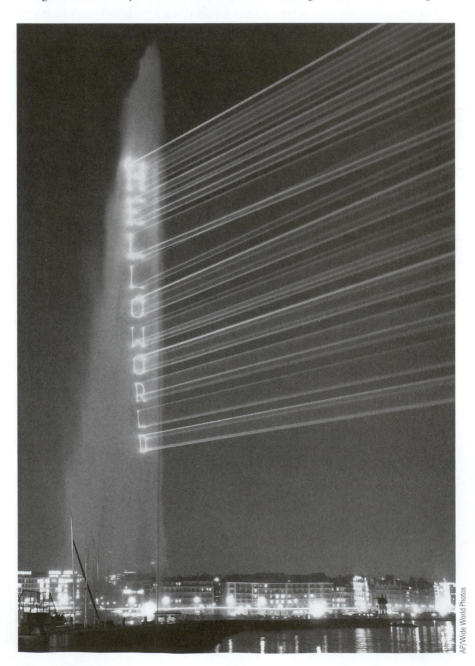

FIGURE 3.24
A light show is projected upon a screen of water.

AP/Wide World Photos

light, either inherent to the instrument or projected, is only visible when the light reaches its target: an object or an actor on stage, the stage floor, backdrop, or scenery. One cannot see beams of light unless there is a particulate in the air that the light can reflect from. If the design intent is to see the shape of beams of light in the air, atmospheric haze or smoke must be introduced to provide a reflecting medium. The light then hits the particles suspended in the air and illuminates them. Haze can create a kind of a screen on which the shape of light is projected. Laser light shows often employ this device to project images into the air, or water may be used to produce a water screen, as in Figure 3.24.

The term "shape" can refer not only to the shape of an individual light or projected effect but also the shape of light as distributed over the whole stage. Distribution of the light over the stage can have a definite shape. By using lights in combination, the designer may create a round or square distribution of light on the stage, or create a more triangular-shaped distribution of light, as Figure 3.25 illustrates.

Color is probably the property of light most people call to mind when thinking of stage lighting. Live performance is one of the few places where colored light is used extensively—and to great effect. As with the other properties, there are a number of different ways to control the color of stage light. The color of light

Linda Essig

FIGURE 3.25
In the preset for *Twelve Angry Men*, the overall distribution of light is of a triangular shape. Directed by Peter Hackett; set design by Bob Schmidt; lighting design by the author.

is primarily the result of the distribution of various wavelengths of electromagnetic energy across the visible spectrum. The most common way to control the color of light on stage is through filtration. Polyester gel or glass filters are placed in front of the light source or the instrument to filter out selected wavelengths of light and allow others to pass through, causing the light to appear colored.

Because different light sources produce different amounts of each wavelength of the visible spectrum, different light sources have unique color signatures based on their "spectral distribution" (see Chapter 8). As noted earlier, the color of incandescent light is relatively warm and results from a filament being heated to incandescence. If that filament is not heated to its fullest possible wattage, it does not burn as brightly, and its color is warmer, more amber. Thus, by dimming an incandescent (or halogen incandescent) light, its color shifts from white toward amber. The color properties of the discharge sources, fluorescent, HID, and cold cathode, result from the makeup of the gases within their lamps and/or the phosphor coating on the lamp. Even sunlight and skylight have variable color properties depending on atmospheric conditions, latitude, time of day, and even season.

Like brightness, human perception of color is very relative. Our perception of color can be manipulated and changed through its relationship with the colors around it. And, just as brightness is a result of both the light source and the object, so too is perceived color. The elements on stage have "object color," which have the ability to reflect light of certain wavelengths. Therefore, the colors the audience sees are the result of both source color and object color.

The quality of light on the stage refers to the hardness or softness of a specific light and of the overall composition. Quality is a very difficult term to quantify, although illuminating engineers have been trying to do so for some time.[2] However, just as it is not necessary to "measure" light for live performance (as opposed to film or video, where it is necessary to provide illumination minimums and contrast maximums to accommodate the film or camera resolution), it is not necessary to measure quality, but rather to develop a vocabulary for describing light quality.

The quality of light can be described as the hardness or softness of light, which results from the scattering of the light source. For many types of theatrical lights, quality of light can be adjusted through the use of diffusion media, also known as frost. Similar to gel media in that they are filters placed in front of the lens of a lighting instrument, diffusion media can be used to scatter light uniformly, creating a moderately soft light or a fully diffused light. Certain frosts can be used to scatter light primarily in one direction. Such media is called "directional frost" or "silk." Diffusion media cannot make light sharper, although there are some optical tricks that can make some instruments appear to have a sharper edge by restricting the halo of light around the beam edge (halation). Donuts or snoots can have this effect.

Different lighting instruments have differing distributions and therefore differing qualities. The aforementioned ellipsoidal reflector spotlight has a very hard, defined edge whereas washlights such as PARs or fresnels (see Chapter 10) have a softer, more diffused edge. A sheet source, such as the sky or a luminous ceiling, has a very diffuse distribution. The quality of the light source affects the quality of the shadow. Shadows cast by diffuse sheet sources, if visible at all, appear quite diffuse, as on a cloudy day.

Light quality is not just a function of one light or another—it is also a function of the overall value and color contrast that make up the entire stage composition. If there is very little value contrast and/or recessive or gray colors are used throughout, then an impression of an overall diffuse composition results. If, on the other hand, there is a high contrast composition with bright highlights and well-defined shadows, the overall quality could be perceived as hard or harsh.

Quality of light can also be said to encompass the subjective responses that result from a reaction to a light source. For example, the metal halide floodlights used to light a sports arena have a harsh quality. Fluorescent sources, although diffuse, may likewise be perceived as being harsh. The harshness of these sources is due as much to their color properties as to their distribution. Because discharge sources do not emit a full spectrum of wavelengths of light, our perception of object color under those sources can be distorted.

The overall quality of light on stage is a function of the hardness or softness of the light as well as the combination of direction, distribution, intensity, and color that produce subjective impressions in the audience.

Movement through space is a powerful property of light because it is very obvious to the audience. Because automated moving lights have become prevalent in almost all types of performances, the lighting designer must carefully consider if and to what extent visible movement is an appropriate design element to employ. Automated lights can pan and tilt to adjust their position and usually can change color, quality, and shape remotely, as well. In a discussion with the author, Tom Littrell described the development of the first commercially viable moving light: "It was only after we hung the first few lights that we got working in a row in the shop, and addressed them all as one and started moving them in unison that we realized the power that that kind of movement could have."[3]

Long before there were automated lights, movement still existed on stage. The use of follow spots, or manually controlled moving lights, predates the age of electricity. Figure 3.26 shows a limelight follow spot being use on a nineteenth-century stage. Today, a follow spot is usually a large, intense lighting unit mounted on a special stand that enables an operator to freely move the light to track the action on the stage. In many types of performances, follow spots are used to single out the lead performers from the others in a bright circle of light. In

FIGURE 3.26
Follow spots have been in use since the advent of the limelight in the nineteenth century.

Special Collections, University of Bristol, UK

opera, or other large venues, extra visibility may be provided by a soft-edged follow spot that is not very noticeable to the audience. This allows for an overall dark or moody stage picture in which the main performer can still be adequately seen.

Another way to create a sense of movement through space is by cuing lights focused at different points on the stage to cross-fade from one to the next. To cross-fade is to take one light out as the next is brought up. This is done by recording a series of linked cues or an effect so that as one dimmer or control channel is brought down, the next is brought up.

Movement is a unique type of change of light. "Change" in lighting is accomplished through cuing. Cues are changes in the lighting composition from one state to another. Each change has a placement in the script, score, or blocking and a duration of time over which the change occurs. The lighting designer must make choices about these cue attributes as much as about the actual look of the lighting.

When any one or all of the components of light are altered throughout the course of an event, the lighting designer can create a rhythm with the lighting. This rhythm may be repetitive and quick, as with a strobe light, or slow and subtle, as with a series of cues that mimic the setting sun. One may decide to have no perceptible change in light at all; stasis is also a choice.

The properties of direction, intensity, shape, color, quality, and movement, when adjusted individually or in combination provide the lighting designer with a nearly limitless palette of choices in the creation of lighting compositions. Every dimmer reading, lens adjustment, or color choice affects the stage picture. Therefore, before the first instrument is specified, the first gel color chosen, and long before the lights are plugged into circuits in the theatre, the lighting designer must decide what the stage should look and feel like—and why.

KEY TERMS

AIMING ANGLE	COLOR
AUTOMATED LIGHTS	CONTROL CHANNEL
BACKDROP	CROSS-FADE
BACKLIGHT	CUE
BILLINGTON, KEN	DIFFUSION MEDIA
BOOMS	DIMMER
BRIGHTNESS	DIRECTIONAL FROST, OR SILK
CANDELAS	DISTRIBUTION
CANDLEPOWER	DONUTS

DOUSER	LUX
DOWNLIGHT	NEUTRAL DENSITY FILTERS
ELECTROMAGNETIC ENERGY	PAN
ELLIPSOIDAL REFLECTOR SPOTLIGHT	PARs
FILTERS	QUALITY OF LIGHT
FOCUS	SHUTTERS
FOLLOWSPOT	SIDELIGHT
FOOTCANDLES	SILK
FRESNEL	SNOOTS
GENRE	SPECTRAL DISTRIBUTION
GOBO	STROBE LIGHT
HALATION	STYLE
HEAD-HIGH	TILT
HIGH SIDELIGHT	TOPLIGHT
ILLUMINANCE	UPLIGHT
INCIDENT LIGHT	VALUE
INTENSITY	VISIBLE SPECTRUM
INVERSE SQUARE LAW	VISIBILITY
LUMINOUS FLUX	WAVELENGTHS

NOTES

1. McCandless, Stanley, *A Syllabus of Stage Lighting,* Eleventh Edition. New Haven: Drama Book Specialists, pp. 2–3.

2. See J. Veitch and G. Newsham's paper "Quantifying Lighting Quality Based on Experimental Investigations of End User Performance and Preference" published in *Proceedings of Right Light Three,* The Third European Conference on Energy-Efficient Lighting, Newcastle-upon-Tyne, England, June 18–21, 1995 (Vol. 1, pp. 119–127). Newcastle-upon-Tyne, UK: Northern-Electric PLC.

3. Essig, Linda, *The Speed of Light: Dialogues on Lighting Design and Technological Change.* Portsmouth, NH: Heinemann, 2002, p. 49.

4

ELEMENTS OF COMPOSITION

ONE sometimes hears the phrase "to paint with light" to describe the role of the stage lighting designer. Like a fine art painter or sculptor, a lighting designer has compositional tools available to her or him with which to achieve the functions explained in Chapter 3. This chapter introduces these tools and then goes on to develop a verbal and graphic vocabulary for describing stage lighting composition specifically.

ELEMENTS OF COMPOSITION

When an audience member looks at the stage, what they are seeing is a "composition"—an ordered arrangement of people, places, shapes, and forms made visible by specifically chosen and articulated light. In performance, the focus of the composition is, more often than not, the performer. There are many graphic elements at the lighting designer's fingertips that can be used to help focus a composition, as well as to establish atmosphere and environment. Among these elements are value, contrast ratio, line, mass and space, balance, texture, rhythm, framing, and even blocking.

FIGURE 4.1
A value scale
indicates steps of
gray between white
and black.

Value, as noted in the preceding chapter, means the position on the gray scale between the lightest light and the darkest dark. Figure 4.1 depicts a value scale based on that developed by Albert Henry Munsell at the turn of the twentieth century. His system for describing color and value is still in use today.

We saw earlier that light intensity is one of the important ways that the overall value composition is created on stage. The surface color and the value relationship between areas of the stage also affect the overall perception of the value composition. Use of the full range of the gray scale is one of the most valuable tools available to the lighting designer.

Differences in value create a contrast ratio between the lights and the darks. Contrast is the basic mechanism for seeing. Without contrast—or difference—between subject and ground we would not be able to distinguish detail. As Figure 2.6 showed, it is easier to read text when it is black text on a bright background than when there is gray text on a gray background—that is, a lower contrast ratio. A person's perception of a space is based largely on value relationships. Consider the way in which you perceive the space of a room. There are no lines defining the corners of the room and the wall surfaces. Rather, it is the variation in value that enables us to perceive the walls as separate planes enclosing a space. The wall opposite a window appears to be the lightest in value, the window wall, the darkest, and the other two fall somewhere between, as Figure 4.2 illustrates.

The human eye is naturally drawn to areas of high contrast, as it is to high brightness. Areas of high contrast therefore tend to pull forward in a composition. Subject/ground relationship and the sense of depth are a result, therefore, of value composition (as well as color). Renaissance artists such as Giovanni Battista Piranesi used value contrast to help create a sense of aerial perspective, just as his contemporaries used color relationships (see Figure 4.3). On stage, designer Steve Woods used contrast relationships to draw focus to Pirate Jenny in *The Threepenny Opera* in Figure 4.4. He has made her significantly brighter than the upstage performers who are still well sculpted, although less bright and lighted to a lower contrast ratio.

Line is a graphic element one may not immediately associate with lighting design but it, too, can be a powerful tool for the lighting designer. Although more obviously utilized by the set designer, lines of light projected on a background or in haze can be used to draw attention to the performers, or lines of

Robert Van Dehlst/CORBIS

FIGURE 4.2
In a room illuminated by light coming through a window, the window wall is the darkest wall in the room, and the wall opposite is the lightest.

Robert Frew Ltd., London, UK

FIGURE 4.3
Piranesi used a low-contrast ratio in the background and a high-contrast ratio in the foreground to create a sense of aerial perspective in his drawings, etchings, and paintings.

FIGURE 4.4
For *Threepenny Opera*, lighting designer Steve Woods establishes visual focus on Pirate Jenny by lighting her more brightly than the characters in the background. Set design by Russel Parkman; costume design by Claudia Stevens.

Steve Woods

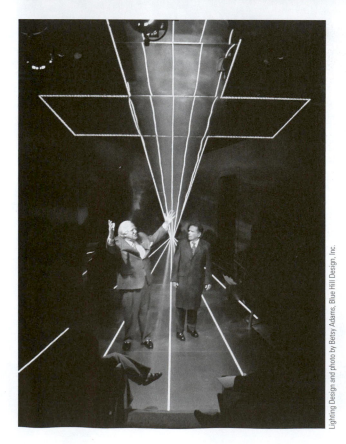

FIGURE 4.5
Lines in light and scenery can help to draw focus as in this production of *God's Man in Texas*. Directed by Steve Rothman; set design by Klara Zieglerova; costume design by Gordon DeVinney; lighting design by Betsy Adams.

Lighting Design and photo by Betsy Adams, Blue Hill Design, Inc.

light can literally be used to point to the performers as seen in Betsy Adams's design for *God's Man in Texas* in Figure 4.5.

Mass and its opposite, space, are also graphic elements. The set designer, costume designer, lighting designer, and director work together to compose the solid shapes (masses) and the empty shapes (spaces) between and around them. Light can fill the empty space invisibly or, with the help of atmospheric haze, visibly. In the production of Shakespeare's *Twelfth Night* depicted in Figure 4.6, lighting designer Chris Parry, set designer Neil Patel, and director Des McAnuff juxtapose the positive mass of an actor within the negative space of a sky drop within another positive space of a floor.

Balance (or its opposite, imbalance) is a graphic element that can be used to express a point of view toward the world of the play—is the world a balanced world or an imbalanced one? Balance can be achieved both symmetrically and asymmetrically. In Figure 4.7, the chorus on stage left balances the mass of the house on stage right.

Texture is yet another graphic element at the lighting designer's disposal. Texture in light can be achieved by projecting patterns of abstract shapes or real symbols, as in Figure 4.8, in which the pattern of windowpanes helps to set the

Chris Parry/Axiom Lighting

FIGURE 4.6
Positive and negative space are juxtaposed in this La Jolla Playhouse production of *Twelfth Night*. Directed by Des McAnuff; set design by Neil Patel; lighting design by Chris Parry.

FIGURE 4.7
The set and the chorus provide compositional balance in this production of *The Barber of Seville.* Directed by Chas Rader-Shieber; set design by Judy Gailen; costume design by Richard St. Clair; lighting design by Boyd Ostroff.

FIGURE 4.8
For *The Dream of the Ridiculous Man,* lighting designer Stephen Quandt creates the impression of moonlight through a window by projecting a window gobo onto the stage. Directed by Russel Reich; set design by Marion Kolsby.

scene as a nighttime interior. Often, the overall texture of the stage is the result of light grazing costume or scenic elements. A grazing angle is one that shallowly scrapes across a textured surface creating highlight and shadow. In Figure 4.9 a very textural image is created when John Ambrosone's lights hit a wave of falling petals.

John Ambrosone

Visual rhythm is also created through the interaction of scenery, costumes, and lighting. Rhythms may be regular or irregular. In Figure 4.10, light grazes across a curtain, creating a rhythm of vertical lines.

The director, more so than any individual designer, bears the responsibility for creating the overall stage composition. One way that focus is achieved on stage is through the blocking of the performers. The stage picture includes the arrangement of people and if all of those people look toward a specific area of the stage, then the audience's gaze is directed there as well. In the Paolo Caliari Veronese etching *The Holy Family* in Figure 4.11, the figures' devotional gaze toward the child does as much or more to achieve visual focus as the value composition and linear perspective.

To make the audience's eye stay within the stage composition, the designers, or the theatre itself, should provide some type of visual frame. The frame also helps to establish scale and proportion in the composition. There are a variety of ways to create a visual frame for the stage picture. In many theatres, a proscenium arch creates an architectural frame. Clear delineation between the lighted and the dark areas of the stage can create a frame. In Figure 4.12, Ken Billington highlights the

FIGURE 4.9
The textural quality of the set is accentuated by light during a petal-drop effect in *Mother Courage*. Directed by Janos Zsasz; set design by Cassandra Antal; lighting design by John Ambrosone.

FIGURE 4.10
Hideaki Tsutsui's lighting design grazes the folds of a curtained backdrop for the Moscow Circus, creating a visual rhythm.

FIGURE 4.11
In Paolo Veronese's etching *The Holy Family*, it is the staging of the figures, all of whom look toward the Infant, that creates the visual focus.

frame of the scenic portal in his Tony-award-winning lighting design for *Chicago*. That portal is a framing device for the whole stage picture, while the strong low backlight creates a frame of light around the lead performer.

ELEMENTS OF LIGHTING COMPOSITION

In the broadest possible terms, lighting compositions fall into two main types: those that have some connection with the light of the real world, and those that are completely abstract. In all cases, designing lighting for live performance is not merely a matter of organizing graphic elements into a pleasing whole. One uses all of the graphic elements and the properties of light to achieve the vari-

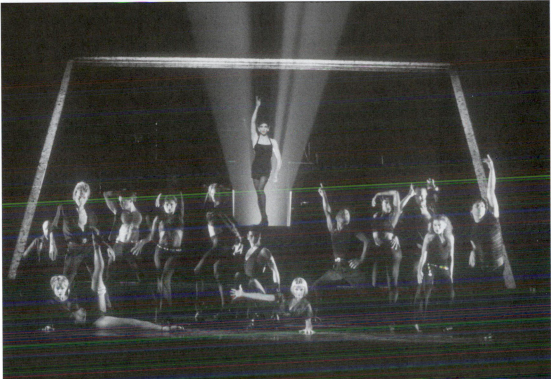

Carol Rosegg

ous functions discussed earlier. Although the end product for any given production is unique, the process by which one develops a lighting composition starts with prioritizing the functions of light and developing ideas about the way light will serve the event as a whole.

For lighting compositions that have some connection to reality, "creating an environment" (time, location, weather, etc.) is very important. For such compositions, there is at least one *motivating* light source. The designer then specifies stage lights that *support* the motivating light source. These lights are said to be *motivated* and become the main source of light in the composition. Even an abstract composition has a lighting idea (sometimes thought of as a "system") that functions as the main source compositionally due to its intensity, color, or quality in relation to the other lights. In a realistically motivated composition, the main source provides the visual clues to the audience that telegraph the time, location, and atmosphere of the scene.

People experience the visual world because of light and its effects. Their perception of the world on stage is colored by their memories and the impressions of the light they experience every day. Much of American lighting design, and

FIGURE 4.12
Ken Billington's lighting highlights the set portal, creating a frame around the action of *Chicago.* Directed by Walter Bobbie; set design by John Lee Beatty; costume design by William Ivey Long.

the American theatrical tradition, is rooted in some degree of realism. How faithfully the reality of any given environmental condition is re-created on stage is the result of the long decision-making process described in the following chapters. Yet, lighting designers should be observant of their real environment in order to appropriately assimilate it into the stage pictures they create.

In order to describe some of the visual clues a lighting design can send to the audience, and develop a way of depicting the lighting composition in diagrammatic form, consider a real-light situation with which most audience members are familiar: a sunlit interior. This simple rectangular room with a single window facing east is lighted at 10:00 A.M. by two sources of light: direct sunlight and skylight, as depicted earlier in Figure 4.2. The sunlight enters the room at an angle unique to the time of day, season, and latitude. Direction of light is the first of the many visual clues a lighting designer can employ in re-creating a specific environmental situation. The quality of the sunlight is also a visual clue about the weather beyond the window. Is it a clear crisp light, parallel in its orientation across the height of the window, or is it slightly diffused—a hazy sunlight on a humid day?

The skylight is also a motivating source in this composition. Skylight is a sheet source, so as it enters this window it is omnidirectional in distribution, has a soft quality, and is cooler (bluer) in color than the direct sunlight.

A person standing in the room is lighted directly by the sunlight on one side. The side of the figure facing the window is the highlight side, the opposite side the shade side. The brightest area compositionally is the highlight side of the figure. The darkest area is not the shade side of the figure, but rather the cast shadow produced when the figure obstructs the path of the light from the window. The shade side, although darker than the highlight side, is lighted by light that bounces off the many surfaces of the room, as illustrated in Figure 4.13. If the room were completely and perfectly mirrored, the light that illuminates the shade side of the figure would be unchanged in color and quality. However, mirrored rooms are a rarity. The *reflected light* would therefore be less intense than the sunlight, as some of it is absorbed by the room surfaces. It is also softer in quality and takes on the color tonality of the room's surfaces as it reflects off of them. The skylight component also reflects off of the surfaces of the room and onto the figure. Therefore, there is some skylight component to the light hitting the figure from all sides.

If this room is placed on a stage as a setting for a play, infinite possibilities arise for the lighting design. The choices the lighting designer makes will be based on ideas about the piece for which the set was designed. However, it is

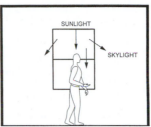

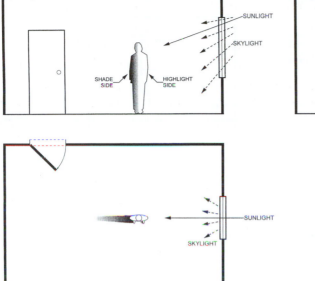

FIGURE 4.13
A schematic diagram indicating how sunlight and skylight may enter a real room.

useful to extend the example we have already begun to develop a stage lighting composition that re-creates the "real" situation described above. Doing so enables us to review the functions and properties of light, introduce some additional stage lighting purposes, and present a method for describing lighting choices in a simple graphic shorthand, the *schematic diagram*.

To re-create this scene on stage, the fourth wall, the one between actor and audience, is removed. Instead of the sun beyond the window illuminating the room, there are now stage lights producing the two main sources of light in the room, sunlight and skylight. Instrumentation that mimics the distribution and color of sunlight should be chosen. The designer can use one large single source or use several lights mounted vertically on a "boom" (a vertical lighting position) so as to provide the parallel configuration of rays of sunlight. A more diffuse source, representing the skylight in the composition, both grazes the window coverings and comes through the window, although at a lower intensity and a softer quality.

In a real room, the light through the window would probably be ample, but on stage, this not the case. The directionality and color of the sunlight need to be "supported" by stage lights as well, to make it appear to the audience that the sun is actually lighting the whole room. The light purpose "sun support" is indicated in Figure 4.14A as coming from basically the same direction as the sun,

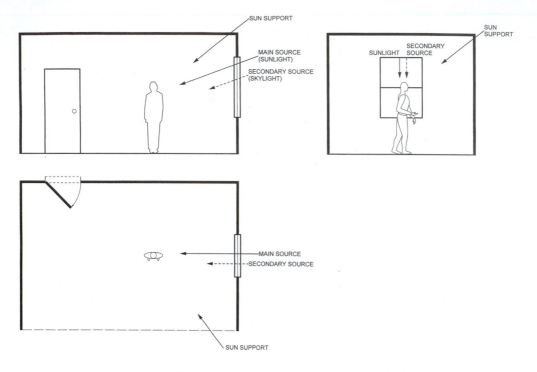

FIGURE 4.14A
To create the effect of sunlight on stage, the main source of light may need to be "supported" by light from a similar angle.

but is pulled out slightly to the front to provide for facial visibility while supporting the idea that the room is lit by the window.

In the real room, light reflected off all of the room's surfaces enables us to see the shade side of the figure's face. On stage, given the width of the set, and the relative weakness of stage lights in relation to real sunlight, more stage lights need to be added to provide this reflected light, as indicated in Figure 4.14B. The direction of this light, the primary reflection, should come from the side of the stage opposite the window. Because the walls of the set are in the way of this direction, the lights can be placed in such a way as to provide a close approximation of this optimal angle. Again, an array of stage lights would be used to achieve the appropriate angle, color, and quality of light across the stage.

Our figure is now lighted by the main motivating sources of light, motivated support light, and reflected light. Because the figure is lighted primarily from two sides, there is still a dark shadow running down the center of the figure. For some productions, this high contrast effect may be desirable. Often, however, more light is required to soften or eliminate this shadow. This can be done with fill light or "shadow fill." This light functions to fill in the shadows on the side of the actors that faces the audience, cast by the main source of light or other lights. In many instances, fill light is necessary for achieving adequate facial visibility because it comes from a frontal angle, as indicated in Figure 4.14C. Light

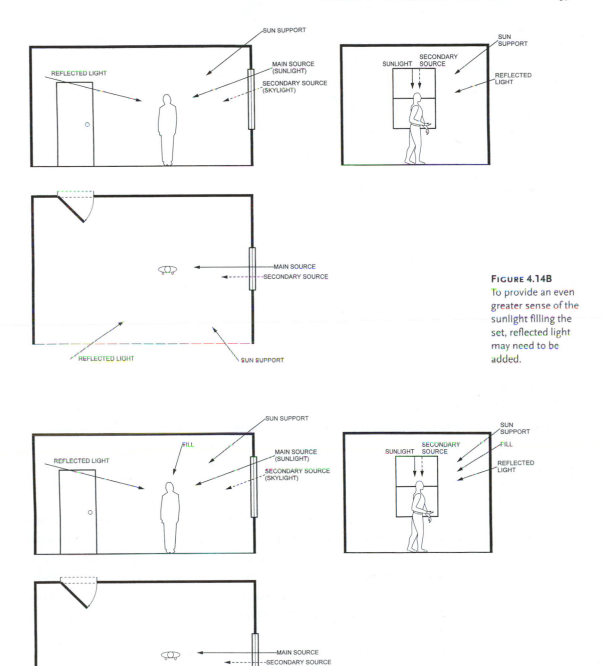

FIGURE 4.14B
To provide an even greater sense of the sunlight filling the set, reflected light may need to be added.

FIGURE 4.14C
Fill light can be added to decrease shadowing caused by the main source of light.

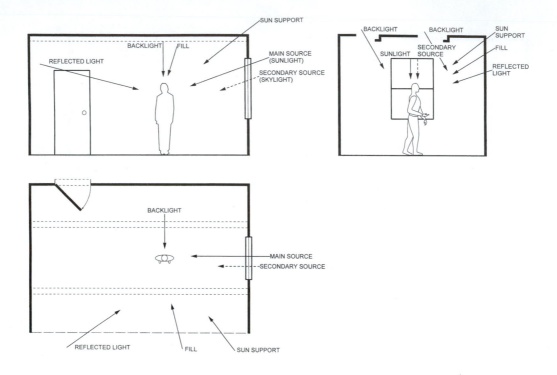

FIGURE 4.14D
Backlight can be added to separate the performer from the background.

that provides visibility may function as more than mere face light. As noted earlier, the "support" light provides some facial visibility, or one can consider the fill light to be a manifestation of the skylight and therefore color it accordingly. In such cases, the light that provides facial visibility is also serving an environmental compositional function.

Perhaps *main source, support, reflection,* and *fill* are all that is required. Yet, there are opportunities to create more striking compositions. For example, to achieve greater separation between the figures and the background, backlight or downlight may be used to highlight the shape of the figure, etching it out and pulling it forward. However, our set, being realistic, has a ceiling. In collaboration with the set designer, some scenic adjustments would need to be made to accommodate backlighting positions. Beams in the ceiling can be added that hide the lighting positions above as in Figure 4.14D, or the walls can be extended higher so they go out of sight of the audience and no ceiling is required.

Perhaps, after consideration of the play and the production's approach, the designer wants to make a statement with color. A tonality of a deep color can be layered over the entire composition. Perceptible only in the darker shadow areas, the audience will subliminally sense the presence of the color. See Figure 4.14E.

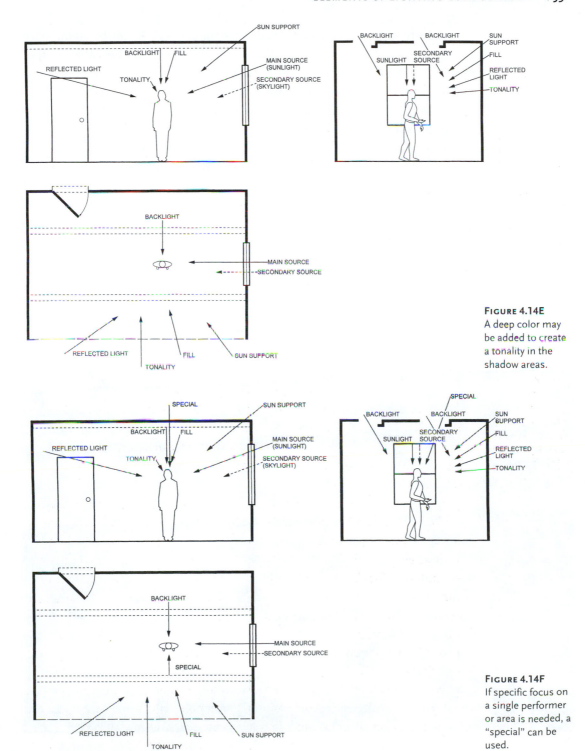

FIGURE 4.14E
A deep color may be added to create a tonality in the shadow areas.

FIGURE 4.14F
If specific focus on a single performer or area is needed, a "special" can be used.

A textural statement can be made in a similar way. A soft breakup, sharp jagged shapes, tree branches, and the like can be layered over the entire composition. Texture can be used to give the impression of a specific location, as when light filters through trees in a forest, for example. In a production that uses stylized scenery, for instance, lights textured with leaf patterns will help set the location, as shown in Figure 4.15. Or, texture can be used to just soften an image abstractly.

An additional specifically focused light, usually called a special, may also be used to distinctively pick out the figure—or another object on stage—in a pool of light. The completed schematic diagram for the realistic interior composition is illustrated in Figure 4.14F. This diagram graphically describes the stage in plan (top), elevation (front), and section (cutaway side) views. The various directions of light are indicated with arrows, and each arrow is labeled with its *compositional purpose*. There are no lights that do not serve a specific purpose in the overall design. These schematic diagrams will be used throughout the design development phase as a means of noting the compositional needs of the production on a scene-by-scene basis and as a whole.

FIGURE 4.15
For the Broadway revival of *Strange Interlude,* lighting designer Allen Lee Hughes textured the abstract clapboard set with foliage patterns. Directed by Keith Hack; set design by Voytek and Michael Levine; costume design by Deirdre Clancy.

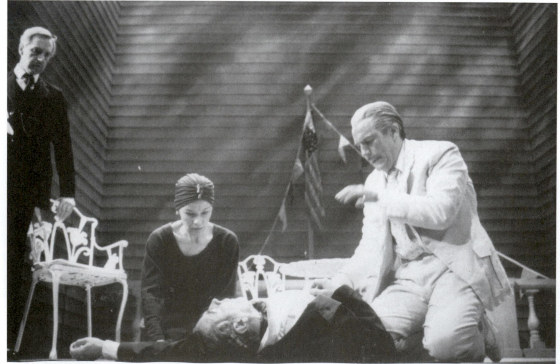

Photo by Peter Cunningham, courtesy Allen Lee Hughes

Main source, support, reflected light, backlight, fill light, tonality, or *specials* are a few common purposes to consider in developing lighting compositions. Light on the stage is not limited to these purposes, however. Many modes of performance are better served by more abstract lighting compositions. For example, in dance, light often functions primarily to sculpt the dancers' bodies in space. A high side light from stage left may be used at the same angle as the sunlight in our realistic composition. It can still be the main source of light and still be sidelight but it no longer has a reality-based meaning. Low sidelight might be employed compositionally as the main source of light to sculpt a dancer's raised arms and legs, as in Figure 4.16.

In concert entertainment lighting, compositions are often designed with a more graphical impact in mind. Lights might be placed to shoot through atmospheric haze, and move and change color in unison, framing the performers with light as in Figure 4.17.

Gert Krautbauer/ffor full credit see page 272

FIGURE 4.16
Low sidelight sculpts the dancers' bodies in *Bad Blood* from the Alvin Ailey American Dance Theater repertoire. Lighting design by Al Crawford.

Robert Laberge/Getty Images

FIGURE 4.17
Concert performers
are framed by light
shooting through
atmospheric haze.

Whether realistic or abstract, as the lighting designer develops compositional ideas for a piece, he or she does so based on an understanding of the material, and a clear point of view toward it. In the next chapter, we explore methods both for analyzing the work being designed and developing ideas about it that will lead toward making design decisions.

KEY TERMS

BACKLIGHT

BLOCKING

BOOM

CAST SHADOW

COMPOSITION

CONTRAST RATIO

ELEVATION

FILL LIGHT

HIGHLIGHT

MOTIVATED LIGHT

MOTIVATING LIGHT SOURCE

MUNSELL, ALBERT HENRY

PLAN VIEW

REFLECTED LIGHT

SCHEMATIC DIAGRAM

SECTION VIEW

SPECIAL

SUPPORT

TEXTURE

TONALITY

VALUE

5

CONCEPTUAL FRAMEWORK

THE development of ideas that drive the visual choices of a production is paradoxically the most individual step in the design process and the most collaborative. Understanding and analyzing the material is the designer's "headwork." Ideas and images start to develop and evolve while reading the material for the first time. Those ideas and images are shared with the creative team, and eventually an overall approach toward the work that will guide all of the design choices develops. Multiple readings and an organized system for analyzing a script can enhance the openness of the imagination and an alertness to the needs of the script and expectations of the creative team.

SCRIPT ANALYSIS

Before meeting with a director for the first time, the designer should assimilate and understand the material. For text-based work, such as drama, musical theatre, and opera, one accomplishes this first by doing a careful analysis of the script and, if applicable, the score. The analysis usually takes the form of a detailed "scene breakdown." The scene breakdown, which necessitates a very close examination of the script, helps the designer to develop a point of view toward the work as well as to take note of the physical requirements of the script as they pertain to lighting, the relationship between the individual characters and their environment, the relationship between the characters, the form of each individual scene, and the form or shape of the piece as a whole. Close examination of the text also helps the designer to assimilate the play's language, both in terms of its rhythm and its style.

The process and format for breaking down a theatrical work espoused here is one of many possible formats. The approach outlined below is meant not just to introduce a way to read a play, but rather a way to approach performance text *as a lighting designer*. The first step in this process is to read the play. Or, if designing for opera or musical theatre, read the libretto or book while listening to the score. (The process for dance, which is not text based and involves direct collaboration with the choreographer creating the piece, is a bit different and will be addressed later.) The initial reading is not a time to take notes, or even to start to develop images. Rather, read the material objectively, as an audience member, to find out what happens and get a first impression.

After this initial reading, the designer may be ready to start the breakdown and analysis, or, if the script is very complex in its language and/or action, may opt for a second reading before committing pencil to paper (or keystroke to computer). Throughout the following, this text uses the classic American poetic realistic play *A Streetcar Named Desire* as an example of dramatic text. The format for the scene breakdown should include—at least—the following categories for each scene:

- ▶ **Scene**—the number or name of each scene, preferably both
- ▶ **Time and place**—where and when the scene takes place
- ▶ **What happens**—the action of the scene
- ▶ **Theme**—what is the scene really about?
- ▶ **Environmental descriptions**—what does the dialogue reveal about the location?
- ▶ **Imagistic language**—images in the dialogue that might speak to the themes, action, or style of the piece
- ▶ **Physical needs**—specific lighting requirements that the designer will need to make decisions about. For example, is there action in which candles are lit or practical lights go on or off in view of the audience?
- ▶ **Form and shape**—does the scene have a "flow" to it, or is it static? Is there a shape to the movement of the scene? Is the scene large or small, casual or intimate, formal or informal?

There is no one right way to break down a scene from *Streetcar*. What follows is an example of how one designer, the author, has done such an analysis. Tennessee Williams writes extensive stage directions, some of which developed out of the original production of the play, directed by Elia Kazan. In reading the play, one should note the stage directions, but of much greater importance is the spoken dialogue, as this is what will be presented on stage.

- ▶ **Scene:** 1
- ▶ **Time and Place:** Exterior and interior of Stella and Stanley's flat in New Orleans. Stage directions: "it is first dark of an early evening in May."
- ▶ **Who:** Primarily Stanley, Stella, and Blanche, other characters include: Mitch, Eunice, Steve, another neighbor, "colored woman" [Williams's description].
- ▶ **What happens:** Blanche arrives, characters are introduced; we learn of the loss of the family home, Belle Reve.
- ▶ **Theme(s):** Isolation, (in)decency, being on the edge of a nervous breakdown, loss . . . tremendous loss.
- ▶ **Environmental descriptions:**
  Eunice: "She's got the downstairs and I got the up." [Stella's apartment is on the ground floor] "its sort of messed up right now but when it's clean it's real sweet"
  Blanche: "Turn that over-light off! Turn that off! I won't be looked at in this merciless glare!" "I thought you would never come back to this horrible place!" . . . "What are you doing in a place like this" . . . "Only Poe! Only Mr. Edgar Allan Poe!—could do it justice! Out there I suppose is the ghoul-haunted woodland of Weir!"
  Stella: "With only two rooms"
  Blanche: "There's no door between the two rooms"
  Stanley: "My clothes're stickin' to me"
- ▶ **Imagistic language:** "Meat"; "Belle Reve" [beautiful dream]; "a different species"; "I took the blows in my face and my body . . . the long parade to the graveyard"; "struggle for breath and bleeding"; Blanche sounds breathless and languid at the same time.
- ▶ **Physical requirements:** Overhead light with switch.
- ▶ **Form and shape:** The public street scene funnels down to a private intensity.

Producing such a detailed breakdown for each and every scene of a play, opera, or musical requires very close examination. Thus, after doing so, the designer is very familiar with the work, its form, and its language. Not all material is easily broken down by scenes. Samuel Beckett's work, for example, set with only a very few characters on a sparse single set with no scene breaks, can still be analyzed and broken down based on thematic or rhythmic changes, changes indicated by stage directions, or by using "French scenes." (French scenes are scenes that begin or end when a character enters or leaves the stage).

POINT OF VIEW

The breakdown of scene 1 of *Streetcar* raises as many questions as it answers. Is the flat as horrible as Blanche says? Is there truly a "merciless glare"? If so, what does Blanche look like in it? What kind of light fills the space when that overhead light is turned off? In answering these questions, one is making design choices—design choices that will color the audience's perception of the rest of the play that follows this scene. Therefore, the designer and creative team need to develop a point of view toward the work.

Given the scene under discussion, the creative team must decide how to present Blanche, Stella, and Stanley. Is Blanche pathetic? A victim? Manipulative? Insane? Or some combination of these attributes? Each of these attributes can be carried through in a different way in terms of the lighting and the relationship of the direction and interaction of the actors with the visual world. For example, if the point of view toward the work is that Blanche is a pathetic victim—and the audience is to know this from the onset—then perhaps the lighting is in fact mercilessly glaring when the overhead light is turned on, but softer and more comforting when it is off. Perhaps the lighting can provide areas of shadow in which to hide (as in Figure 5.1), so that Blanche can be seen as truly cowering in the corner like a caged animal as discussed earlier. Conversely, if the direction runs more toward seeing Blanche as somewhat manipulative who only later truly loses her mind, the lighting in scene 1 might be more neutral, both when the overhead light is on and off. Thus, when Blanche describes the light as "merciless glare," the audience is left to question both her motives and her sanity.

Straight plays are not the only performance mode that necessitates the development of a point of view. All design choices should be based on an idea about the work. Even a musical revue, such as *Ain't Misbehavin',* requires a conceptual approach to guide the design choices. For a recent production of the show, rather than producing the play in its traditional nightclub format, the director and design team developed a point of view toward the work that focused on the

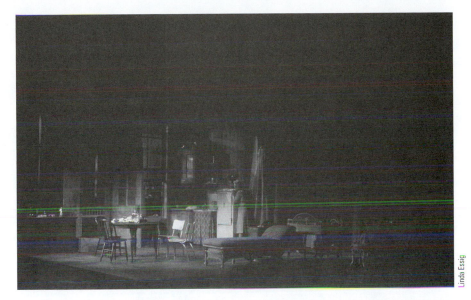

Linda Essig

FIGURE 5.1
In this production of *A Streetcar Named Desire,* Blanche cowers in the shadows like a caged animal before Stanley arrives. Directed by Cynthia White; set design by Thomas C. Umfrid; lighting design by the author.

historicity of the development of the music in the show. That is, they chose to set the piece in a 1930s "rent party" to showcase both the upbeat nature of the music and the reality of life in Harlem in that period. Doing so contextualized the more serious numbers while providing a visual through-line for the others, as seen in Figure 5.2.

In opera, too, where the music is often paramount, a point of view is needed to guide design choices, so, too, in dance. In developing an approach for dance, the designer and the choreographer must discuss what the choreographer is trying to convey with the work. Is there a narrative, toward which there may be a point of view similar to that for *Streetcar,* or is the piece about the geometry of

Melanie Schuessler

FIGURE 5.2
Unlike most productions of the piece, this production of *Ain't Misbehavin'* was conceived to take place in a Harlem brownstone.

FIGURE 5.3
Choreographer
Kevin Wynn
conceived of *Black
Clouds Under My
Feet* as a series of
paintings, and the
lighting was de-
signed accordingly.
Costume Design by
Rosie Kanellis;
lighting design by
Chris Dallos.

form in space, about sexual relationships, or political ones? In the example depicted in Figure 5.3, the dance was about a series of paintings and the lighting
needed to be painterly in its compositions of light and dark, color and form.

FORM, STYLE, AND GENRE

If the point of view provides the skeleton of the conceptual framework, the
form, style, and genre of a piece can provide its outer dressing. Earlier, broad
categories of performance were discussed: dramatic play, opera, dance, musical
revue. More than just these broad categorizations, the form, style, and genre of
a specific work influence design decisions, giving them visual and intellectual
specificity. Rather than limiting this discussion to the often misused term
"style," what follows is a discussion of three allied concepts: the form or shape
of the work, the style of the language, and the theatrical genre to which the
piece belongs.

Upon reading a play and developing a scene breakdown, one starts to develop an understanding of the shape or form of the work, the way individual
scenes are structured and the way scenes relate to one another in terms of the
flow of the overall piece. For example, *A Streetcar Named Desire* consists of
eleven scenes that follow one another chronologically, although there are longer
temporal breaks between scenes 4 and 5 and between scenes 6 and 7 than be-

tween the other scenes. Intermissions and costume changes are often placed here, to mark the longer expanses of time.

Marivaux's *La Dispute,* pictured in Figure 5.4, has a more geometric form as four isolated individuals meet, join, and square off (literally), under the watchful eye of another couple. The play is structured in a way that telegraphs the need to raise the watchers above the others in a space with four corners—a square—from which the young lovers can emerge.

A performance work need not have a linear narrative to have a form or a shape. The modern ballet *Agon* (music by Igor Stravinsky; original choreography by George Balanchine), depicted in Figure 5.5, is a good example of a dance piece with a distinct form but no actual story. "Agon" is Greek for "contest" and as such the piece presents an idealized contest between the moving sculptures that are the dancers. Yet, the piece has a definite shape, having eleven distinct scenes, only the first and last of which include the entire company of twelve dancers. The lighting designer for *Agon* should note that there are distinct scenes, but can question whether the lighting should visually separate each of the segments from one another. If so, should that separation be accomplished through blackouts between or just different looks for each? If the point of view is that this is a contest merely for show, an exhibition in which no one dancer dominates, should each section therefore look exactly the same so as not to throw the visual balance toward one or another? Once the form of the piece is

FIGURE 5.4
The set and lighting for this production of *La Dispute* were based on the form of a square, cubed, with levels of watching and being watched. Directed by Patricia Boyette; set design by Kate Henderson; costume design by Karen Boyer; lighting design by the author.

Linda Essig

FIGURE 5.5
George Balanchine's form-based *Agon,* like many of his ballets, uses primarily white light.

Martha Swope

acknowledged, the questions that that form raises can be answered in collaboration with the choreographer.

As another example, consider works of musical theatre. In discerning the form of a musical, one considers not only the chronological relationship between scenes, but also the relationship between musical numbers and book scenes. Do the musical numbers grow organically from the content of the preceding scene, do they comment on the scene, or are they structurally outside the narrative. The Kander and Ebb musical *Cabaret,* its recent revival pictured in Figure 5.6, is a musical that contains all three types of numbers. A number like "The Pineapple Song" grows out of the book scene set in the fruit shop, whereas "Life is a Cabaret" is more presentational—a performance within a performance that seemingly is outside the narrative but ironically comments upon it.

The form of many plays written since the middle of the twentieth century has been greatly influenced by cinematic conventions such as quick-cutting, dissolves, and fades, as well as by the availability of automated lighting and scenic technologies. Straight plays, musicals, and entertainment extravaganzas alike have been conceived to exploit the newest stage technology to achieve the smoothest transitions and the most breathtaking effects.

The shape of a piece most directly affects the cuing (changes) in light over the course of a performance, but form can also bring to the fore more general considerations about the overall style of the play and its lighting. Style here refers to how faithful to reality the production and its lighting will be; the manner in which the environment will be expressed. In the preceding chapter, a real room was examined to see how light behaves and how it might be re-created on stage if the design were to remain true to reality. In addressing style of production, one considers to what degree a real situation may or may not be executed on stage. Most productions fall somewhere on a continuum between absolute reality and total abstraction. Determining the style of the work and collaborating to decide on the stylistic latitude for a specific production help the designer to locate the design appropriately on that continuum.

The language of a play is perhaps the most important aspect one assesses in determining style. Clearly, there is some stylistic latitude in a piece in which characters periodically break into song. But even in a dramatic play, one can consider the following questions: how do the characters talk to one another? Do they speak in verse? Does the playwright use symbols and images in the language?

Joan Marcus

FIGURE 5.6
Strong use of uplight helps to set the visual style of *Cabaret,* a musical with book and musical scenes, as well as scenes within the "Kit Kat Klub" hosted by the Emcee depicted here. Directed by Sam Mendes; set design by Robert Bill; costume design by William Ivey Long; lighting design by Peggy Eisenhauer and Michael Baldassari.

The passage from *Streetcar* quoted earlier is a good example of the use of imagistic language. Recall the "ghoul-haunted woodland of Weir!" Contrast Williams's language to the grittier realism of Sam Shepard's opening to *True West:*

> **Lee:** So, Mom took off for Alaska, huh?
> **Austin:** Yeah.
> **Lee:** Sorta left you in charge.
> **Austin:** Well, she knew I was coming down here so she offered me the place.
> **Lee:** You keepin' the plants watered?
> **Austin:** Yeah.

Here, the lighting design could function, along with the set, to create an environment in which this dialogue can be believably spoken, although it is worth noting that the language of this particular play does become richer and more imagistic as the play develops.

Other playwrights may use rhythm in their language to help establish the style of a piece. In *Venus,* Suzan-Lori Parks uses rhythmic language and verse rather than dialogue to set up a very presentational style in the "Overture" to her play during which various characters are introduced:

The Negro Resurrectionist
The Venus Hottentot!

The Mans Brother, later The Mother-Showman, later The Grade-School Chum
The Venus Hottentot!

The Man, later The Baron Docteur
The Venus Hottentot!
(*Rest*)
(*Rest*)

The Chorus
The Chorus of the 8 Human Wonders!

The Man, later The Baron Docteur
The Man, later
The Baron Docteur!

The Negro Resurrectionist
The Negro Resurrectionist!

The Mans Brother, later The Mother-Showman, later The Grade-School Chum
The Brother, later
The Mother-Showman! Later
The Grade-School Chum

The Negro Resurrectionist
The Negro Resurrectionist!

The Chorus
The Chorus of the 8 Anatomists!
(*Rest*)
(*Rest*)

In this example, there is no dialogue, per se, but a presentation of characters. In some ways, this scene functions as the other examples to introduce characters, but its language—as well as its form—differs significantly.

As a last example, let us examine the use of verse. Act V of Shakespeare's *The Merchant of Venice* begins like this:

Lorenzo The moon shines bright. In such a night as this,
    When the sweet wind did gently kiss the trees
    And they did make a noise, in such a night
    Troilus methinks mounted the Trojan walls
    And sighed his soul toward the Grecian tents
    Where Cressid lay that night

Jessica   In such a night
    Did Thisbe fearfully o'ertrip the dew,
    And saw the lion's shadow ere himself,
    And ran dismayed away.

Lorenzo   In such a night
    Stood Dido with the willow in her hand
    Upon the wild sea banks, and waft her love
    To come again to Carthage.

Jessica   In such a night
    Medea gathered the enchanted herbs
    That did renew Aeson

Lorenzo   In such a night
    Did Jessica steal from the wealthy Jew
    And with an unthrift love did run from Venice
    As far as Belmont

Jessica   In such a night
    Did young Lorenzo swear he loved her well,
    Stealing her soul with many vows of faith,
    And ne'er a true one.

Lorenzo   In such a night
    Did pretty Jessica, like a little shrew,
    Slander her love, and he forgave her.

Here, as in the first scene of *Streetcar,* the characters describe their lighting environment. They do so, however, in verse, with multiple images drawn from antiquity and a rhythm created not only by the iambic pentameter of the verse, but by the repetitive phrase "In such a night." Because of the verse, the symbolism, and the rhythm, the lighting designer can create a night in which the "moon shines bright" in an infinite number of ways, the language freeing the designer to stray from the reality of moonlight (a cool, high-contrast, dimness) to express the poeticism of the language through color, angle, and texture.

In addition to the form of a piece and the style of its language, one should consider its genre. Genre here refers to the theatrical category or period in which the play was written. Not all plays, operas, or dances neatly fall within a performance genre, but when they do, one should investigate the genre and its design implications (see the following chapter on research methods).

American musicals of the 1940s and 1950s, for example, have numerous design conventions associated with them. Among these are the use of follow spots on lead performers; a color palette based in pinks, blues, lavenders, and ambers; and directions of light available in proscenium theatres. In a contemporary production, the design team must choose whether to adopt, adapt, or reject outright those conventions, and, of course, should base those stylistic decisions on a point of view toward the work. The production of *Cabaret* pictured earlier, as directed by Sam Mendes, subverted the conventions of book musicals by placing all of the action within the Kit Kat Klub. In the original production, shown in Figure 5.7, which itself subverted many conventions of musical the-

FIGURE 5.7
Boris Aronson's set for the original production of *Cabaret* subverted the theatrical traditions of its time by including a mirror that intentionally reflected the audience.

atre (not the least of which was a large mirror in the set designed by Boris Aronson), the club was juxtaposed against more traditional book scenes.

A nineteenth-century melodrama originally would have been lighted by gas fittings in the wings, footlights, and overhead battens as shown in Figure 5.8.

FIGURE 5.8
This nineteenth-century stage shows some typical gas fittings including wing lights, gas battens, and footlights.

FIGURE 5.9
The Illusion mixes elements from many different periods. Directed by David Esbjornson; set design by Karen ten Eyck; costume design by Claudia Stevens; lighting design by Brian MacDevitt.

Will a contemporary production suggest this lighting look using modern electrical equipment or opt to set the play in a different theatrical period? Or, will it mix periods by using contemporary-looking lighting with period costumes on a period-neutral set as seen in the production of *The Illusion* shown in Figure 5.9, which in Corneille's time would have been lighted by candlelight.

Research is a necessary tool in establishing the genre of a piece and the lighting conventions associated with that genre. Often, too, theatrical genres have associated with them genres or styles of decorative arts that can be used as visual flashpoints for the design.

THE GESTURE AND FLOW OF THE LIGHTING

Stage lighting can be an active participant in performance. As such, it communicates meaning. The term gesture means an action that communicates nonverbally, and so lighting can be gestural. What is the impact of the lighting? What is the story of the lighting? And, how will the lighting help to tell the story of the play?

In the production of *Ain't Misbehavin'* mentioned previously, color was used in a gestural way to punctuate both the celebratory and more thoughtful songs of Act 1. Furthermore, the use of color evolved over the course of the event so that more realistic colors were used at the beginning of the piece to establish the Harlem 1937 setting, and splashier color was used as the piece progressed through Act 2, as seen in Color Plate 8, and the Archibald Motley painting that inspired that palette in Color Plate 7.

In developing an approach to *A Streetcar Named Desire,* one consideration was the nature of the overhead light in the main room of the flat. This main light can also convey meaning in a gestural way by being harsh, or confining, or conversely flattering and warm.

Considering the flow, or evolution of the lighting over the course of the performance, is another important element of the conceptual framework for a production. If the lighting changes over time, that change can be read by the audience in relation to the play as a whole. Perhaps the light in *Streetcar* becomes more and more fractured as the play progresses, echoing the breakdown of Blanche's mind. Or, perhaps the lighting can be designed to become more confining for Blanche as the play progresses, communicating the impression that Stanley is somehow keeping Blanche under his control.

A lighting designer should consider how light functions overall for a production by weighing the balance between the various functions of stage lighting and how the properties of light can be used to achieve those functions in a steady state and over time. The following chart (Figure 5.10) can be a helpful tool for organizing those ideas.

KEY TERMS

BOOK SCENE	MUSICAL NUMBER
DRAMA	POINT OF VIEW
FRENCH SCENES	SCENE BREAKDOWN
GENRE	STRAIGHT PLAY
GESTURE	STYLE

	Properties of Light						
Functions of Light	Direction	Intensity	Shape	Distribution	Color	Sharpness	Movement Through Space	Change
Visibility							
Environment							
Image							
Atmosphere							
3D Form							
3D Space							
Visual Focus							
Style							

Linda Essig

FIGURE 5.10

The beginning lighting designer may find it helpful to use this chart to represent the relative importance of the various functions of light in a production and which properties of light can best be used to achieve those functions.

6
LIGHTING DESIGN RESEARCH

THE conceptualization of the overall lighting design approach does not happen in a vacuum. Collaboration with the director and other designers is necessary to develop that approach, as is the synthesis of other forms of external input gathered through thorough research. Research materials of various types can and should be brought in to the designer's thinking throughout the design process from the second reading of the play through technical rehearsals (if needed). Different types of research are used in different stages of the process. Early on, before even meeting with the collaborative team, the designer may do dramaturgical and historical research. As ideas start to form, the designer seeks images, both from external sources and from his or her own personal experience. In the implementation phases of the design, technical research is necessary.

DRAMATURGICAL RESEARCH

Dramaturgical research is research that delves into the critical history of a piece and its playwright, composer, or choreographer. This knowledge, as well as some research into other works created by the same au-thor(s) can aid in determining the literary or musical style of a piece and devel-oping the production's style. For example, Tennessee Williams has been termed a "poetic realist" by many and this idea of "poetic" realism may be useful in de-veloping a design approach.

Many directors and dramaturges look at previous productions when formu-lating their own production concept. It is particularly useful and interesting to look at the original production of a play because the playwright was most likely involved with that initial production. Although this author by no means advo-cates re-creating a previous production, insight into the text and context of an original production is useful in developing new production ideas. A director may even choose to formulate design ideas in reaction *against* the choices of the original production. Witness these director's notes from a production of *A Streetcar Named Desire*:

> I find it easy (especially in thinking back to the productions I saw of *Streetcar* ten years ago or more) to be put off by the scrimmy, atmospheric moody ele-ments suggested in the stage directions [of the original production]. . . . I do not want to sugarcoat the violence or the brutality. Nor do I want to under-play the very real passion and tenderness which also exists in the Stanley/ Stella relationship.[1]

In not-for-profit professional as well as academic theatres, there is often a production dramaturg. The dramaturg can be a wonderful resource for the de-sign team. Among other duties, he or she will probably collate biographical in-formation about the playwright and the production history of the piece. The dramaturg also assists the director in researching elements of the performance text. The dramaturg may also provide other types of background research to help contextualize the piece but the designer should not count on someone else to do his or her work.

HISTORICAL RESEARCH

Finding the appropriate conceptual context for a piece can be aided by good historical research. Historical research, research into the historical context in which the play was written and in which it is set, like dramaturgical research, is most useful in developing initial ideas about a play and its style and the subse-quent development of a point of view toward the work as a whole.

An understanding of the social, cultural, political, and economic times in which a play was written gives the design team insight into the world of the playwright. Such knowledge aids in developing an approach and in assimilating contemporary parallels between the playwright's time and our own. For example, in designing *The Marriage of Figaro,* either the Beaumarchais play or the Mozart/da Ponte opera *Nozze de Figaro,* one should consider the social, cultural, and political upheaval of the latter part of the eighteenth century during which the piece was written and is often—although not always—set, as in Figure 6.1. The conflicts between the upper and lower classes and the bourgeoisie that helped fuel the French Revolution are present in the relationships among Figaro, Susanna, the Count and Countess, and their entourage. Given that political climate, a production team might decide to focus on the socio-economic conflicts of that period. Lighting can help set the period through choice of color and angle and/or accentuate the contrast between Figaro's room and the world of the Count.

A director and his or her designer/collaborators may *choose* to set a piece in a period other than that for which or in which it was written. In the Glimmerglass Opera production of *Figaro* in Figure 6.2, the director and design team set the piece in a far more abstract space.

Often, a piece is meant to be played in a period other than that in which it is written. In such cases, both periods should be thoroughly researched. Take, as an example, Bertolt Brecht's play *Galileo.* Research into the historical Galileo is very important, but it is research into Brecht and the censorship and exile he faced as Hitler rose to power in Germany that gives some insight into this play.

The Metropolitan Opera, New York, NY

FIGURE 6.1
An eighteenth-century setting for Jean Pierre Ponnelle's production of *The Marriage of Figaro* for the Metropolitan Opera.

FIGURE 6.2
A visually abstracted production of *The Marriage of Figaro*. Directed by Stephen Lawless; set design by Benoit Dugardyn; costume design by Johann Stegmeir; lighting design by Paul Pyant.

An understanding of the revisions to the script Brecht made in light of the use of the first atomic bomb provides further insight into some of the play's major themes, including the morality of scientific advancement, from which one can draw further connections to contemporary scientific and ethical debates.

VISUAL AND IMAGISTIC RESEARCH

Visual research is by far the most directly applicable form of external input to the designer's decision-making process regarding composition, color, texture, and the like. Visual research may be specific to a particular period in history of fine and decorative arts or may be more visceral and inspirational in nature.

It is fairly easy to find visual materials based on the decorative arts of a specific period. Anyone with access to the World Wide Web can use a search engine to find images from broad historical categories. (The author finds www.artcyclopedia.com to be an invaluable art search engine.) The traditional book—so easy to transport to a production meeting—should not be discounted. Art survey books such as Hutter's *Styles in Art: An Historical Survey* or Canady's *Modern Art* are good references. After finding a broad category of decorative style or an art historical period, which need not be limited to Western art forms, one can fine-tune the research to specific movements or artists of a period, and from there hone in on a few images that are particularly appropriate or useful. Books usually prove more useful for "collaborative browsing," that is, at a creative team meeting, than does Internet browsing.

To again use *Ain't Misbehavin'* as an example, given the 1930s Harlem setting, the design team looked to painters of the Harlem Renaissance for visual inspiration. As Color Plates 7 and 8 show, the high chromaticity color palette of the paintings of Archibald Motley made their way into the design in the magenta tonality of the second act lighting, as well as into the costume designer's palette.

Another avenue of visual/pictorial research that can also be classified as historical or dramaturgical is research into the theatrical conventions of a period. Set and costume designers must use their historical research not only to help formulate ideas about a play but also to find out what a specific period looked like in art, dress, and decoration. Similarly, pictures of what theatres looked like and how they were lit when a play was written can be quite helpful. For example, in designing *She Stoops to Conquer,* one might look at the configuration of a post-Restoration theatre (see Figure 6.3) and then adapt some of that pre-electric lighting into a contemporary vernacular. What was the color of the light in the eighteenth century? What lighting positions were used?

Mary Evans Picture Library

FIGURE 6.3
The view from the audience toward an eighteenth-century stage.

Not all visual research material must be rooted in a specific place or period in the decorative arts. Some of the most useful visual material for the lighting is not specific to the way a particular scene precisely looks but rather is an inspiration for the lighting design as a whole. Visual inspirations for the lighting design can be more visceral, imagistic flashes one might come upon by chance. A flower, happened upon during an evening walk, could provide the impetus for the design choices of *As You Like It* or *Dancing at Lughnasa*. Advertising art can also be a fertile source for striking images. Extraordinary lighting images may be encountered while browsing through magazines.

Because some of the most relevant images may be stumbled upon by chance, the designer should keep an open mind not only about where to look for images, but also about what images may be useful. If, in the search for visual material one has a set and concretized idea about what they are looking for, the risk of bypassing something new, different, and totally unexpected arises. Lighting images need not be two-dimensional pictures but can be objects in our lives that evoke a sense of atmosphere as well as light. Such visual material may seem more metaphoric than actual.

In employing such visceral, emotive visual material, the lighting designer and director or choreographer must decide which aspects of the object or image are relevant to the piece. After this collaboration, the lighting designer can proceed to determine how those attributes of the image or images can make their way into the design in practice. Consider the controllable properties of light. In what ways are the found visual materials to guide the choices of direction, contrast, color, movement, change, shape, and so on? Even a piece of fruit can function as an appropriate lighting inspiration in this way. A navel orange, with its round shape, stippled texture, and orange-tinged-with-green color provided both inspiration and a visual structure for the lighting of Cliff Keuter's dance piece *Women Song,* shown in Figure 6.4. Individual lighting compositions, as well as the movement of the main source of light in an arc from one side of the stage to another were based on the round shape of the orange. The color palette for the piece was drawn directly from the colors found on the orange as well as the freshness of spray as the peel was broken apart. Most of the lights were textured with a delicate stippling which, inspired by the texture of the orange, evoked a leafiness appropriate to the piece, and a similar texture was projected on the background.

In addition to visual research materials that provide a visual inspiration or image for a specific moment or moments in a performance, one may also find that these visceral visual responses provide metaphors for the way light functions and evolves over the course of an entire event. A fading white rose might

Linda Essig

FIGURE 6.4
An orange was used as visual inspiration for the lighting design of *Women Song*. Choreography by Cliff Keuter; lighting design by the author.

be an appropriate "lighting metaphor" for *Streetcar,* the light starting out pale, soft, and pretty, but by the end of the play being brown and crackled.

These forms of visual research are useful not only for the lighting designers in their decision-making processes about color, composition, and cuing, but are also effective for communicating design intent to directors and other designers. Many designers and directors find it difficult to use words to describe what is essentially an abstract and rather ephemeral composition of light, dark, and shadow. Visual research materials can be a basis for director/designer communication because they can be brought in to a design conference and discussed.

PERSONAL EXPERIENCE

In addition to (but not in place of) research materials that can be brought to design meetings, the lighting designer can draw on the rich bank of their own experience. Primary to the development of a point of view is the designer's own personal "take" on a piece. How do one's own experiences relate to those of the characters? How does the music make one feel? Similarly, visual memories from a designer's own life can be a useful source of visual inspiration. The childhood memory of a morning spent in a grandparent's barn may provide some ideas for the look of the hayloft scene in *Spring Awakening,* for example.

Lighting designers should also learn to observe, store, and recall their impressions of the natural and artificially lit world so that they have a virtual storehouse of images, a mental picture file to draw from. Observing sunsets over the course of a month—or over a summer month and a winter month—in differing weather conditions can provide a mental catalog of images to use for lighting backdrops, for example. Take note of the oppressive nature of institutional fluorescent lights, or the warm shadowy light of a candlelit dinner. All of these impressions, especially if noted verbally or pictorially, can be used in subsequent designs.

TECHNICAL RESEARCH

The last type of research discussed here has more to do with the implementation of the design than the conceptualization of it—technical research. The lighting designer needs to ascertain what technological tools are available from a theatre's stock or via rental, what that equipment might do, and what equipment might be appropriate for a given lighting need or effect.

It is in the area of technical research that the World Wide Web can be most useful. Manufacturers of lighting equipment publish data sheets (or "cut sheets") for their equipment and most manufacturers post this information to the Web in some downloadable format. Data sheets, and manufacturer's sites as a whole, usually include general information and photographs geared toward sales and, more importantly for the practicing designer, technical information about the equipment. This information includes details on physical size, wattage, materials, ventilation, special features, and accessories, as well as photometric data. The photometrics, or light measurement statistics, include information on the beam spread and the footcandles at a given distance—the distribution and amount of light. By comparing data sheets for comparable equipment from different manufacturers, the designer can make informed decisions about the similarity or differences from manufacturer to manufacturer.

Figures 6.5, 6.6, and 6.7 are sample data sheets for some commonly used theatrical luminaires from different manufacturers. The first page of each usually includes descriptive information and the size of the unit, and the second page covers the photometric information and other performance data. These fixtures, or similar ones, are found in many professional and academic theatre inventories. Sometimes, however, specialized accessories are required for special effects and so further research is needed. Trade publications such as *Lighting Dimensions* or *Theatre Design and Technology* often include new product

ETC, Inc.

Source Four® 36°

436 Series

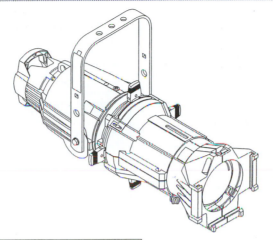

SPECIFICATIONS

Ellipsoidal lighting fixture

PHYSICAL Die cast aluminum construction
Rotating shutter assembly ±25°
20 gauge stainless steel shutters in a tri-plane assembly
Interchangeable lens tubes with smooth–running teflon guides provide six user-fit field angle options
Thermally insulated rear handle
High impact, thermally insulated knobs and shutter handles
Two accessory slots, and a top mounted, gel frame retainer
Steel yoke with two mounting positions
Positive locking single-clutch fixture body
Slot for glass or stainless steel patterns
Slot with sliding cover for motorized pattern devices or optional iris
UL and cUL listed

ELECTRICAL 115-240V, 50/60Hz
High temperature 3–conductor 36" leads in a glass fiber outer sleeve
Supports ETC Dimmer Doubling™ technology

LAMP 750W maximum
HPL — compact tungsten filament contained in a krypton-filled quartz envelope (see table for suitable lamp types)
Patented filament geometry makes for extremely efficient light collection and transmission
Integral die cast aluminum heat sink lamp base

OPTICAL Projector-quality, high contrast meniscus front lens and bi-convex rear lens
Faceted borosilicate reflector with multi-layer dichroic coating
95% of visible light reflected through the optical train
90% of infrared radiation (heat) passes through the reflector
Reflector secured with anti-vibration shock mounts
Lens(es) secured with anti-vibration shock mounts
Tool free lamp centering (X/Y) and peak/flat (Z) adjustment knobs
Positive locking X, Y and Z adjustments, unaffected by relamping
Beam edge continually adjustable hard–to–soft
Interchangeable lens barrels permit selection of 5°, 10°, 19°, 26°, 36°, and 50° field angles

ORDERING INFORMATION

Source Four

Model#	Description
436	36° ellipsoidal (black)
436-1	36° ellipsoidal (white)

ETC Source Four are supplied with C-clamp, color frame and 3' (96cm) leads as standard

Connector Designation
Use Suffixes below to specify Factory–Fitted Connector type

Model#	Description
A	Parallel-blade U-ground connector
B	Two-pin and ground, 20 amp connector
C	Grounded, 20 amp, twistlock connector
M	Dimmer Doubling™ Connector (NEMA L515P)

Source Four Accessories

Model#	Description
436LT	36° lens tube with lenses installed (black)
436LT-1	36° lens tube with lenses installed (white)
400CC	C–clamp (included)
400PH–A	Pattern holder (A size)
400PH–B	Pattern holder (B size)
400PH–G	Glass pattern holder
400SC	Safety cable
400RS	Drop–in iris
400CF	Colorframe (6.25") (included)
400DN	Donut (6.25")
400TH	Top hat
400HH	Half hat
400GE	Gel extender
407GE	Conical gel extender
407CF	7.5" Square color frame
400FB	Source Four Fixture Body, Single Clutch

Note: For colors other than black or white, please call ETC.

FIGURE 6.5
A data sheet for an ETC Source Four. (Used with permission of Electronic Theatre Controls.)

Source Four® 36°

436 Series

PHOTOMETRIC

All photometric data in this document was prepared using standard production fixtures, and the Prometric™ CCD measurement system. Fixtures were adjusted for cosine distribution, and were tested with a calibrated HPL 750/115V 21,900 lumens lamp at its rated voltage. All data were normalized to nominal lamp lumens.

36°

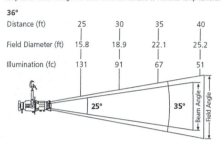

Distance (ft)	25	30	35	40
Field Diameter (ft)	15.8	18.9	22.1	25.2
Illumination (fc)	131	91	67	51

For illumination with any lamp, multiply the candlepower of a beam spread by the multiplying factor (mf) shown for that lamp.

To determine illumination in footcandles or lux at any throw distance, divide candlepower by distance squared.

For Field diameter at any distance, multiply distance by .63
For Beam diameter at any distance, multiply distance by .45

Metric Conversions: For Meters multiply feet by .3048
For Lux multiply footcandles by 10.76

PHYSICAL

Lamp code	Watts	Volts	Initial Lumens	Color Temp.	Average Rated Life	MF
HPL 750/115	750	115	21,900	3,250°	300	1.00
HPL 575/115	575	115	16,520	3,250°	300	0.87
HPL 575/115X	575	115	12,360	3,050°	2000	0.66
HPL 575/120	575	120	16,460	3,250°	300	0.87
HPL 375/115	375	115	10,540	3,200°	300	0.55
HPL 375/115X	375	115	8,060	3,000°	1000	0.43
HPL 550/77*	550	77	16,170	3,250°	300	0.87
HPL 550/77X*	550	77	12,160	3,050°	2000	0.66
HPL 750/230	750	230	19,400	3,200°	300	0.90
HPL 750/240	750	240	19,400	3,200°	300	0.90
HPL 575/230	575	230	14,900	3,200°	400	0.76
HPL 575/240	575	240	14,900	3,200°	400	0.76
HPL 575/230X	575	230	11,780	3,050°	1500	0.61
HPL 575/240X	575	240	11,780	3,050°	1500	0.64
HPL 375/230X	375	230	7,800	3,050°	1000	0.38
HPL 375/240X	375	240	7,800	3,050°	1000	0.38

*77V lamps are intended for use with the ETC Dimmer Doubler™.

Warning: Use of lamps other than HPL will void UL/cUL safety approval and product warranty. Source Four is rated for 750W maximum.

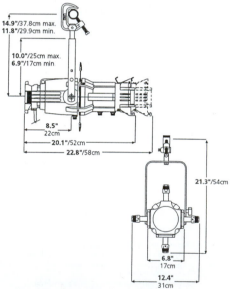

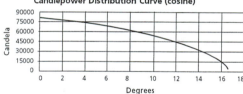

Candlepower Distribution Curve (cosine)

Source Four 36° cosine

Degree	Candlepower	Field Lumens	Beam Lumens	Efficiency
36°	82,000	12,300	8,030	56.2%

Source Four Weights

Model	Fixture Weight*		Shipping Weight	
	lbs	kgs	lbs	kgs
36°	14	6.3	20	9.1

* Add 2.3 lbs for C-clamp

Americas ▪ 3030 Laura Lane, P.O. Box 620979, Middleton, WI 53562-0979 USA ▪ Tel: +608 831 4116 ▪ Fax: +608 836 1736 ▪ Toll free: 800 688 4116 ▪ Toll free fax: 800 555 8912
Europe ▪ 5 Victoria Industrial Estate, Victoria Road, London W3 6UU, UK ▪ Tel: +44 (0)20 8896 1000 ▪ Fax: +44 (0)20 8896 2000
Asia ▪ Room 605-606, Tower III Enterprise Square, 9 Sheung Yuet Road, Kowloon Bay, Kowloon, Hong Kong ▪ Tel: +852 2799 1220 ▪ Fax: +852 2799 9325
Web: www.etcconnect.com ▪ **Email:** (US) mail@etcconnect.com ▪ (UK) mail@etceurope.com ▪ (Asia) mail@etcasia.com

FIGURE 6.5
(continued)

Coolbeam Spotlight

Strand Theatre Lighting

SL19 / SL26 / SL36 / SL50
Coolbeam spotlights 575W

Features

Excellent light output, superb distribution and the smoothest soft edge
while maintaining beam size. Sharp gobo, edge and shutter focus.
Very compact and narrow with the smallest dimensions in their category.
Easy to use and maintain with many features for increased safety.

- ❏ High efficiency dichroic glass reflector and coated aspheric computer-designed lenses
- ❏ Coolbeam operation for extended gobo, shutter and gel life
- ❏ Optimized for energy efficient, high performance GLC 575W lamps;
  GLA long life lamps also available
- ❏ Fast and easy lamp centering with positive screw driver lock so that it won't move in transit
- ❏ Fast positive peak/flat adjustment via screw drive mechanism for smooth, tool-free
  field settings
- ❏ Bayonet action lamp changing system for simple lamp changes without affecting
  field setting
- ❏ Compact and lightweight, allowing closer hanging in tighter spaces
- ❏ Smooth 360° body rotation for quick and easy gobo and shutter positioning
- ❏ Shutters in three planes for triangular shutter cut
- ❏ Highly versatile rigging by combining 360° rotation with two balance positions for yoke
- ❏ Large rear handle for easy positioning
- ❏ Quick and easy access for reflector and lens cleaning
- ❏ Common lamp house with easily interchangeable tubes
- ❏ Wide gate will fit 2 gobo holders, including glass gobo holder, drop-in iris or rotating
  gobo holder
- ❏ Safety cable attachment point for the luminaire and accessories
- ❏ UL, cUL listed

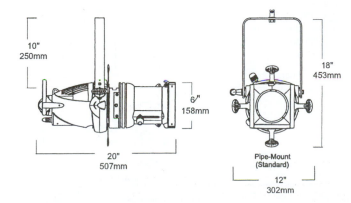

Weights and dimensions

Weight	15 lb
Packed weight	20½ lb
Packed volume	2½ cu ft
Filter cut size	6¼" x 6¼"

FIGURE 6.6
A data sheet for a Strand Lighting SL series ERS. (From Strand Lighting, Inc.)

Coolbeam Spotlight

Strand Theatre Lighting

Photometric data

Typical performance based on: 575W GLC 115V lamp

SL19

Distance (ft)	35	40	45	50	55
Beam Ø (ft)	11.7	13.4	15.1	16.7	18.4
Illum (fc)	184	141	111	90	74

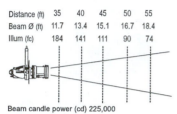

Beam candle power (cd) 225,000

SL26

Distance (ft)	25	30	35	40	45
Beam Ø (ft)	11.5	13.9	16.2	18.5	20.8
Illum (fc)	310	216	158	121	96

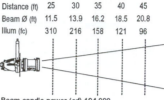

Beam candle power (cd) 194,000

SL36

Distance (ft)	20	25	30	35	40
Beam Ø (ft)	13	16.2	19.5	22.7	26
Illum (fc)	218	139	97	71	54

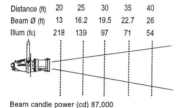

Beam candle power (cd) 87,000

SL50

Distance (ft)	15	20	25	30	35
Beam Ø (ft)	14	18.7	23.3	28	32.6
Illum (fc)	227	128	82	57	42

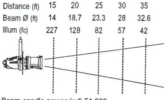

Beam candle power (cd) 51,000

Performance at any distance: divide beam candle power by distance²

For beam diameter at any distance: 19° multiply 0.32 x distance
26° multiply 0.46 x distance
36° multiply 0.64 x distance
50° multiply 0.93 x distance

Operational features

Focus adjustment

By moving the burner assembly using a simple screw drive mechanism.

Lamp Adjustment

Lamp centering by use of a screwdriver

Electrical & mechanical data

Construction

Die cast aluminum housing with black epoxy powder coat. Stainless steel shutters.

Gate

Plated steel

Lens

Crown glass coated aspheric lens

Lamp

TP22 medium 2-pin base
GLC	400 hours	3200°K
GLA	1500 hours	3100°K

Supply voltage

115-230V, 50/60 Hz

Standards compliance

UL, cUL listed

Max operating ambient temperature

115°F/ 45°C

Ordering information

Supplied complete with 3 ft cable with bare ends (be) or fitted connector as specified, color frame, 360° rotation yoke & c-clamp.

Cat No	Description
11321	SL19, 115V, be
11331	SL26, 115V, be
11341	SL36, 115V, be
11351	SL50, 115V, be

Optional accessories

Cat No	Description	Cat No	Description
18045	Gobo holder size B	18403	19° lens tube
18049	Iris (24 leaf)	18404	26° lens tube
18114	Color frame	18405	36° lens tube
		18406	50° lens tube

For connector options please specify GR, GP, or GTL when ordering.

Strand Lighting Inc
6603 Darin Way, Cypress, CA 90630, USA
Tel: +1 714 230 8200   Fax +1 714 230 8173

**Strand Lighting (Canada)
Inc/Eclairages Strand (Canada) Inc**
2430 Lucknow Drive No 15
Mississauga Ontario L5S 1V3 Canada
Tel: +1 905 677 7130   Fax: +1 905 677 6859

BERLIN · HONG KONG · LONDON · LOS ANGELES · MOSCOW · NEW YORK · PARIS · ROME · TORONTO

FIGURE 6.6
(continued)

ELLIPSOIDAL LIGHTING

Catalog Numbers
S6-1535Z
S6-3055Z

Fixture Type:

The SHAKESPEARE Series Zoom ellipsoidals are the state of the art in variable focus theatrical luminaires for function, style, and efficiency. These ellipsoidals have been designed and engineered with a number of innovative details and features enhancing versatility and efficiency without sacrificing performance. The dichroic coated glass reflector removes heat from the beam, resulting in longer gel and pattern life. The super smooth, variable focus lens system, which operates with Teflon bearings on stainless steel guide rails, produces wide-to-narrow beams offering a sharp, full field and distortion free pattern projection. The generous accessory slot, the two-slot accessory·holder, and self-closing, self-locking retaining latch for the accessory holder are just some of the special features provided. The aesthetic appearance and ergonomically designed function controls only add to its appeal. With a wide range of non-proprietary lamps to choose from, the low wattage, high output SHAKESPEARE zooms are ideal for theatres, nightclubs, television studios, or wherever superior, energy efficient lighting performance is required.

S6-3055Z
pictured

Specifications subject to change without notice

750 WATT
SHAKESPEARE® Series ZOOM ELLIPSOIDAL

Features

- Compact, rugged die-cast aluminum construction
- Spring mounted dichroic coated glass reflector provided with heat shield
- Lockable, 180° indexed rotation of shutter assembly and lens barrel, optional 360° rotation
- Color Coded lens and lens barrel identification system
- Tempered crown glass lenses have anti-reflective coating
- Zoom focus lens carriers use Teflon glide bearings on stainless steel guide rails
- Tool free operating lamp centering knob and peak to flat field adjustment knob
- Replaceable two-slot accessory holder provided with self-closing and self-locking accessory retaining latch
- Accessory slot provided with locking cover that will accept rotating gobo accessories, glass pattern holder and drop-in-iris
- Removable lens access panel

- Tool free removable heavy gauge stainless steel shutters mounted in separate planes equipped with oversized insulated handles, and spring pressured shutter assembly
- Dual positioning yoke supplied with dual positive locking dogs and tilt angle markings
- Protective insulated rear mounted ring handle serves as a cord wrap, stand, and focusing aid
- G9.5 medium two-pin lampholder provided with heat shield that accepts a wide variety of non-proprietary lamps
- Uses standard 7 ½" accessories
- Three 36" Teflon lead wires
- Up to 25' of Hi-Temp rubber cable optional
- Pipe clamp, color frame and safety cable included
- U.L., c.U.L. and CE listed for 750 watts
- Made in the USA

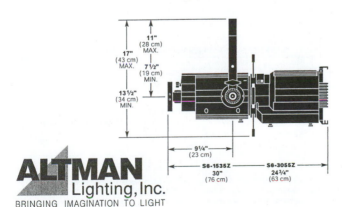

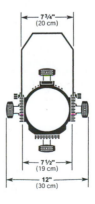

ALTMAN Lighting, Inc.
BRINGING IMAGINATION TO LIGHT

FIGURE 6.7
A data sheet for an Altman Shakespeare ERS. (From Altman Lighting, Inc.)

750 WATT SHAKESPEARE Series ZOOM ELLIPSOIDAL

Catalog Numbers
S6-1535Z
S6-3055Z

Specifications

Housing: Die-cast aluminum construction.

Materials: Construction employs all corrosion-resistant materials and hardware.

Yoke: Rigid flat steel with dual locking dog tilt handles, two mounting positions, indexed pivot angle markings.

Reflector: Spring mounted dichroic coated glass, elliptical design, provided with heat shield.

Lenses: Color coded crown glass (white plate) lenses provided with anti-reflective coating.

Lens Barrel: Die-cast aluminum construction, color coded and marked, rotates 180° with shutter assembly.

Socket: Altman G9.5 medium two-pin, axially mounted, supplied with heat shield. Tool free relamping.

Rating: 120/240 volts AC/DC operation, 6.3/3.1 amps, 750 watts maximum.

Cable: 36" Teflon leads encased in black fiberglass sleeving, rear cord wrap provided. Hi-Temp rubber cable optional, up to 25'.

Shutters: Four provided, .037" stainless steel, fully adjustable and removable. Constructed with oversized Valox heat resistant handles.

Shutter Assembly: Spring pressured, 180° indexed rotation on Teflon glides, provided with locking knob.

Access Door: Removable, allowing access to lens.

Focusing Lamp: Fully adjustable in three axis with two concentric Ultem 2100 heat resistant knobs.

Focusing Fixture: Zoom lens movement contained within body. Lens carriers travel on Teflon glide bearings along stainless steel guide rails, each lens carrier provided with heat resistant lock knob. Ring shaped rear mounted aiming handle provided, constructed of Ultem 2100.

Accessories: Accessory slot provided with cover, rotates 180° with shutter assembly, accepts drop-in iris and rotating gobo accessories. Removable Lexan front end accessory holder equipped with two slots and accepts standard 7 ½" accessories. Accessory holder retaining latch is self-closing and self-locking for safety.

Finish: Black epoxy sandtex, electrostatic application.

Weight: Approx; 22 lbs. (9.9 kg.) for S6-1535Z.
Approx; 21 lbs. (9.5 kg.) for S6-3055Z.

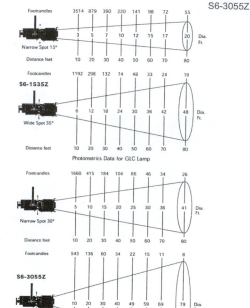

Photometrics Data for GLC Lamp

Photometrics Data for GLC Lamp

ACCESSORIES	
Supplied with Luminaire	
510-HD	Heavy-Duty Malleable Iron Pipe Clamp
6-CF	Color Frame, 7 ½" x 7 ½"
SC	Safety Cable with Spring Clip

ADDITIONAL ACCESSORIES	
6-CFB	Black Color Frame, 7 ½" x 7 ½"
360-PH	Pattern Holder with Channels, 2 ¾" diameter opening, 3 ⅜" wide
1KL6-PH	Pattern Holder with Slots, 2 ¾" diameter opening, 3 ⅜" wide
S6-GPH	Pattern Holder for Glass Patterns
6-SN	Snoot
404.6	Motorized Color Wheel
6-DN	Donut, 7 ½" x 7 ½" w/3" diameter opening
SDii	Drop-in iris

LAMP DATA

Watts	Volts	ANSI Code	Manufacturer Lamp Code	Color Temp (°K)	Rated Life (Hours)	Rated Lumens	Correction Factor
400	115	—	HX400	3200°	300	10,000	.69
400	115	—	HX401	3050°	1500	8,500	.59
575	115	—	HX604	3250°	400	15,500	1.14
575	115	—	HX605	3100°	1500	13,500	.88
600	230	GKV	HX600/HV230	3200°	400	14,500	1.00
575	115	GLC	HP600/6989P	3200°	400	15,500	—
575	115	GLA	HP600/6992P	3100°	1500	13,500	—
750	115	—	HX754	3200°	300	21,500	—
750	115	—	HX755	3050°	1500	18,250	—

SHAKESPEARE PERFORMANCE CHART WITH GLC LAMP

Fixture Type	Candlepower (Candela)	Beam Angle (Degrees)	Field Angle (Degrees)	Efficiency (%)
Narrow Spot				
S6-1535Z	351,000	9°	15°	48
S6-3055Z	166,000	13°	30°	60
Wide Spot				
S6-1535Z	119,000	15°	35°	65
S6-3055Z	55,000	15°	55°	65

BRINGING IMAGINATION TO LIGHT

57 Alexander Street, Yonkers, NY 10701 Tel: 914.476.7987, 212.569.7777, Fax: 914.963.7304, Toll free: 800.4.ALTMAN or Visit our website at http://www.altmanltg.com © 2003 Altman Stage Lighting Company, Inc. Altman Lighting, Inc. is a subsidiary of Altman Stage Lighting Company, Inc.

120302

FIGURE 6.7
(continued)

profiles. They also contain lots of advertising for equipment that may be useful in the future.

As an example, imagine a situation in which a small academic theatre department is considering purchasing two automated spotlights. To decide what specific luminaire would be appropriate, the following questions should be asked:

- What pan and tilt range is needed to cover the whole stage space?
- How wide (or narrow) should the maximum and minimum beam spreads be for the throw distance?
- Would an incandescent source or an HID source be more appropriate given the potential uses of the fixtures?
- How can the lights be controlled? Can the extant control system control them or will a separate console be required?
- Does the fixture have all of the features required in terms of iris capability and diffusion, as well as gobo and color wheels?

The answers to all of these questions can be found on a manufacturer's data sheet for a moving light, as shown in Figure 6.8.

When a lighting designer is using a new type of equipment for the very first time, it is a good idea to actually do a mock-up with the real thing. This is a type of technical research that can be critical to the success of a special effect. For example, can a specific atmospheric haze effect be achieved in a theatre with a ventilation system over which the stage manager has no control? Only an on-site test, in simulated show conditions can answer that question. Preproduction testing can save both time and money on a tight technical rehearsal schedule.

Even color choices can be mocked up, either in a lighting lab or simply over the designer's drawing table using one or more incandescent light sources. Color specifications will eventually be made using specific numbers from sample books, but early mockups of color compositions can save time, trouble, and money later in the process.

With some visual research in hand, and after much discussion with the director and other designers, the lighting designer can start to develop what the lighting will actually look like. However, the research process can continue throughout the design development phase. Technical research may continue well into the technical rehearsal process. One should keep an open mind to incorporate new images and new visual ideas throughout the entire process.

SPECIFICATIONS
MAC 2000 PERFORMANCE II

GOBOS

Outside diameter: . . . . 37.5 +0/-0.3 mm (1.48 +0/-0.01 in.)
Image diameter: . . . . 30 mm (1.18 in.)
Thickness: . . . . .1.1 mm in static slots, up to 7 mm in rotating slots
Material: . . . . high-temperature Borofloat or better glass
Coating: . . . . dichroic or enhanced aluminum

GOBO ANIMATION WHEELS

Outside diameter: . . . . .133 mm +0/-0.25 mm)
Image outer diameter: . . . . .130 mm (5.12 in)
Image inner diameter: . . . . .16 mm (0.63 in)
Thickness: . . . . 0.5 mm (0.02 in)
Construction: . . . . .Aluminium

CONTROL AND PROGRAMMING

Protocol: . . . . USITT DMX-512
Control channels: . . . . 28 or 31
Receiver: . . . . Opto-isolated RS-485
Data I/O: . . . . .locking 3-pin & 5-pin XLR, pin 1 shield, pin 2 cold (-), pin 3 hot (+)
Setting and addressing: . . . . LED control panel, remote w/ MP-2 uploader
Pan/tilt resolution: . . . . .8- or 16-bit
Gobo indexing: . . . . .8- or 16-bit
Movement control: . . . . tracking and vector
Software installation: . . . . serial upload (MUF)

ELECTROMECHANICAL EFFECTS

Cyan: . . . . 0 - 100%
Magenta: . . . . 0 - 100%
Yellow: . . . . 0 - 100%
Color correction: . . . . 0 - 178 mireds
Gobo animation wheel: . . . . Animation effects at any angle
Gobo wheel: . . . . 5 rotating and indexable slots
Four-blade framing system: . . . . Blade tilting +/- 31°, frame rotation +/- 45°
Effect wheel: . . . . .wide-angle converter lens, non-rotating 9-facet prism, variable frost
Iris: . . . . .motorized
Dimmer/shutter: . . . . .full range dimming and variable speed flash
Focus: . . . . .2 m (6.5 ft.) - infinity
Zoom: . . . . .10° - 28°
Pan: . . . . 540°
Tilt: . . . . 267°

DESIGN STANDARDS

EU EMC: . . . . EN 50 081-1, EN 50 082-1
EU safety: . . . . EN 60598-1, EN 60598-2-17
Canadian safety: . . . . .CSA C22.2 No. 166
US safety: . . . . ANSI/UL 1573

CONSTRUCTION

Housing: . . . . UV-resistant fiber-reinforced composite
Colors: . . . . black
Protection factor: . . . . .IP 20

FIGURE 6.8
Performance data
for Martin's MAC
2000 Performance
automated
luminaire. (From
Martin.)

KEY TERMS

BEAM SPREAD	GOBO
CHROMATICITY	PAN
COLOR WHEEL	PHOTOMETRICS
CUT SHEET	RESEARCH
DATA SHEET	THROW DISTANCE
DRAMATURG	TILT

NOTE

1. Cynthia White, director's notes for *A Streetcar Named Desire,* Utah Shakespearean Festival, 1993.

7

DESIGN
DEVELOPMENT

THE preceding chapters explained and detailed the medium of light and discussed methodologies for developing ideas about a performance work. At this point in the process, one starts to consider how the first, the medium of light, will be applied in service to the second—ideas about the piece. One can now start to develop more specifically what the lighting environment will actually look like—what it will *be*. Consideration should be given not only to what individual moments of a piece look like but also to how the lighting flows overall and how it functions to serve the broader conceptual ideas driving the production. Following is a discussion of means for thinking of the design implementation as a whole, communicating the look of the lighting to the director and other designers, and developing the design for eventual translation into a lighting plot and subsequently realized design.

THE FUNCTION, GESTURE, AND FLOW OF THE LIGHTING

To begin to develop specific compositional choices about the lighting, the designer needs to answer a critical question: How does the light function for this specific production and how will that function be implemented? The functions of light discussed earlier—visibility, environment, image, atmosphere or mood, three-dimensional form, three-dimensional space, visual focus, and style—all play a part in any design, but in varying proportions. The key is to link the functions of light to the production ideas.

For example, in designing *The Gin Game* pictured in Figure 7.1, light was used to help create the realistic environment of the retirement home so that the situation of the play was believable and to subliminally focus attention on the two characters. However, the goal of the concept overall was to present the relationship between the characters in a neutral way, not to favor one character over the other in their many arguments. Another goal was to enable the audience to see the home not as some over-bearing oppressive place, but as a place that one could be comfortable in if one chose to be.

These ideas could then be manifested in the lighting "gesture" or overall thrust of the lighting. To express the environment, realistic angles of light were employed, including a significant amount of textured light to simulate light through trees. To subtly focus attention on the characters, specific control of individual lights was necessary. And finally, a neutral color palette, neither too chillingly cool nor too invitingly warm was used to express the neutrality of the environment.

FIGURE 7.1
The lighting design for *The Gin Game* was meant to appear realistic, as well as to subtly focus the audience's attention. Directed by Ira Cirker; set design by Vicki Smith; lighting design by the author.

Bob Barrett photo

In designing an abstract contemporary dance piece such as that pictured in Figure 7.2, the primary thrust of the lighting (the "gesture") is to reinforce the spatial and musical rhythms of the piece while defining three-dimensional form and space.

The light within the three-dimensional space of the stage can create a sense of confinement or escape, relaxation or tension, and so on, all of which can change over time to express the conceptual ideas of the production. This overall evolution or "flow" of the lighting is another way that the gesture of the lighting can be expressed. In the color plates of *The Physicist* (Color Plates 2, 3, and 4) the changing light sources themselves are an expression of the increasingly institutional look of the lighting.

The overall gesture of the lighting can be developed using two-dimensional or three-dimensional means but the flow of the lighting can be discovered and communicated to the director and the rest of the design team through the creation of storyboards. Storyboards visually track the evolution of light over the course of the play. They may be used to figure out how the light might function for a piece, develop ideas for what the play may look like, and communicate those ideas to others.

One of the most useful types of storyboards for achieving all of these goals is the research storyboard. In a research storyboard, the lighting designer collects images—photographs, paintings, and so on—that express the lighting idea for each scene. The images are then presented in order so that the overall flow of the lighting can be seen and assessed. Sometimes, the lighting flow is

James Seawright

FIGURE 7.2
Brightly lighted vertical elements frame individual dancers and create visual rhythm.

not pre-determined, but rather discovered in examining the research story-board.

Another discovery type of storyboard is more abstract, but very useful for the lighting designer. In an abstract storyboard, the designer sketches an impression of each scene, in a color or value study. The designer can use this type of storyboard to find patterns of light and dark, color, or shape that exist in the piece. This type of abstract storyboard (Figure 7.3 is an example) may be of more use to the designer in her or his own design process than to communicate with others, yet can also be a good exercise in visualization.

The designer might find it useful to graphically chart individual properties of light across a play to help ascertain how those properties may be used. The designer may find such a chart useful for evaluating the way certain properties of light evolve over the course of a piece in relation to others, as the example in Figure 7.4 indicates.

Lastly, one can actually produce thumbnail sketches of each scene and locale. This type of storyboard, pictured in Figure 7.5, synthesizes the other storyboard types and is particularly useful for communicating the flow of the lighting to the director and other designers. Because of the potential volume of sketches one may need to produce for a storyboard, the goal should be to *evoke* the lighting rather than to render it faithfully. The storyboards are *not* the design; rather, they are a step toward developing specific lighting choices. For storyboards that investigate only value (light/dark) progression, a soft drawing pencil on heavy bond paper can be an appropriate—and inexpensive— medium. Ink and wash, although harder to control than pencil, is a good wet medium for storyboards. A line drawing of the set can be photocopied multiple times to create a basis for the lighting sketches. If the space will be primarily dark, it might be more effective to use light media on black, dark gray, or navy paper, as in Figure 7.6. For storyboards that explore the color dimension, chalk pastels or colored pencils can be very effective.

RENDERINGS AND VISUALIZATION

An important step in the design process is to visualize what the stage will actually look like and, if feasible, share that visualization with the collaborative team. There are a number of methods for creating a stage visualization that can be used both to work out the graphical composition of the lighting and explain the lighting ideas to others. Traditional rendering may involve watercolor, gouache, pastels, or other media—even collage. Digital tools can be used to

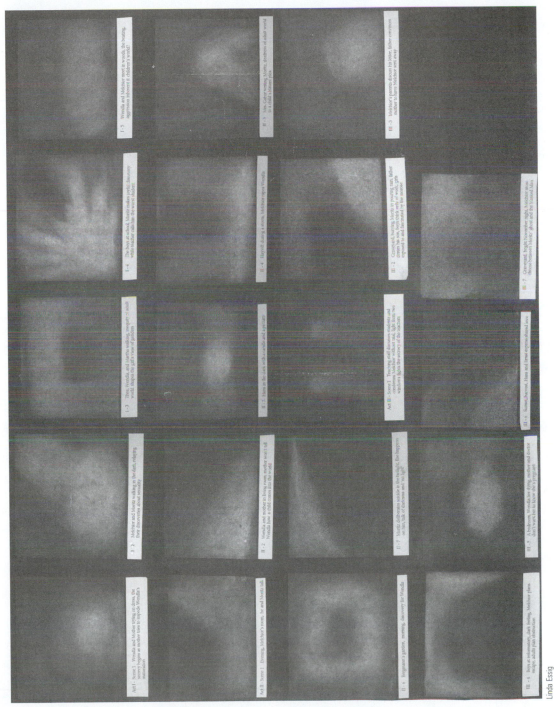

Linda Essig

FIGURE 7.3

In this abstract storyboard for Brecht's *Galileo*, the designer explores the shape of light in space.

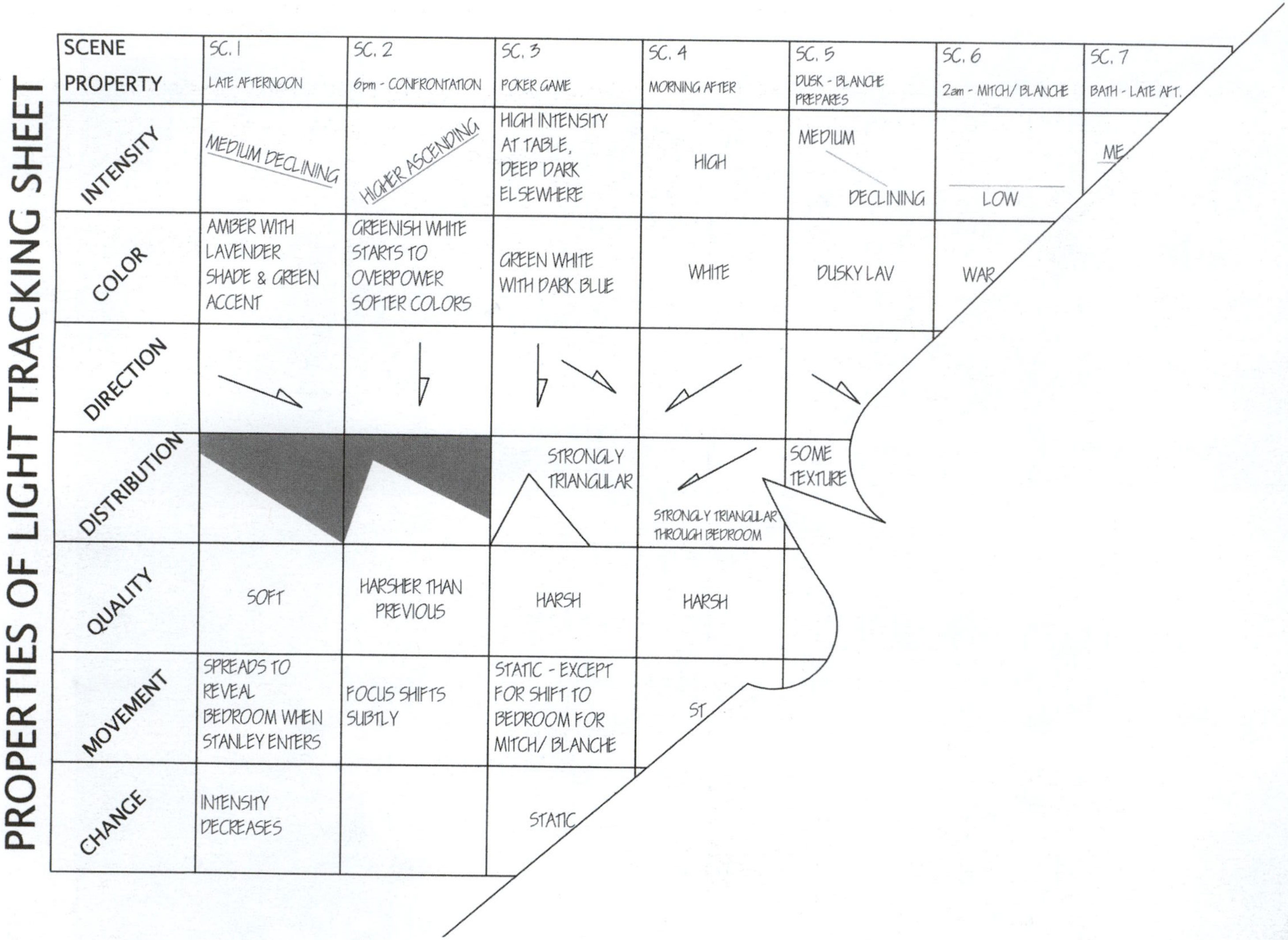

PROPERTIES OF LIGHT TRACKING SHEET

SCENE / PROPERTY	SC. 1 LATE AFTERNOON	SC. 2 6pm - CONFRONTATION	SC. 3 POKER GAME	SC. 4 MORNING AFTER	SC. 5 DUSK - BLANCHE PREPARES	SC. 6 2am - MITCH/ BLANCHE	SC. 7 BATH - LATE AFT
INTENSITY	MEDIUM DECLINING	HIGH ASCENDING	HIGH INTENSITY AT TABLE, DEEP DARK ELSEWHERE	HIGH	MEDIUM DECLINING	LOW	ME
COLOR	AMBER WITH LAVENDER SHADE & GREEN ACCENT	GREENISH WHITE STARTS TO OVERPOWER SOFTER COLORS	GREEN WHITE WITH DARK BLUE	WHITE	DUSKY LAV	WAR	
DIRECTION	*(arrow)*	*(arrow)*	*(arrow)*	*(arrow)*	*(arrow)*		
DISTRIBUTION			STRONGLY TRIANGULAR	STRONGLY TRIANGULAR THROUGH BEDROOM	SOME TEXTURE		
QUALITY	SOFT	HARSHER THAN PREVIOUS	HARSH	HARSH			
MOVEMENT	SPREADS TO REVEAL BEDROOM WHEN STANLEY ENTERS	FOCUS SHIFTS SUBTLY	STATIC - EXCEPT FOR SHIFT TO BEDROOM FOR MITCH/ BLANCHE	ST			
CHANGE	INTENSITY DECREASES		STATIC				

FIGURE 7.4

It is sometimes useful to track individual properties of light over the course of a piece, as in this chart for *A Streetcar Named Desire*.

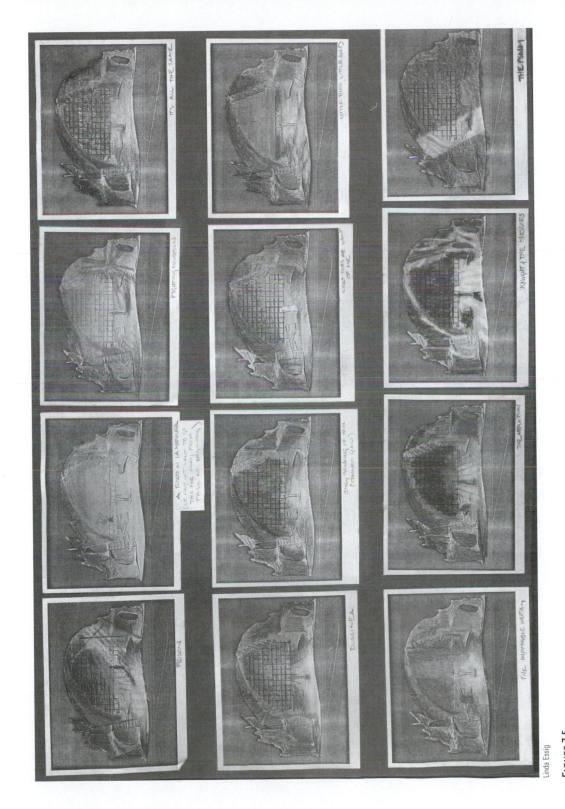

Linda Essig

FIGURE 7.5

A line drawing or photo of a set model can be copied numerous times to create the underlayment for thumbnail sketches such as these for *Man of La Mancha*.

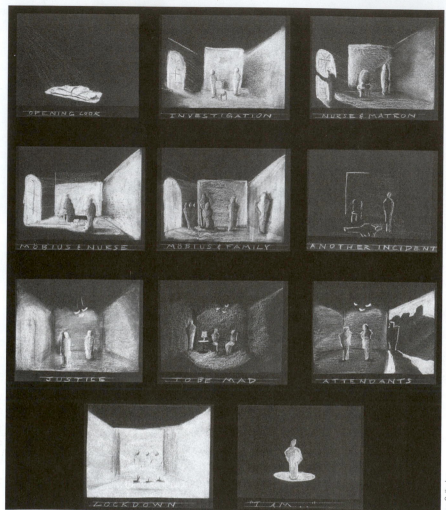

FIGURE 7.6
Lighting designer
Daniel Gallagher
used white media
on black board to
sketch his lighting
ideas for *The
Physicists*.

Dan Gallagher

"sketch" the stage in two dimensions or model the stage in three dimensions, and scale models of the set can be lighted to evoke the look that will be implemented on the full size set.

Set designers often sketch their sets as they envision the stage space under light. More frequently, the set designer works almost exclusively in model form, leaving the lighting designer more room for his or her own compositional creativity. The lighting designer can use the model, or even a photo of the model, as a basis for sketching the light. Unlike the thumbnail sketches one might produce for a storyboard, a full rendering is larger and more detailed. In the example in

Color Plate 9, one sees highlights, shade, and shadows indicating the direction of light. A sense of softness and humidity results from overlaying watercolor washes. Sketches such as this can be used as a stepping stone toward determining precise angles, colors, and qualities of light (see also Figure 7.12). Digital tools are very useful in the design development phase as well, as long as one remains mindful that digital techniques are part of the design process rather than the end product. Two-dimensional programs such as Painter or Adobe Photoshop are popular with set and costume designers. A very effective technique for lighting designers is to take a digital photograph of a set model, then manipulate it in Photoshop to communicate an impression of what the set would look like under light, as seen in Figure 7.7.

Three-dimensional rendering and modeling programs such as 3DS Max or Maya can be used to create photo-realistic renderings, and programs such as Lightscape or Radiance can be used to produce photo-accurate renderings. A photo-realistic rendering program uses algorithms that imitate the behavior of light but do so in a way that creates an impression of what the stage will look like. A photo-accurate rendering calculates the actual effect of light using both ray-tracing (direct light) and radiosity (indirect and reflected light) algorithms derived from the photometrics of the luminaires in a model and surface finishes of the setting.

Linda Essig

FIGURE 7.7
In this rendering for the same production of *The Physicists,* Photoshop was used to manipulate a photograph of the set model to show how a scene might be lighted. Set design by Jenny Nehls; sketch by the author.

In both types of renderings and models, each pictured in Figures 7.8 and 7.9, the lighting designer can relatively quickly alter the direction, color, or quality of light to show the director various lighting options and to assess those options for himself or herself. However, for presentation purposes, as these two renderings show, the photo-accurate rendering appears more "luminous," more light-filled. Because 3DS Max has become fairly popular for modeling with set and lighting designers, especially in academic theatres, that particular program has adopted much theatre "lingo" and even includes gobo catalogs in its image libraries. Thus the lighting designer can evaluate various options for using texture or other projected effects.

Two words of caution, one practical and one more philosophical, regarding computer visualization: If one needs only to produce a rendering or two, it is likely that sketching by hand using traditional media will take significantly less time than it takes to build a computer model, light it, and render it. It is also easy to get caught up in the virtual world of the computer model at the expense of time spent in analyzing the material and visiting rehearsal where the live performers are speaking, singing, and/or dancing. What makes live performance so exciting and interesting is its very live-ness. If one finds that one is enjoying the time spent in creating virtual images more than the time spent creating the images in the theatre, one should consider the more lucrative fields of computer rendering or animation.

FIGURE 7.8
The 3DS Max program was used to create a photo-realistic rendering of Bob Schmidt's set for *Twelve Angry Men*. Rendering by Andrea Bilkey. (Used with permission of Andrea Bilkey.)

Andrea Bilkey

Maggie Bailey

FIGURE 7.9
Lightscape software
was used to create
a photo-accurate
rendering of Bob
Schmidt's set for
Twelve Angry Men.
Rendering by
Maggie Bailey.

One last way of visualizing the lighting design is simultaneously traditional and avant-garde. Rather than lighting a virtual model of the set, the lighting designer can light the actual scale model of the set to explain how light may affect the stage space. Traditionally, this has been done with a few small focusable lights. Recently, designers in both Florida and Boston have developed systems that use fiber-optic emitters with optical accessories that provide the same beam spreads and qualities, albeit in a miniaturized scale, as the actual stage lights. With these systems, such as that used to light the model depicted in Figure 7.10, the design team can predict fairly well what the set will look like under light—however, what the actors will actually look like moving through the space still needs to be addressed in the theatre. A similar system, called Studio 4:1, is used in Europe. This system actually builds a 1-to-4-scale model of the set (much larger than the 1-to-24 scale usually used in America) and lights the set in a studio, complete with control console.

SCHEMATIC DIAGRAMS

Developing a point of view, synthesizing research materials, and visualizing the lighting lead the designer to make clear and specific choices about what the lighting looks like. Eventually, those ideas need to be translated into the actual lighting plans so that the design ideas can be implemented in the theatre. The step that bridges between the ideas and the plot is the development of schematic

The Nuckols Fund for Lighting Education/for full credit, see page 273.

FIGURE 7.10
Lighting designer Stan Kaye uses a fiber optic system to light a scale model of a set to communicate his lighting ideas to the director and set designer.

diagrams of the lighting compositions. Specific angles and colors of light, as they appear in plan (top), section (side), and elevation (front) views, can be worked out diagrammatically, and, from there, exact placement of lights in the theatre can be determined (see Chapter 9 on lighting positions). Some designers may call these diagrams "magic sheets," "effects charts," or even "color keys." A color key, it is worth noting, is used only when there is uniform lighting across the stage and so can be both limited and limiting in its use.

In Chapter 4, a real room was translated into a simple series of line drawings indicating direction and compositional function of light in that room. A similar process can be used to turn the lighting designer's sketches, renderings, or storyboards into the schematic diagram form. Figure 7.11 shows how various angles of light may be shown in the schematic diagrams.

The rendering of *Streetcar* in Color Plate 9 can be translated into the schematic format by examining what purposes of light one observes in the rendering and articulating them graphically on the schematic diagram:

- ▶ Steamy warm afternoon light through the jalousied windows
- ▶ Soft lavender skylight
- ▶ Darker purple tonality
- ▶ Green highlight
- ▶ Light through portieres
- ▶ Recessive textured break-up in the unused bedroom

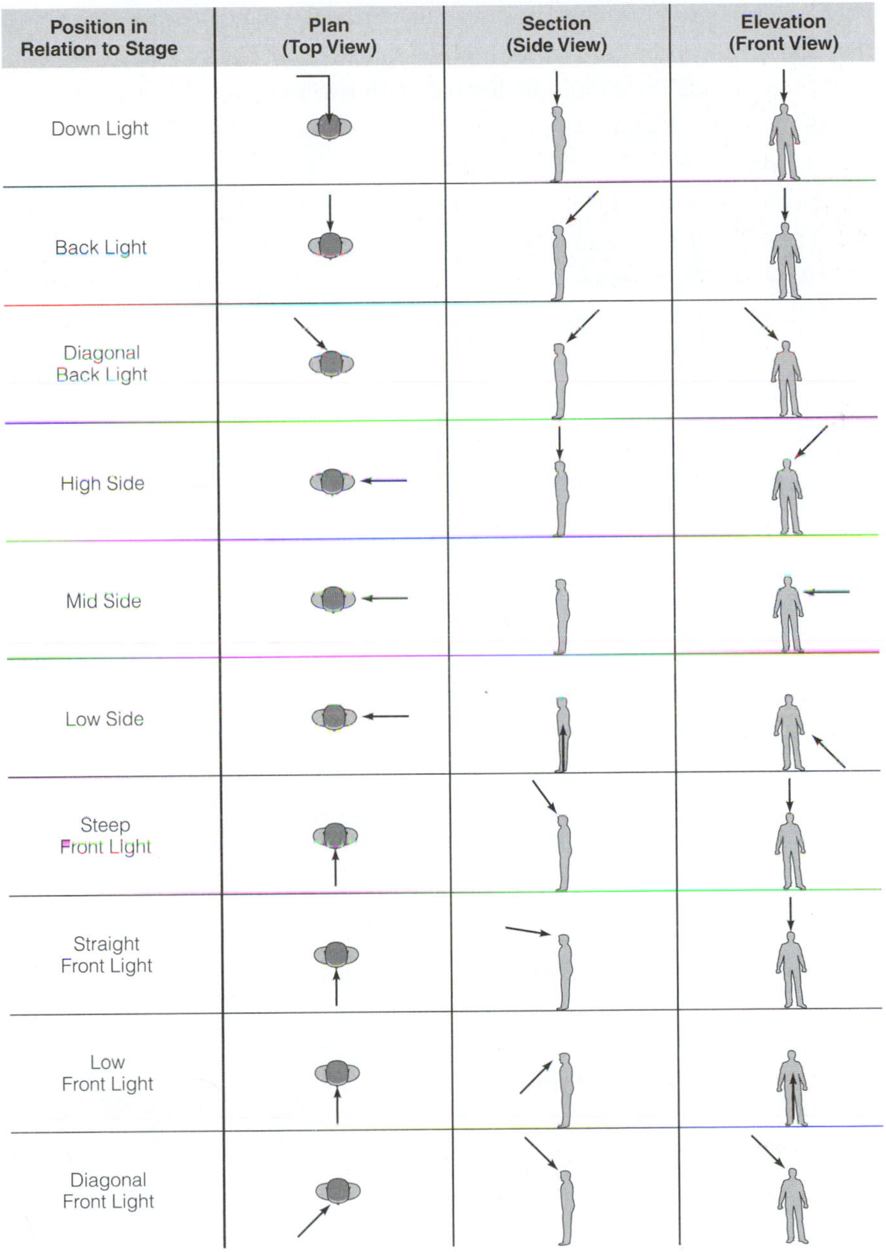

Position in Relation to Stage	Plan (Top View)	Section (Side View)	Elevation (Front View)
Down Light			
Back Light			
Diagonal Back Light			
High Side			
Mid Side			
Low Side			
Steep Front Light			
Straight Front Light			
Low Front Light			
Diagonal Front Light			

FIGURE 7.11
This "key" can be used to indicate light from various directions on the schematic diagrams. Note that light should have a compositional purpose as well as direction noted on the schematic diagrams.

A reduced, but still scaled ground plan, section, and elevation of the set (designed by Thomas Umfrid) is used to generate the schematic diagrams. Because schematic diagrams are used not only to work out what the specific angles of light are and how the lighting positions may need to relate physically to the set, they should always be done in all three views, as seen in Figure 7.12.

This scene is fairly specifically lighted, with two motivating sources and the architecture of the set dictating some of the potential angles of light. For other productions, and for repertory situations or for dance, one might need to design a composition that is more general in nature that can be infinitely adaptable throughout the event. Figure 7.13 is a schematic diagram for a dance repertory plot. It indicates the use of multiple angles of light that can be utilized singly, in pairs, or groups to design individual moments in the dances.

The translation of the pictorial image, whether sketched by the designer or expressed using research images, collage, or even words, into the schematic dia-

FIGURE 7.12
This schematic diagram for the first scene of *A Streetcar Named Desire* is beginning to turn the lighting ideas expressed in the sketch into the lighting plot.

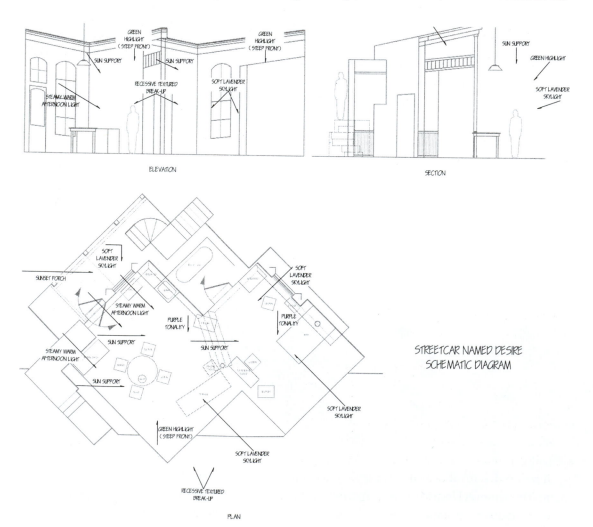

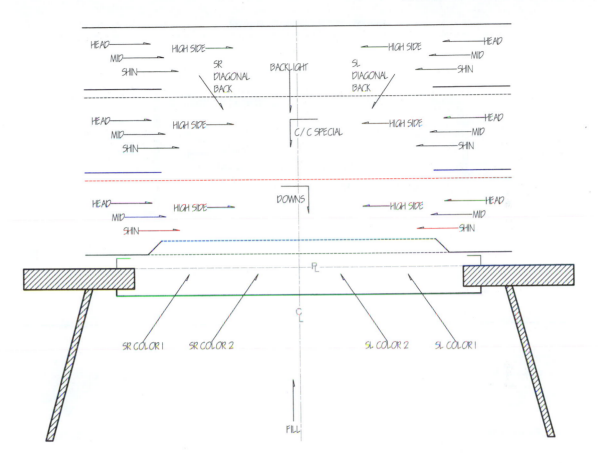

grams is a seminal step in the design process. It is the beginning of turning *what it looks like* into *how to make it look that way.*

In lighting a play that is dependent on the reality-based functions outlined in Chapter 4, one uses the schematic diagrams to work out from where the main motivating source of light is emanating. Then, one must decide how, compositionally, all of the other functions of light relate to that motivating source (or sources) and the scenery. The main source of light may, for example, be coming directly from stage right at a fairly high angle, as in *Twelve Angry Men* (plan →, section ↓, elevation ↘) but how will the supporting light, reflected light, and any other subsequent compositional functions of light relate to that main source?

Reflected light, for example, may enter the stage space at an angle directly opposite the main source or at some angle diagonal to it. The former implies a rigidity to the environment that may (as in this case) or may not be present in the design of the set. The choice of angle, as illustrated in Figure 7.14, should be made based on the designer's point of view—that is, is rigidity the appropriate

FIGURE 7.13
In developing a repertory lighting plot, especially for dance, maximum flexibility of lighting angle is usually desirable.

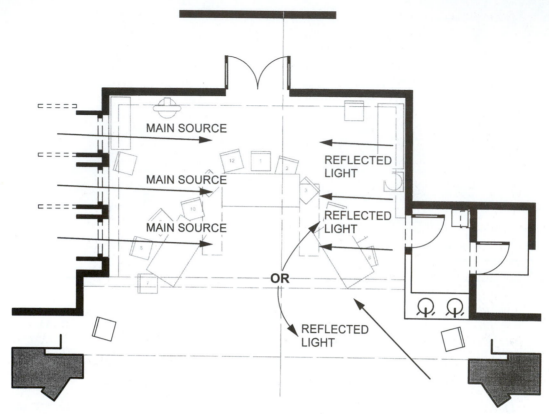

FIGURE 7.14
As this partial schematic diagram indicates, the lighting designer must make choices about the angle of reflected light based on the production's point of view.

design choice for this specific production? The "reflected light" may be at a high angle, causing higher contrast and more shadowing of facial features, or a lower angle, filling in more completely the shadows cast by the main source of light. This light may be from any one of a number of different luminaires providing differing color and distribution of light. One can ask the critical question of every lighting idea one considers putting on to the schematic diagrams: Given the point of view toward the piece and the style of production, which angle, color, and quality of light will produce the appropriate modeling of facial features, human form, and stage space?

In designing a composition based less in reality, the designer should decide what the structure of the design is going to be. In other words, the lighting designer must come back to that all-important question of "how will the light function for this production and what will it look like?" For example, a lighting composition may be based on circles or spheres of light if the visual inspiration for the piece is the work of painter Aaron Douglas (Figure 7.15). Or if the set is based on ideas of translucency and transparency, as in Figure 7.16, how will the lighting help to support those visual ideas?

FIGURE 7.15
The lighting designer may create compositions based on the circular shapes of this Aaron Douglas painting.

FIGURE 7.16
The lighting and set designs must work together to implement the ideas of translucency and transparency found in this composite image of New Orleans interiors.

Throughout the history of modern stage lighting, a number of methods that are based primarily on formulae and technique have been espoused for providing adequate illumination on the stage. The design development process advocated here—taking conceptual ideas, turning them into pictorial representations and from there into schematic diagrams—is a more open construct, providing a structured process for developing visual choices for all types of live performance.

KEY TERMS

COLOR KEY	RENDERING
ELEVATION VIEW	SCALE MODEL
MAGIC SHEETS	SECTION VIEW
PLAN VIEW	STORYBOARD
RADIOSITY	THUMBNAIL SKETCHES
RAY-TRACING	

8
COLOR

IN developing the lighting compositions schematically, the lighting designer makes some preliminary color choices. Research materials, personal intuition, collaboration with the set and costume designers, one's own sketches, or some combination thereof inspire those choices. For example, amber sunset light, lavender skylight, or purple tonality were used in the schematic diagrams found in the preceding chapter. These color names are not actual color specifications, however. There are many amber, lavender, or purple color filters available for the designer's use from multiple color media manufacturers. How, then, can a precise color specification be made that will achieve the desired result in performance?

Research, sketches, and intuition (and a little talent and experience), when combined with an understanding of vision, the color properties of light, and their associative characteristics, provide the tools and vocabulary necessary to answer that question. The way a color appears on the stage is not only the result of choosing the appropriate color from a sample book; it is also a matter of relating that color to the other colors in the total visual picture. Therefore, it is important to understand the *relative* nature of color, how the relationship between different colors and values can create compositional focus, establish a sense of environment, and support the overall conceptual framework.

THE PHYSICAL PROPERTIES OF COLOR IN LIGHT

Light behaves in a way that can be explained by both particle theory (photons) and wave theory. For the explanation and study of color, the wave model of light is more useful. As noted in Chapter 2, light is "visually evaluated radiant energy." As such, light is part of the electromagnetic spectrum that includes gamma rays at one extreme and induction heating at the other. As Color Plate 10 indicates, the visible part of this spectrum is just that small part of the electromagnetic spectrum that the psycho-physiological system of eye and brain can detect and interpret. All of this electromagnetic energy, be it in the form of radio waves or cosmic rays, travels in waves of distinct length, amplitude, and frequency. The spectrum of visible light is that part of the electromagnetic spectrum whose wavelengths measure from approximately 380–700 nanometers of wavelength. A nanometer is 10^{-9} meters in length and so can only be measured with specialized instruments.

Refraction occurs when light passes from a medium of one density through a medium of a different density. A prism refracts light in a unique way that enables us to see the visible spectrum of light as each wavelength is "bent" by the prism at a slightly different angle. (See Color Plate 11.) The colors one sees when sunlight is refracted by a prism are the same as those seen in a rainbow: red, orange, yellow, green, blue, indigo, and violet. To produce a rainbow, water vapor in the air refracts and reflects sunlight, creating an arc of color.

Colored light is achieved on stage most commonly through filtration, rather than refraction. When a light source is passed through a color filter, only certain wavelengths are transmitted. Figure 8.1 shows the percent transmission of the wavelengths of the visible spectrum through a piece of "gel." The color filters are most commonly and inexpensively made from a deeply dyed heat-resistant polyester film. They are usually called "gels" because in the early days of color filtration, the filters were actually made from gelatin, but gelatin proved to be too delicate. Other filters may be tinted glass, or, as in most automated lights, dichroic glass. A dichroic filter makes use of the principles of refraction and selective reflection to allow much smaller ranges of wavelengths to be transmitted than is possible with the less costly gel media. Keep in mind that regardless of the material, filtration *subtracts* light so that there is less actual light emitted from a luminaire with a color filter than from a luminaire without.

Color Figure 1

In this photograph of a sunlit interior, note the two colors of light—the warmer direct sunlight emanating from the right side of the picture and the bluer ambient light most in the shade and shadows.

Color Figure 2

In this scene from *The Physicists*, incandescent lights are colored to create the impression of late afternoon light in the interior. Directed by Nicholas Tamarkin; set design by Jennifer Nehls; costume design by Karen Boyer; lighting design by Daniel W. Gallagher.

COLOR FIGURE 3
Later in *The Physicists*, the lighting designer uses exposed fluorescent tubes to wash the set walls with light. Note the color, linear distribution, and diffuse quality of this source.

COLOR FIGURE 4
By the end of this production of *The Physicists*, the stage is lighted by a single high intensity discharge (HID) source with its greenish hue and harsh quality.

COLOR FIGURE 5
Ultraviolet light from "black light" luminaires reacts with fluorescent paint and makeup, causing them to fluoresce in intense colors for special effect in the 2002 *Olympic Games* closing ceremony.

COLOR FIGURE 6
Painter Raphael employed cooler colors in the background than the foreground to create a sense of depth, technically known as "aerial perspective."

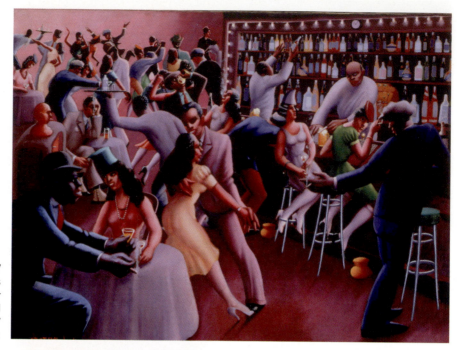

COLOR FIGURE 7
Archibald Motley's *Nightlife* inspired color choices for the second act of *Ain't Misbehavin'* pictured below.

COLOR FIGURE 8
Note the deep magenta tonality of the lighting, drawn from the Motley painting.

COLOR FIGURE 9
This lighting sketch for *A Streetcar Named Desire* was produced with watercolor, colored pencil, and chalk on top of a line drawing of Thomas Umfrid's set design.

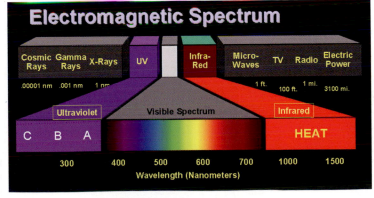

COLOR FIGURE 10
Visible light is one small part of the spectrum of electromagnetic energy.

COLOR FIGURE 11
When light is refracted by a prism, each discrete wavelength is bent at a slightly different angle, enabling individual colors to be distinguished.

COLOR FIGURE 12
The spectral distribution of an incandescent light source at three different color temperatures. Note the amount of long red wavelengths in relation to the shorter wavelengths at the blue end of the spectrum.

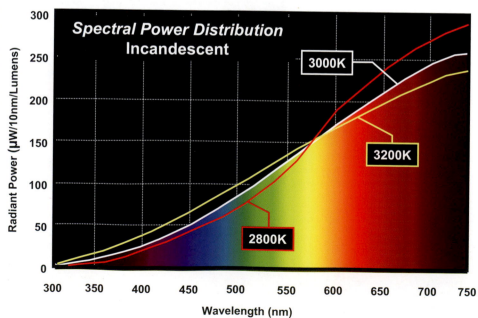

Spectral Power Distribution
Incandescent

3000K

3200K

2800K

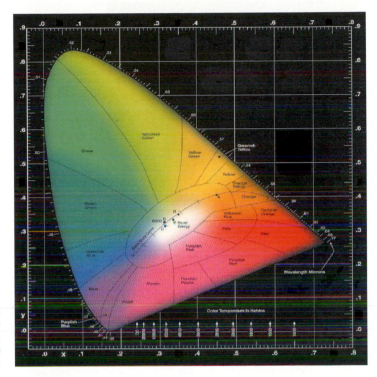

COLOR FIGURE 13
The CIE Chromaticity diagram plots all visible color on an *xyz* coordinate system.

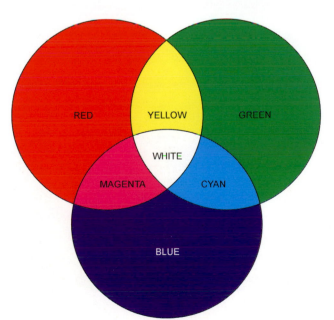

COLOR FIGURE 14
The three primary colors of light—red, blue, and green—can be additively mixed to create the three secondary colors—yellow, cyan, and magenta, as well as white light.

COLOR FIGURE 15

For the Mabou Mines production of *Flow My Tears the Policeman Said*, lighting designer Anne Militello used intense colors to create colored shadows and blue and yellow sources to create the white light seen on the stage left wall of the set. Directed by Bill Raymond; set and costume design by Linda Hartinian.

COLOR FIGURE 16

For *She Loves Me*, the author used a palette of pinks and lavenders to help support the period quality of the show. Directed by Jim Tucker; set design by Kenneth Kloth.

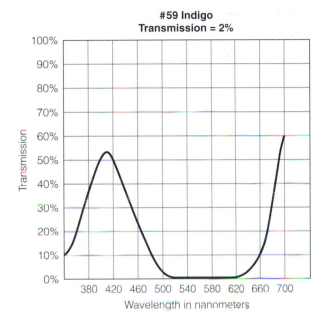

FIGURE 8.1
This chart shows the amount of each wavelength of light that is transmitted by Roscolux59 gel medium. Similar transmission charts are available for every color. (From Rosco Laboratories Limited, www. rosco-ca.com. Used with permission.)

In considering light color, one should also consider object color. Object color is the pigmentation of the performers, costumes, and scenery. Our perception of object color is analogous to our perception of object brightness in that it is a function of the wavelengths of light emitted and the ability of the object to reflect those wavelengths. For example, a red dress under unfiltered incandescent light appears red. It likewise appears red under an incandescent light with a red filter in front of it. However, under a luminaire with a green dichroic filter that transmits no red light, the dress looks black because there are no red wavelengths of light to be reflected back to our eyes.

COLORIMETRY: THE MEASUREMENT OF COLOR

There are a number of ways to actually quantify the color of a given light source. One such method of quantification is to examine the spectral distribution of a light source. As the term implies, spectral distribution is essentially the amount of radiant energy of each distinct wavelength of light across the visible spectrum emitted by a source or a luminaire. Different light sources have differing spectral power distributions and it is these differences that give sources their unique color qualities. Mixed sky and sunlight has a continuous spectrum of light, making it appear white. In light, white is made from the combination of all wavelengths, so daylight, with its continuous spectrum, is a very white source. Incandescent light sources are also continuous spectrum sources but, as Color Plate 12 shows, there is more spectral power in the red wavelengths than in the blue. Discharge sources such as fluorescent or HID sources do not emit a continuous spectrum of light. Instead, they emit many wavelengths that, when perceived together, give the appearance of white light, even if some wavelengths may be missing. Understanding the spectral distribution of the sources in theatrical luminaires is important when choosing gel media. For example, fluorescent sources emit very few wavelengths at the blue/violet end of the visible spectrum. A gel that appears deep blue when fluorescent light passes through it may look purple when incandescent light passes through it. Thus, one should examine gel samples using sources of the same type as the luminaires that will be used in the theatre. (One can see this effect by looking through Roscolux59 at fluorescent light and then incandescent light.)

Another means for quantifying color is with Kelvin color temperature. The Kelvin temperature scale uses Celsius degrees (the metric system measurement of temperature) but starts the temperature scale at absolute zero (−459°F). To assess color using the Kelvin scale, a standard "black body radiator" is heated to incandescence and its temperature measured. The black body radiator is actually tungsten so that the color of an incandescent lamp, which has a tungsten filament, will be the same as the standard black body radiator heated to a given temperature. At 1900 K, the color is amber like a candle flame, at 2750 K it is the color of a household lamp, and at 3200 K or 3250 K we have the color of most stage and studio incandescent lamps. The lower the color temperature, the more amber the light, and the higher the color temperature, the less amber (or more blue). Daylight has a color temperature of 4500 K to more than 10,000 K as seen in Figure 8.2.

Color temperature, therefore, is a measurement of the "warmness" or "coolness" of a given source. Warmness and coolness here, however, refer to the emotional connotations of the light color, rather than its physical properties because as color temperature rises, the color goes from amber through white to blue-white. When an incandescent lamp is taken down on dimmer, its physical temperature and therefore its color temperature decrease. An incandescent lamp becomes warmer, more red/amber until its filament has just a faint orange or red glow when dimmed. In order to achieve a cool white light, such as daylight at 5600 K with an incandescent lamp, one usually employs "color correction filters," so called because they filter out some of the red end of the spectrum, making the incandescent light appear closer to daylight in color and spectral distribution.

9500° K	Clear Blue Sky
7000° K	Overcast Sky
5500° K	Sun at Noon
4100° K	Cool White Deluxe Fluorescent
3200° K	Studio Incandescent
3000° K	Halogen
2700° K	100W Incandescent/Warm Fluorescent
2250° K	40W Incandescent
1800° K	High Pressure Sodium
1500° K	Candle Light

FIGURE 8.2
This graph shows the color temperature of various light sources from candlelight through clear blue sky. (From www.islandreef.com. Used with permission.)

Discharge sources, because they do not produce light through incandescence, are said to have a "correlated color temperature." That is, the color of a fluorescent or HID source is compared to the standard black body radiator at a given temperature. Some common fluorescent correlated color temperatures are 3200 K (warm white) and 4100 K (cool white). Remember, though, that the spectral distribution of the fluorescent light with a correlated color temperature of 3200 K is different than that of an incandescent light at 3200 K.

More and more, designers and other color specialists are using the CIE Chromaticity Diagram (see Color Plate 13) to describe color in light. This diagram is a representation of all visible colors of light, with the pure spectral colors located around the curved edge and the color produced by heating the standard black body radiator located along the black line labeled "black body locus." To understand this diagram, it is necessary to understand that the normally sighted human eye has three types of cones in the fovea, each particularly sensitive to a range of wavelengths, as shown in Figure 8.3.

The CIE (Commission Internationale d'Eclairage or International Commission on Lighting) first developed this diagram in 1931 and revised it more recently in 1976. The diagram acknowledges that the human eye has three different types of cones. The x-axis represents the relative sensitivity of the cones most attuned to red wavelengths, the y-axis represents the sensitivity of the cones most reactive to green wavelengths and the z-axis, which does not

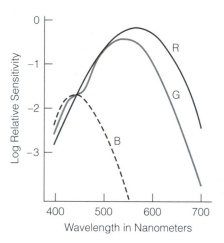

need to be pictured because $x + y + z$ always equals 1, represents the relative sensitivity of cones attuned to the blue wavelengths. In a normally sighted person, all visible color is "seen" to varying degrees by at least two of the three types of cones.

The diagram is a fabulous tool for predicting the effects of additive color mixing. If one draws a line between two points on the outside edge, then adding just those two wavelengths of light can produce all the colors along that line. One can also predict the limitations of the color response of film and video media because they cannot sense all of the wavelengths of light to the extent humans do. If the camera's extremes of red, blue, and green are plotted on the diagram, only those colors within the triangle formed by connecting those three points can be seen on that particular medium.

Another way of quantifying the color of light, and in this case light sources, is with the color rendering index (CRI). The color rendering index compares a test source to a standard source (incandescent or daylight) of the same color temperature to assess the ability of the test source to render pigment colors accurately. This color metric is used extensively by architectural lighting designers as a light source selection criterion, especially those working in retail applications where seeing merchandise color accurately is critical to a successful lighting design.

USING COLOR THEORY

Looking at the chromaticity diagram can explain why red, blue, and green are considered to be the primary colors of light. These three colors of light, when mixed in varying proportions from different sources produce the greatest number of other colors. When all three primaries are mixed together, white light results, as illustrated in Color Plate 14, showing the color wheel of light. The primary colors of red, blue, and green are on the outside, the secondary colors of yellow, cyan, and magenta are indicated where the primaries overlap, and white is found in the center. Because the secondary colors result from *adding* light, the secondary colors are lighter in value than the primaries. These color relationships are the reverse of those in pigment. In mixing pigment, one relies on *subtractive* mixing to achieve darker and darker colors. The subtractive primaries are therefore cyan, yellow, and magenta or, more commonly stated, blue, yellow, and red.

Theatrical gel media also operate through the principle of the subtraction or filtering of light. For purposes of explanation, let's assume we are using a white light source emitting only the spectral primaries of red, blue, and green. When passed through a red gel (as in Figure 8.4), only the red wavelengths of light are transmitted. The blue and green wavelengths are absorbed or dissipated as heat. If a piece of green gel is now placed in front of the now spectral red light, there is no transmission because there are no longer any green wavelengths to be transmitted.

If one were to try this with the polyester gels labeled "primary green" and "primary red" in a lab, one would see the imperfections of theatrical gel. The green gel actually does transmit a small amount of red light. This can be predicted in advance by looking at the transmission chart for the gel, although it is best to evaluate color options with one's own eyes.

Often in theatre, opera, and dance one uses tints or tones rather than the pure hues of the primary and secondary colors. A tint is a color plus white. If we were to use the theoretical RGB light source discussed earlier and pass it

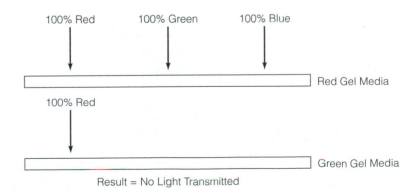

FIGURE 8.4 Theatrical gel media operates through filtration, selectively transmitting only some wavelengths of the visible spectrum.

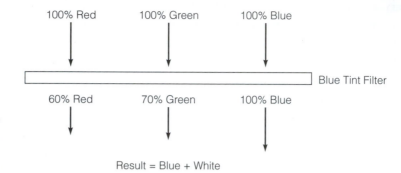

FIGURE 8.5
When light passes through a tint of color, some amount of all wavelengths is transmitted.

through a pale blue tint such as Roscolux61 or GAM820, all of the blue light would be transmitted because the hue of the filter is blue. Much of the green and red would be transmitted as well because if white light is to be transmitted (as it is when using a tint) then some of all wavelengths must be transmitted, as illustrated by Figure 8.5.

Tones are also often used in gel media. Tones are a color made grayer by the inclusion of its complement. How is it possible to have gray light? On the color wheel of light in Color Plate 14, one finds complementary colors opposite one another. By subtractively mixing complementary colors—a pale blue and a pale yellow gel in front of the same light for example—one can produce a grayish light, as illustrated in Figure 8.6. Many gels are actually tones to begin with. Some good examples of tones are Roscolux17, a tone of amber or Roscolux38, a tone of magenta.

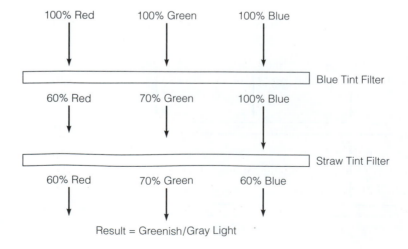

FIGURE 8.6
By subtractively mixing complementary tints, grayish light—a tone—is transmitted.

When colored light is additively mixed from two sources, a third color, or, if complementary colors are used, white light is produced. Because the colors are coming from two different sources and therefore slightly different locations, the shadows cast by the individual lights take on the strong coloration of the other light. This effect can be clearly seen in Anne Militello's design for *Flow My Tears the Policeman Said*, depicted in Color Plate 15. Note the shadows of the lampshade on the stage left wall. There are blue and yellow lights coming from stage right producing white light on the opposite wall, except in the area where the lampshade casts its shadow. Here the blue and yellow are quite clearly visible.

More often, designers additively mix tints of colors, or additively mix deeper colors only on a backdrop where there are no three-dimensional objects to cast tell-tale shadows. For example, a designer may specify a bright medium blue, an amber, and a dark warm blue to light a sky drop. By additively mixing the medium blue and amber at full intensity, a bluish-white can be achieved; by additively mixing the deep blue with the amber at a low level, magentas or purples may be produced. Yet, when a bright medium blue is needed, the designer has that pure color at the ready.

COLOR COMPOSITION

In finally deciding on specific colors, the lighting designer considers a number of factors. These include the hue of the color—the color name; the chromaticity of the color—how close to a pure hue the color is; and its value—how much white light (in the case of tints) will be allowed to pass through or how much will be blocked (in the case of shades). For example, compare Lee213 ("white flame green"), Roscolux88 ("light green"), and Lee124 ("dark green"). All of these gels are of similar hue, although Lee213 has more blue than the others, therefore it is cooler, and the three are listed in ascending order of chromaticity. Each of these colors has a different value as well, with the Lee213 being the palest. One can compare colors of differing chromaticity but the same value by looking at Lee158 ("deep orange") and Lee134 ("golden amber"). The Lee134 has significantly more gray in it and so is considered a tone.

Warmness and coolness, value, chromaticity, and comparative effects combine to establish the overall color composition. Certain colors have a tendency to dominate in a composition while others have a tendency to recede. The light that is the highest in value (brightest, with the palest color) often appears to be the main source of light in a composition. Hue, however, effects this impression as well. Warm colors tend to dominate over cooler colors, causing the warmer color to appear to be the main source of light in a composition, just as sunlight is warmer and brighter than light from the sky. The exception to this is within the blue family where blues with a green component (cool blues) tend to dominate over blues with more of a red component (warm blues). The lavender color family is the most recessive of all, the hardest color for our eyes to see. As one might expect, colors that are tones tend to recede when compared with colors of higher chromaticity.

Painters use these dominant/recessive qualities to evoke the aerial perspective discussed previously. Just as a painter can make the background of a painting recede by using lavenders and warm blues, so too can a lighting designer. A lighting designer can also use these recessive and dominant color characteristics for atmospheric effect. For example, a misty impression can be created on a translucent backdrop by lighting it from behind with a more dominant color and then interrupting that transmission with a recessive color on the front, creating a sense of heavy atmosphere. Placing a transparent gray scrim in front of the translucent drop and lighting the front of that with an even more recessive color, creating more and more layers of "air," can enhance this effect even further. An overall dusky impression can be achieved by using recessive lavender colors on the figures downstage, as well.

In addition to creating a sense of depth and atmosphere, dominant/recessive color relationships help to establish visual focus in the overall stage composition. An object or performer in warm light tends to draw the audience's attention more than an object or actor lighted with a more recessive color, much in the same way that a more brightly lighted performer does.

One can use color to create specific conceptual and/or physical environments, as well as to achieve graphic effect. For example, the color of walls can be implied even when no walls exist by orchestrating the color of "reflected light" and/or "fill light" in the composition.

Color and color relationships can support the conceptual framework within which the design is created through reinforcement of production style. References to daylight and its color are anchored in the human subconscious. Using colors close to daylight white and building the composition around "real" colors of light establishes a high level of reality, as does using gel colors that render human skin "normally." How far the design diverges from what we see every day in the real environment establishes differing levels of reality for the audience.

In addition to the associations the audience brings in regarding natural light sources, there are colors and color palettes that can be used to make reference to theatrical genres or styles of visual art. Both the colors and lighting positions common to the gaslight era may be used within the context of a specific production for a play written in the 1880s, for example. Many American musicals written in the 1950s and 1960s were originally lighted with shades of pink and lavender that are still available today. If the intention is to exploit the "period" quality of these shows, then it is appropriate to use these colors today, as in Color Plate 16, much as a set designer uses period furnishings. Even no-color can have this type of stylistic significance. The original productions of Bertolt Brecht's plays employed exposed un-gelled lighting instruments. This mode of presentation has been popular in re-creating his works. Although he was originally able to produce an alienating effect with this type of design, it would no longer have quite the same impact (see Figure 8.7). To produce that level of alienation today would take more than just a few exposed spotlights. With all three of these examples, the color choices of specific genres should be considered as one of the many factors that go into making design decisions.

Although color responses differ greatly across cultures, some colors do have a tendency to elicit emotional responses from the audiences—to draw out a "mood" that can enhance the dramatic impact of the moment on stage. Red, for example, is a color often associated with anger (or other passions), blue

FIGURE 8.7
For the Berliner Ensemble's production of Brecht's *Caucasian Chalk Circle,* under his own direction, white light and stage scenery made from real materials such as wood and raw canvas were used. Set design by Karl von Appen.

with romanticism, green, which is the complement of the pink undertone in much Caucasian skin, can be used to create a sense of sickliness, yet when textured with leaves can create a sense of sunlight through trees. Despite the associations of certain color and compositional choices, color should never be chosen "by the book."

As with value contrasts, color contrasts can be exploited in light. Juxtaposing colors that are opposite one another on the color wheel creates a jarring, high-contrast composition, whereas using a palette drawn all from within the same color family produces a softer impression.

In the latter case, one should consider how the "main source" of light in the composition will be read by the audience. In a monochromatic palette, the audience tends to read the palest color as white. The visual perceptual system wants to try to find a reference white against which to measure the other colors in the visual field. Thus, monochromatic palettes are tricky for the lighting designer. Often, an accent from outside the color family is needed. For example, a purple accent may be used in an otherwise all-pink palette to maintain the sense of "pink-ness" in the palette.

Another perceptual factor in color response is the desaturation of color. Due to retinal fatigue, over time, very intense color will look less and less intense. If, however, the eye is reminded of what "white" truly is (the presence of all wavelengths) then the fatigue factor can be corrected.

Warmness and coolness are also perceived in a relative way. For a color or composition of colors to be perceived as being warm, there must be some light in the visual field that is cooler. For example, Roscolux07 appears to be a warm "straw" color when juxtaposed against a pale blue such as GAM820, but when compared to a warmer straw such as Roscolux08, it appears so cool as to be almost green.

Keeping in mind both the physics of light and color and the relative nature of color perception, the lighting designer should be able to translate the hue names in the schematic diagrams into actual gel color choices. Experimentation may be necessary but that experimentation can be done in the studio rather than the theatre, to save the time and expense incurred by bringing in a crew.

KEY TERMS

ADDITIVE MIXING

AMPLITUDE

BLACK BODY LOCUS

BLACK BODY RADIATOR

CHROMATICITY DIAGRAM

COLOR RENDERING INDEX

COLOR TEMPERATURE

COLORIMETRY

CORRELATED COLOR TEMPERATURE

DICHROIC FILTER

ELECTROMAGNETIC SPECTRUM

FILTRATION

FREQUENCY

GEL

HUE

KELVIN

NANOMETERS

OBJECT COLOR

PHOTONS

PRIMARY COLORS

REFERENCE WHITE

REFRACTION

SCRIM

SHADE

SPECTRAL DISTRIBUTION

TINT

TONE

TRANSLUCENT

VALUE

VISIBLE SPECTRUM

WAVELENGTH

9

LIGHTING POSITIONS

IN addition to hue names and compositional purposes, schematic diagrams of lighting compositions imply an optimal location for positioning lights in the theatre in order to achieve the desired direction of light. The property "direction"—crucial to the revelation of form and texture, establishment of environment and style, and orchestration of contrast ratios—is controlled by the placement of the lights in relation to the stage and the performer.

Many theatres have unique configurations for their lighting positions, others have configurations more common or standard to the industry. Some performance spaces don't have any lighting positions at all and the production must bring everything into the space. Because lighting is a three-dimensional medium, the plan, section, and—if available—elevation views of a theatre must be carefully examined to determine the location or potential location for lighting positions. Because instrumentation choice will be affected by throw distance, only after decisions about instrument location are made can the lighting designer determine precise luminaire specifications.

THEATRE TYPES

To ascertain the location of potential lighting positions ("hanging positions") the lighting designer examines both the set designer's plans for the scenery and drawings of the theatre space itself. Often, it is necessary to perform an on-site theatre survey to discern the potentialities of a space. A site survey would include measuring the stage space and the distance from permanent lighting positions to the stage as well as determining the angle between those positions and the stage. Although each theatre is unique, there are five basic theatre configurations: proscenium, thrust, arena, flexible, and "other."

Proscenium theatres became the norm in Europe, and subsequently in North America, during and after the Renaissance. Most commercial theatres, most theatres built in the U.S. prior to 1960, and almost all opera houses and dance theatres are proscenium theatres. A proscenium theatre is characterized by fixed seating, a permanent archway framing the stage, and a stage that does not protrude significantly into the seating area. The audience, therefore, has a fixed single point of view in relation to the stage. Until Adolphe Appia wrote eloquently about the paradox of placing a three-dimensional human figure in front of two-dimensional scenery, most scenery designed for proscenium stages consisted of flat painted wings, drops, and borders. With the advent of theatrical realism came three-dimensional scenery, as well. Many of the lighting positions characteristic of proscenium theatres, including "box booms," "balcony rails," and "overhead electrics" are also found in other theatre types. Usually, the lighting positions in front of the proscenium, known as "front-of-house positions" are fixed and permanent while the lighting positions over and around the stage itself are more flexible.

The thrust stage configuration, in which the stage is at least partially surrounded on three sides by the audience, was developed by the ancient Greeks. Once theatre moved indoors during and after the Renaissance, the three-sided thrust configuration fell out of favor until Tyrone Guthrie opened the Guthrie Theatre in Minneapolis in 1963, as shown in Figure 9.1. Thrust theatres often adopt the Greek vomitory or "vom" exit for downstage entrances and exits. In many theatres, these voms can also be used to hide low angle lighting positions. A modified thrust theatre is one in which there is a proscenium arch but the bulk of the playing space protrudes downstage of the arch to be surrounded by the audience. Lighting positions over the "apron" area are often fixed and unique to an individual space, with positions upstage of the arch being similar to those in a proscenium theatre. Thrust or modified thrust theatres are prevalent among American not-for-profit professional theatres.

The Guthrie Theater, Minneapolis, MN

FIGURE 9.1
The original Guthrie Theatre in Minneapolis was distinguished by a deep and relatively narrow thrust stage.

Arena stages are stages that have audience seating on all sides. Lighting positions in such spaces, many of which are reclaimed through adaptive reuse of existing structures, are almost always idiosyncratic. One of the very first "regional" not-for-profit theatres was Arena Stage in Washington D.C., which opened its first in-the-round performance space in 1950 in a converted movie house. Figure 9.2 shows the current Arena Stage seating plan.

Flexible theatre spaces are those in which the seating is not in a permanent fixed relationship to the playing space. The playing space is configured specifically for each production. In such theatres, lighting positions often take the form of an overhead grid throughout the entire theatre so that lights can be hung almost anywhere to accommodate the shifting configurations of the performance space.

Other types of performance spaces might include concert venues such as a sports coliseum or even found spaces such as abandoned buildings, parking garages, piers, and the like. In such cases, there is no permanent lighting rig and all of the lighting positions need to be brought in by the production. The lighting rig might be quite elaborate, as in the case of a stadium rock concert, as shown in Figure 9.3, or an avant-garde, site-specific performance might choose to use "found" lighting positions to go with the found space.

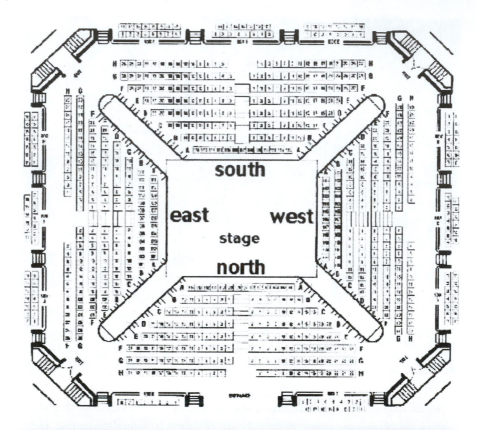

FIGURE 9.2
Arena Stage in Washington D.C. has audience seating on all four sides of the stage.

FIGURE 9.3
For a stadium rock concert, the entire lighting rig is brought in on trucks and installed temporarily.

Graham Steans/Camera Press/Retna, Ltd.

PERMANENT LIGHTING POSITIONS

Many theatres have unique and idiosyncratic lighting positions with unique names. In such cases, a theatre's staff electrician will know the nomenclature and share it with the designer. There are, however, many positions that are fairly standard and can be found in one or more theatre types. Common fixed positions in proscenium and modified thrust theatres are the balcony rail, cove or beam, box booms, and torms. Other theatre types may have permanent catwalks or a grid over both the playing space and the audience area.

A balcony rail is located on the front face of a balcony of most proscenium theatres, and some larger modified thrust theatres. Even theatres that do not have a balcony may have a permanent position called a "rail" that mimics the angle from a balcony rail. Because the balcony rail may be as little as 6 to 20 feet above stage level, that angle is usually fairly shallow, as shown in the section of the new performance space pictured in Figure 9.4. This flat angle has both advantages and disadvantages. Fill light from a rail position serves to fill in performers' eyes quite well, even creating a sparkle. However, this may also cause the performer's shadow to be cast on to the background and furthermore tends to flatten the stage picture. Yet, the rail is still a good position from which to introduce a tonality of color over the stage or fill the entire proscenium opening with texture. Lights hung at this low angle off to one side of the rail or another can be used to provide an impression of setting or rising sun and the rail is probably the optimal position from which to hang curtain warmers. (Curtain warmers are lights used to provide a glow of light on the house curtain before and after the performance.)

Because lights from the balcony rail can provide an even, intense field of illumination that fills in the performers' eye sockets, the balcony rail position is used extensively in musical comedy. The use of this angle of frontlight has become somewhat of a stylistic convention in the musical theatre. There are, however, no rules that say the rail must be used in musicals or cannot be used in other modes of performance.

Some larger proscenium theatres have a second balcony with a second balcony rail. This position can provide for slightly steeper and therefore more controllable front light. Light from a second balcony position (some theatres may call it a "gallery") can light the performer without spilling quite so much on the background, maintaining a clearer figure/ground distinction.

A cove or beam is a position not found in older proscenium theatres, but it is a position designed into most newer spaces, as noted in Figure 9.4. The cove or

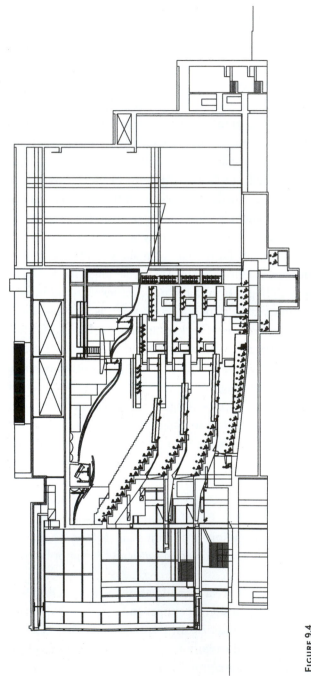

FIGURE 9.4
This new performing arts facility in Madison, Wisconsin, will include three balcony rails as well as substantial cove and box boom positions.

beam, like the balcony rail, is a front-of-house horizontal position, however it is located in the ceiling of the theatre. The most useful positions are those that extend the whole width of the theatre, although many theatres have only "slits" in their ceilings to accommodate just a few lights. These positions provide for even steeper, more sculptural front light than a second balcony rail. This is often a good position from which to achieve that all-important function of facial visibility, while still maintaining some sculptural integrity. In some houses, the beam or cove nearest to the stage may be so close so as to be useful for downlight isolation of the actor on the downstage part of the stage or an apron, rather than for frontlight visibility.

In thrust theatres, beams and coves may wrap around or be parallel to the profile edge of the thrust stage itself. In such cases, various angles of light are possible including even high side light if the position extends fully around to the side (see Figure 9.5).

FIGURE 9.5
At Milwaukee Repertory Theatre, catwalks follow the profile edge of the stage.

Linda Essig

Box booms are vertical front-of-house positions located on the side walls of the theatre or in side boxes of older proscenium theatres (hence the name of this position). Depending on the architecture of the theatre, the distance from the proscenium arch and the stage edge varies. Some theatres have only one set of box booms that may be quite close to the stage or farther away, but many larger theatres have two sets, usually called a "near box boom" stage left or right and a "far box boom" stage left or right. Alternative names are "#1 Box Boom" (for the position closer to the stage) and "#2 Box Boom" (for that farther away).

Because box booms are so far off to one side, and are also likely to be above the stage level, the angle of light from them can be somewhat more compositionally interesting—that is, sculptural—than that from a balcony rail position. If the box booms are far enough from the stage, the box booms are an excellent position from which to provide for facial visibility while still sculpting three-dimensional form and defining the shape of a figure in space. A box boom nearer to the stage can be used for motivated light and/or sidelight on the downstage portion of the stage. For example, light from a near box boom might mimic or support light from a stage practical placed near the downstage corner of a set or support light from a window on the side of a set further into the width of the stage.

There are some drawbacks to the box boom position. It is almost impossible to make a shot (get the light to where it needs to go on stage) from a near box boom on to the near side of the stage adjacent to the position. Also, the closer the box boom is to the stage, the more oblique its angle, making distortion of the beam a certainty. Although most contemporary spotlights have rotating shutters for beam shaping, it may still be difficult to achieve the desired beam shaping because of the oblique aiming angle.

In proscenium theatres, the upstage side of the proscenium arch is known as the "plaster line." When a vertical lighting position is attached to the plaster line, it is called a torm. "Torm" is short for "tormentor," the obsolete name of the vertical masking piece that was usually placed just upstage of the proscenium. Lights on torms are hung off of side arms and can be used to sidelight the downstage plane of the stage. Not all theatres have torms, but if that position is needed, one can usually add a temporary "boom" in its place (see more on booms later in this chapter).

Catwalks are another type of permanent lighting position, though usually found in thrust, arena, and flexible spaces rather than in proscenium theatres. The easy access available with a catwalk system reduces the hang and focus time of the production period considerably. Catwalks may run parallel to the stage edge, parallel and perpendicular, or follow the profile of a thrust stage, as in Figure 9.5. Lights are usually hung off of the knee rail or handrail of the catwalk. By doing so, adjacent catwalks may become obstructions to the focusability of a given light. Careful attention to the section view of the theatre, and construction of a section view parallel to the center line of the proposed beam of light will prevent this problem from occurring.

Many flexible or arena spaces have a permanent lighting grid over the stage. The grid is usually made up of crossing pipes on 4-foot to 6-foot centers. Lights can then be hung anywhere on this grid. A hidden complication in using a permanent grid is that in a flexible or arena space where there is no definitive upstage, downstage, left or right, one may not know how to label the lighting positions. One common practice is to number all of the pipes going in one direction and use letter names for those pipes that run perpendicular. The key is to choose one orientation and maintain it consistently throughout the design drawings. Because the grid, like catwalks, covers all or most of the playing space, lights positioned there can be used for almost any purpose from almost any direction—except uplight of course.

FLEXIBLE POSITIONS

Not all lighting positions are fixed and permanently located in the theatre. Many positions are more flexible and/or temporary. The most common of these are stage electrics. Generally, in proscenium or modified thrust theatres, pipes are rigged parallel to the proscenium arch on the linesets of a counterweighted or winched rigging system. These pipes may be used for scenery, masking, or lighting equipment. When they are used for lighting equipment, they are called "electrics." The electrics are numbered "#1 Electric," "#2 Electric," and so on, starting at the proscenium and working upstage. This numbering convention may change slightly in thrust theatres in that numbering may begin at the stage edge rather than the proscenium. Or, a theatre may have pipes that are permanently dedicated to being electrics because they have circuit raceways attached to them. In such cases, the theatre will probably have permanent numbers for their electrics and any additions become a lettered addendum. "#1A Electric" would, for example, be a production-specific hanging position located between the #1 and #2 Electrics in a house with permanent electrics. If there is no fixed line set in the theatre where an electric is required, then the sheaves and head block need to be moved or new rigging installed.

The height of the pipe above the stage floor, the "trim height," is completely variable, within the limitations of the height and location of the set. The position of the electrics in relation to the plaster line is determined by the lighting designer in consultation with the set designer to best achieve the angles of light required. Onstage electrics can be used for a wide variety of overhead angles of light including steep front light, backlight, downlight, and high sidelight. Figure 9.6 shows an electric from the National Tour of *Thoroughly Modern Millie*.

FIGURE 9.6
The #1 Electric on *Thoroughly Modern Millie—National Tour* is actually rigged from truss to make loading in and out of the theatre as efficient as possible.

Linda Essig

Lighting units can be hung from C-clamps (pipe clamps) anywhere along the length of an electric. Most fixed-focus units are designed to hang at a minimum of 18-inch centers while automated lights generally take up more space. The length of electrics can vary, but 42 feet is a common length as pipes are purchased in 21-foot sections and coupled together.

Booms are vertical lighting positions that are fastened to the stage floor on a boom base or a flange and tied off to the overhead grid for safety. Lights on booms are rigged off of side arms, as shown in Figure 9.7, or from C-clamps hanging from cross-pipes. (Note that when lights are hung directly from a C-clamp attached to the vertical boom, the axes of movement are limited.) Booms are rarely taller than 21 feet, the length of a single piece of pipe. Often, booms are shorter, depending on the needs of the design and space availability. To accommodate the vertical height of the lighting units, side arms are generally hung on 2-foot centers on booms.

Booms are often placed in side wings to provide low side light, head-high light, or mid-high sidelight. Booms can also be tucked behind scenery to light hard-to-reach areas of the stage, provide light through windows or other openings in the set, and so on.

A dance tower is sometimes placed in the wings instead of a single boom pipe. Popular in touring and depicted in Figure 9.8, dance towers consist of an 8- to 12-foot section of square box truss on end with lights placed within.

Ladders can also be placed in the wings to provide for mid-high sidelight, but ladders are rigged from the grid or tailed down from a batten and do not go down to the stage floor as booms do. Rather, ladders are used when there is significant movement of people or scenery through the wings that would be obstructed by

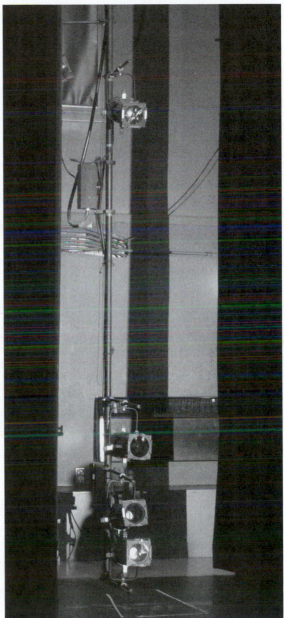

Linda Essig

FIGURE 9.7
Lights on booms are hung from side arms rather than C-clamps or from C-clamps off of horizontal crosspipes.

FIGURE 9.8
A dance tower is a piece of vertical square truss in the wings with lights rigged within it to prevent them from being knocked out of focus as dancers exit. Dance towers are also used in touring productions.

Linda Essig

booms. As the name implies, a lighting ladder is a position consisting of horizontal rungs from which the lights hang on C-clamps, between vertical members.

A lighting position with its roots in the Renaissance that has been making a comeback recently is the footlight position. Rather than the fixed, permanent position of the seventeenth through nineteenth centuries, footlights today can refer to any low front light position. Traditional footlights, such as those in Figure 9.9, may be placed in a trough near the downstage edge of the stage, on brackets affixed to the front of the stage or on the stage itself. Specific low frontlights, that is individual units, can be placed on floor bases at the edge of the stage. Footlights are useful for filling in the eyes of the actors as well as highlighting legs and feet. Because of their historical associations with theatre of the Late Renaissance through the nineteenth century gaslight period, footlights can also be used to help achieve a period stylistic effect.

In thrust and arena seating configurations, footlights, as well as low sidelights, can be problematic. The lighting designer needs to consider not only the angle of light hitting the performer from these positions, but also where the lights can feasibly be placed and where the light itself ends up (or "buries") after it hits the actor.

In any theatre configuration, the lack of lighting positions should not stifle the designer's imagination. Lights can be mounted on table bases, also known as floor bases, such as that in Figure 9.10, tucked in and around the stage or set. The lights can be set-mounted using a wall flange. Fiber optic cables can even be used to pipe light to the really hard-to-reach areas of a set.

Richard Feldman

FIGURE 9.9
A view of footlights.

FIGURE 9.10
A stage light attached to a table base such as this one can be placed almost anywhere on the set.

When moving into a concert venue or any type of empty space, the designer may opt to use lighting truss rather than more traditional pipe rigging. A truss is an assembly of pipe welded together to make a rigid structure. Lights can then be hung from or within the truss, depending on its configuration. Concert tours may be designed with very complex truss structures that are designed to support the entire lighting and scenery systems.

INTEGRATING THE SET DESIGN INFORMATION

Schematic diagrams imply angles of light in relation to scenic elements designed by the set designer. The layout of the lighting positions to achieve those angles must coordinate with the set design in all three dimensions. Therefore, the set design drawings and their implication for the lighting design, although two-dimensional, must be understood in their three-dimensional form.

The plan, section, and elevation views of the set need to be fully examined. If one thinks of the stage space as a three-dimensional box, it is simple to understand these views. The plan view is a drawing of the set looking straight down on the set as if it were cut through a horizontal plane at eye level. In order to emphasize the placement of walls and other vertical elements on the ground plan, scenic and architectural elements that fall below this cut line are usually shown in bold solid lines, often double lines cross-hatched, and those elements above the line, such as crown moldings, are shown as lighter solid lines. Scenic elements that hang above the stage or are placed below the deck are indicated in broken or dashed lines, as indicated in Figure 9.11.

The ground plan indicates the placement of furniture and other important prop elements, as well. The lighting designer should note the location of these as action and blocking tend to gravitate to or between sittable items. These might indicate important playing areas of the space that will need to be highlighted or specifically controlled with light.

In addition to placement of walls and furniture, the ground plan includes offstage masking elements such as legs (vertical masking elements). The lighting designer can use the ground plan to devise horizontal sightlines. By drawing a

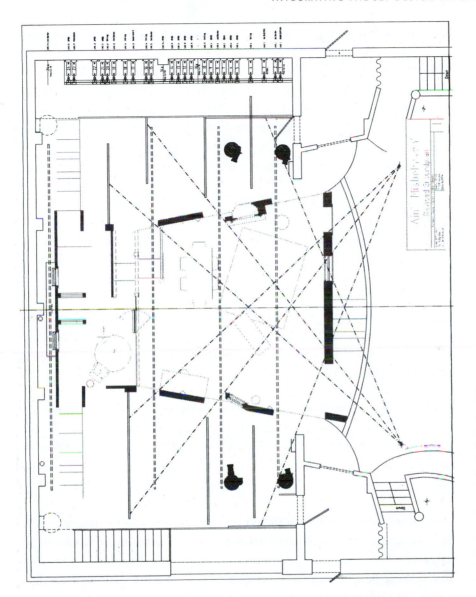

FIGURE 9.11
The lighting designer examines the ground plan of a set, such as this one for *Ain't Misbehavin'*, to assess sightlines and determine possible on-stage lighting positions. (Adapted from ground plans by Megan Wilkerson. Used with permission.)

line from the sidemost seat in the front row to the onstage edge of a leg and then continuing that line, one sees where lights will be visible to the audience—onstage of that line—and where they will be masked from the audience—offstage of that line.

The section view of the set is often the most important to the lighting designer, particularly early in the design process, because it is in this view that the lighting designer can figure out the potential overhead lighting positions, the angle of light to be achieved from them, and their trim heights. The section shows the stage from a side view as if it has been cut along a vertical plane perpendicular to the stage floor, usually at the center line of the space. Items that fall on this plane are indicated in bold or dark lines, those beyond the center line appear in a lighter solid line, and those that are on the near side of the line are indicated in dotted lines, or omitted. To have a complete understanding of the implications of the set design for the lighting, it may be necessary to have a center line section looking both stage left and stage right. (In fact, the lighting designer should examine all the drawings submitted for the set design, including detail drawings.)

Vertical sight lines, and thence trim heights, can be determined in the section view. By drawing a line from the first row center seat sight line through the bottom of the show portal or first header and each subsequent border or scenic element, the lighting designer can see how high the overhead electrics will have to trim to be out of sightlines (see Figure 9.12). Or, if the intent of the production is to see the lights from the entire house, the lighting designer can see what the maximum trim should be by drawing a sightline from the highest rearmost seat through the bottom point of the masking. The lighting designer, in collaboration with the set designer, is often the person to establish exact placement and trim heights of the overhead masking elements in order to facilitate the lighting design.

Obstructions created by ceiling pieces, flying scenery, or portals are also identified in the section view. When there is the potential for serious obstructions of a particular lighting angle from a specific position, the lighting designer needs to construct his or her own sections along the path of the beam of light to make sure that light is not obstructed. See Figure 9.13.

The elevation view is the view looking straight into the front of the stage space. A full stage frontal elevation is rarely produced by the set designer, so the lighting designer may need to construct one from the elevations of the individual scenic elements and the information found on the ground plan and section. The lighting designer uses a full stage front elevation to determine sidelight angles—that is light that will be essentially parallel to the front of the stage. For example, on the front elevation of *Ain't Misbehavin'*, potential low sidelight angles are indicated on a front elevation produced by the lighting designer (see Figure 9.14). This drawing is not necessary for communicating design intent to the electricians but rather is part of the design development process, determining exactly where lights need to be in the theatre.

In all three of these drawing types, there is no indication of the perspective of the view; there is no vanishing point. Instead, all elements are drawn to scale on

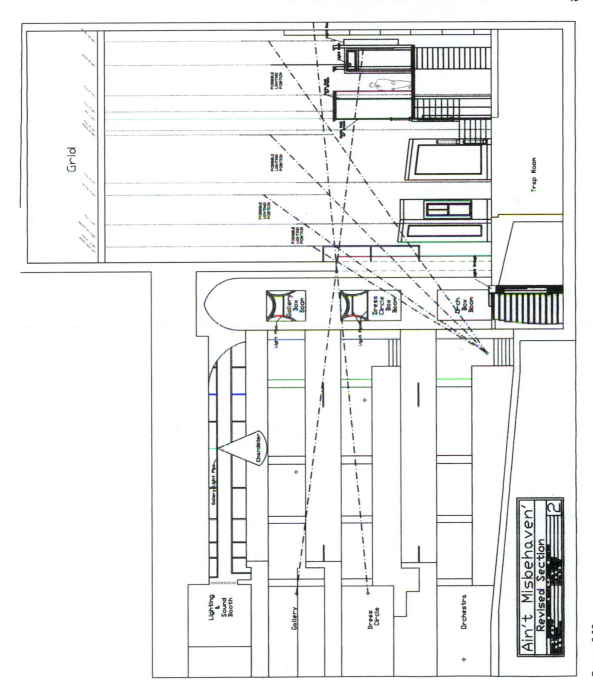

FIGURE 9.12

To determine vertical sightlines and trim heights of overhead electrics, the lighting designer closely examines the scenic section. (Rendered by Megan Wilkerson. Used with permission.)

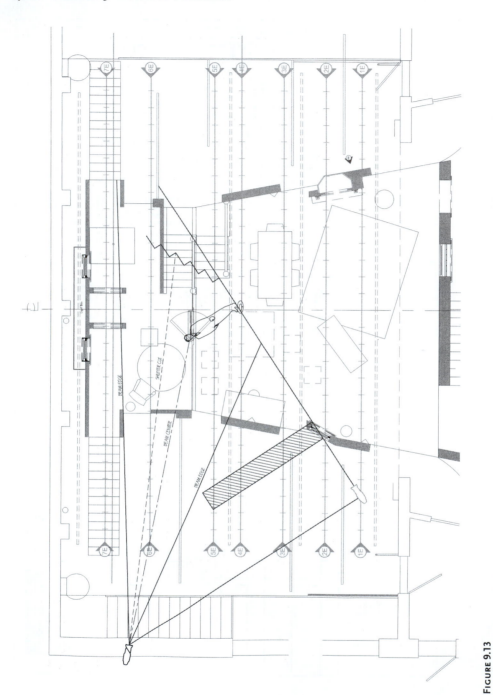

FIGURE 9.13

The lighting designer will often need to construct a section parallel to the direction of light in order to assess whether a light from a particular location can "make its shot."

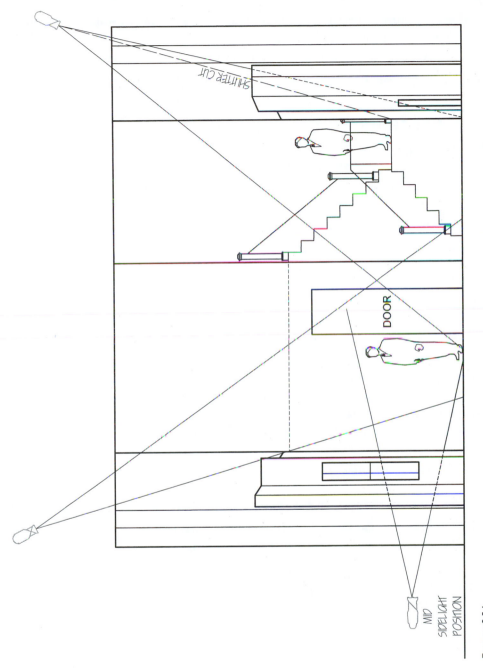

FIGURE 9.14
To determine the height of sidelight from booms, the lighting designer probably needs to construct a front elevation, if one is not provided by the set designer.

the picture plane. Doing so means that dimensions can be scaled directly from the drawing regardless of the depth of the stage.

With lighting positions determined in a preliminary fashion at least, the design development phase can proceed to the specification of exact luminaire types.

KEY TERMS

APRON

ARENA STAGE

BALCONY RAIL

BATTEN

BEAM

BOOM

BOOM BASE

BORDER

BOX BOOMS

C-CLAMP

CATWALK

CIRCUIT RACEWAY

COUNTERWEIGHT

COVE

CURTAIN WARMER

DANCE TOWER

ELECTRICS

ELEVATION VIEW

FIXED-FOCUS

FLANGE

FLEXIBLE SPACE

FOOTLIGHT

FRONT-OF-HOUSE

GUTHRIE, TYRONE

HEAD BLOCK

HEADER

HORIZONTAL SIGHTLINES

LADDERS

LEGS

MODIFIED THRUST

PLAN VIEW

PLASTER LINE

PORTAL

PROSCENIUM

SECTION VIEW

SET-MOUNTED

SHEAVES

SIDE ARM

SIGHTLINE

TABLE BASES

THROW DISTANCE

THRUST STAGE

TORM

TRIM HEIGHT

VOM

10
INSTRUMENTATION

IN order to harness light to achieve the various functions necessary for a successful design, the lighting designer must, of course, have a thorough understanding of the luminaires available to them and what unique characteristics each luminaire type may have. The lighting designer must decide which type of luminaire is the best choice for achieving the desired quality, quantity, and shape of light. The first part of this chapter details common types of both fixed-focus and automated luminaires, as well as follow spots. The latter portion outlines methods for choosing between the various types of lights, whether lighting the acting area or the scenic space.

Theatrical luminaires fall into three primary categories based on their distribution: spotlights, wash lights, and flood lights. There are both fixed-focus and automated luminaires of each type of distribution. Fixed-focus luminaires are dealt with first as they generally make up the bulk of the inventory of a resident and/or academic theatre. Commercial productions usually use a mix of both fixed-focus and automated lights.

FIXED-FOCUS SPOTLIGHTS

The workhorse of fixed-focus theatrical luminaires is the ellipsoidal reflector spotlight. Developed in the early 1930s simultaneously by Kliegl Brothers and Century Lighting, the ERS, although it has since been redesigned for far greater efficiency, is still very widely used. Century's "Lekolite" brand of ERS became so popular that the term "leko" was used for many years to mean any type of ERS. In 1992, Electronic Theatre Controls introduced its "Source Four" brand of ERS. With its vastly improved optics, higher efficiency and lower wattage, it has become the most popular brand of ERS in the U.S. and the term "leko" has

FIGURE 10.1
The light from an ERS is conical in shape. The light is made visible here through the use of atmospheric haze.

Linda Essig

fallen out of favor, having been replaced by the generic terms "ERS" or "ellipsoidal."

The conical, well-defined beam shape, as shown in Figure 10.1, characterizes the light emitted from an ERS. As with any spotlight, the light has a beam and a field. The beam is that area of the light distribution that is from the most intense center of the beam to where it is 50% of the most intense. The area between 50% of maximum intensity and 10% of maximum intensity is called the "field," as illustrated in Figure 10.2. Most modern ERSs are specified by their field angle in degrees, as this represents the spread of usable light from the luminaire. Common spreads are 5°, 10°, 19°, 26°, 30°, 36°, 40°, and 50°. Older ERSs may be specified by the diameter of the lens in inches times its focal length, such as 6×9, 6×12, 6×16, or 6×22. These units have field angles of approximately 36°, 26°, 19°, and 10°, respectively.

The optical system of an ERS consists of an ellipsoidal reflector, a lamp whose center is placed at the first focal point of the ellipse, and two plano-convex (or similar) lenses. Large units may have one step lens instead of two lenses. The lamp can be aligned along the axis of the reflector to produce either "peak beam candlepower" distribution—the brightest light at the center of the beam—or "flat field distribution" (also called "cosine distribution") in which the lamp is aligned (or "trimmed") to make the light output as uniform as possible over its entire field.

The reflector focuses light through a plane inside the luminaire known as the "gate" before the light passes through the two lenses, converging at a focal point some inches beyond the lenses, as illustrated in Figure 10.3. The image of gobo patterns, shutters, or other shaping devices placed in the gate can be clearly projected if the lamp, reflector, and lenses are aligned for sharp focus.

The edge of the beam of light can be adjusted between very sharp to fairly soft, particularly in units with a wider field angle. The beam size changes when this adjustment is made, achieved by "running the barrel"— moving the lens train forward or back. When hard-focused, an ERS tends to have a more even field; when soft-focused, the differentiation of the bright beam within a less bright field is more distinguishable. When projecting gobo patterns or other images, the sharp focus is useful; if blending multiple lights to achieve uniform illumination across the stage, a softer focus may be useful.

A critical feature of the ellipsoidal reflector spotlight is the shutter assembly. Shutters sit in the gate of the unit and have straight edges. They are used for beam shaping and perhaps most importantly for "cutting" the light beam off of scenery, out of the audience, or to the edge of a scenic detail, such as molding. An optional framing device available for many ERSs is an iris. This too sits in the gate of the unit, but frames the beam of light in a circular shape, rather than

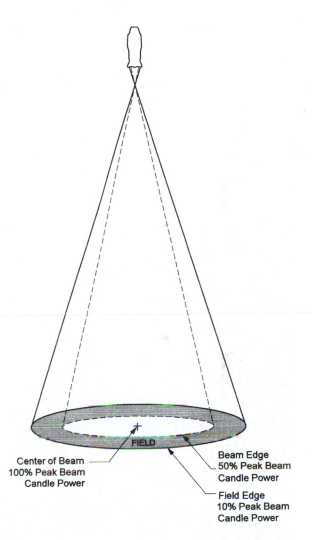

Center of Beam
100% Peak Beam
Candle Power

FIELD

Beam Edge
50% Peak Beam
Candle Power

Field Edge
10% Peak Beam
Candle Power

FIGURE 10.2
An ERS, like all spotlights, has a beam and a field as diagrammed here.

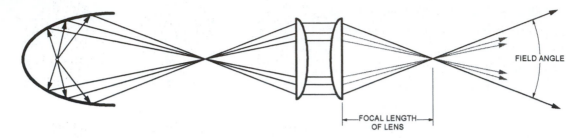

FIELD ANGLE

├── FOCAL LENGTH ──┤
OF LENS

FIGURE 10.3
The optical system of an ERS consists of the lamp, the elliptical reflector, and two (or sometimes one) lenses.

with straight edges. An iris is very useful for framing specific round objects such as a full moon on a painted drop, and is a necessary accessory if an ERS is used as a small followspot.

The ability of an ERS to project template patterns and its controllability are other characteristics that have made them so important to stage lighting. Figure 10.4 shows a sampling of the literally hundreds of template patterns available from a variety of manufacturers for use in ERSs.

The ellipsoidal reflector spotlight, like many common stage lighting luminaires, is designed to be hung off of a "C-clamp" (see Figure 10.5). Alternatively, they can be hung off of a side arm from a vertical position or mounted directly onto a table base or rolling floor stand. Many other optional accessories are available for an ERS, including automated devices such as a movable yoke, moving mirror attachment, or color scroller that can be used to turn an ERS into a low-end automated light. Other accessories are more mundane but equally useful, including top hats for reducing halation, donuts for sharpening a projected image, and the gel frame itself.

The fresnel is another fairly common type of lighting unit, although it is more popular in film and video lighting than in theatre because it is not as controllable as an ERS but has a flatter, more uniform field, which makes it desirable for video production. This unit type is named for the Fresnel-type lens used in these units, originally designed (on a much larger scale) for use in lighthouses. Like the ERS, the fresnel emits a conical shape of light, but its edge is not as well defined. Overall, the quality of light from a fresnel is softer than that from an ERS.

The optical system of a fresnel is fairly simple; it consists of a small spherical reflector, a lamp, and the single Fresnel lens. By adjusting the relationship between the lamp and the lens, the luminaire can go from a spot focus, as shown in Figure 10.6 (page 155) when the lamp is far back from the lens, to a flood focus, as shown in Figure 10.7 (page 156) when the lamp is closer to the lens.

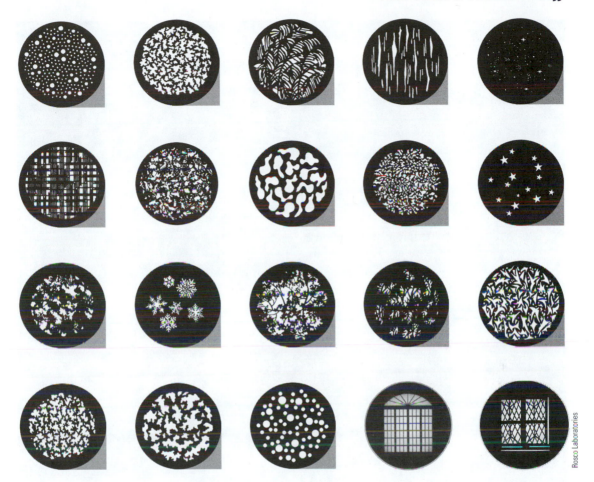

Rosco Laboratories

FIGURE 10.4
A sampling of stock template patterns (gobos) available for a lighting designer's use.

Notice that when the unit is in spot focus, it has a fairly tight, defined beam with a visible field surrounding. In flood focus, a fresnel spreads the light quite evenly over its field. Although considered a spotlight when in spot focus, in flood focus, the fresnel can be used for creating broad washes of light on scenery or sky-like overhead light.

Fresnels are usually specified by the diameter of the lens and the wattage of the lamp. The most common sizes are 6-inch (6") and 8-inch (8") fresnels, while 3-inch (3") fresnels (also known as "inkies") are useful for set-mounted, hard-to-light locations. HID-sourced fresnels are popular in Europe and are becoming more popular in the United States, especially in opera, such as in the Glimmerglass Opera production of *Agrippina* depicted in Figure 10.8 (page 157). The

Linda Essig

FIGURE 10.5
An ERS is usually hung from a C-clamp as pictured here.

intense clear light HID fresnels produce is, due to its discharge source, cooler (higher color temperature) than incandescent lights and may require a mechanical douser or shuttering device rather than an electronic dimmer.

The mounting accessories for a fresnel are the same as for an ERS, but the optical accessories differ. The lighting designer can shape the soft field of light from a fresnel when in flood focus by adding a barn door, such as that depicted in Figure 10.9 (page 157). In such usage, the barn door acts as an external shutter for cutting light from areas of the stage where it is unwanted. When a "top hat" is used on a fresnel, it creates a defined circle of light that cannot be altered in size.

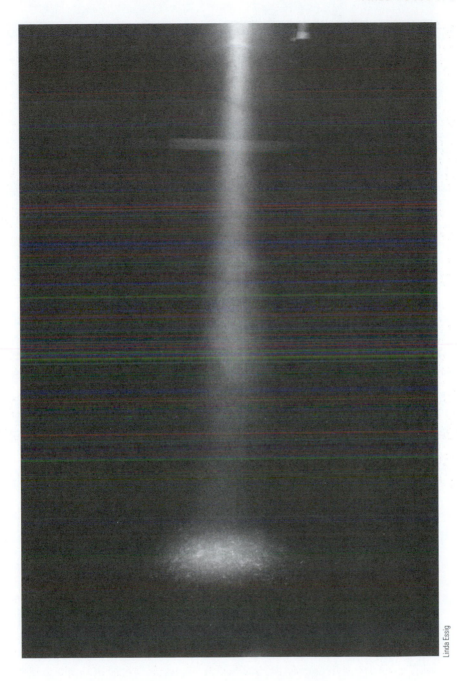

Linda Essig

FIGURE 10.6
In spot focus, a fresnel has a tight, defined beam with a visible field surrounding it.

FIGURE 10.7
In flood focus, a fresnel emits a uniform field of light (compared to other luminaire types) with a very soft edge.

Linda Essig

FIGURE 10.8
Fresnels with HID sources are used extensively in Europe and are popular for use in opera in the U.S. as in this production of *Agrippina* at Glimmerglass Opera. Set design by John Conklin; costume design by Jess Goldstein; lighting design by Mark McCullough.

© 2001 George Mott/Glimmerglass Opera

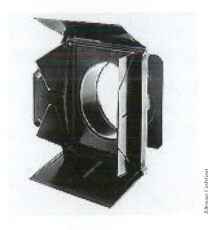

FIGURE 10.9
A barn door is an optional accessory for a fresnel that enables some beam shaping when the luminaire is in flood focus.

Altman Lighting

WASH LIGHTS

Although fresnels can be used as wash lights, they are categorized here as spotlights because of their optics. PARs, or parabolic aluminized reflector luminaires, are considered wash lights here because they are often used to create washes of light over the stage and they have simpler optical assemblies.

PAR luminaires come in two types. The older type consists of a sealed-beam PAR lamp in a simple housing. The sealed-beam lamp consists of a reflector, an incandescent or HID lamp capsule, and a lens all fused together in a single optical assembly. The second type, developed in the 1990s, has a parabolic reflector and lamp capsule with interchangeable lenses. Theoretically, when a source is placed at the focal point of a parabolic lens, the resulting reflected light is parallel in configuration, as shown in Figure 10.10. The lens may be clear, in which case a tight parallel beam results, or may be striated to produce a variety of beam spreads. Common beam spreads of PAR lamps include VNSP (very narrow spot), NSP (narrow spot), MFL (medium flood), WFL (wide flood), and VWFL (very wide flood).

Because of the interchangeability of lenses on the newest generation of PARs, those fixtures are specified by manufacturer brand name and the lens distribution desired. Traditional PAR "cans" are specified by wattage, lamp size, and beam spread. The standard way to specify lamps is by lamp shape and lamp diameter in eighths of an inch. PAR56 and PAR64 lamps are the most common sizes used in performance, although the much smaller PAR16 (also known as a "birdie") is used for specialized applications, such as set mounts or footlights. Consequently, the specification for a PAR fixture might be: 1K PAR64 MFL, the light from which is pictured in Figure 10.11.

Unlike the ERS and fresnel, the PAR does not emit a round, conical beam of light. Rather, its beam shape is oval, or even rectangular. A soft-edged beam surrounded by a bright, diffuse field characterizes the light emitted from a PAR. No focus adjustment can be made on a PAR except to orient the axis of the oval shape in one direction or another. This is done by rotating the lens or the whole lamp inside a can. The designer should consider the axis of the light in advance and indicate it on the light plot. Having the lamp axis preset in the shop or at the hang saves time at the focus session.

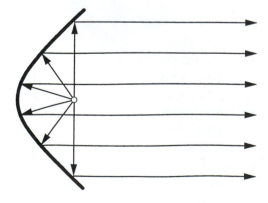

FIGURE 10.10
When a lamp is placed at the focal point of a parabolic reflector, light rays are reflected in a parallel configuration.

Linda Essig

FIGURE 10.11
The light emitted from a PAR is rectangular or oval, rather than round or conical.

Control of the field of light from a PAR is difficult. There are no shutters, and barn doors do not work very well. In addition, barn doors make the unit exceedingly front-heavy, making it hard for the PAR can to maintain its focus position. Because of the difficulty in controlling the field from a PAR, be cautious about using PARS in front-of-house positions.

PARs in groups can be used for many applications, but one of the most popular is in an array of multiple units to create a color field over the stage. PARS became very popular in the 1970s in the concert touring industry for this effect because they are lightweight and durable. Consequently, one can see many PARs on tour even today, often used to supplement an extensive moving light rig as shown in Figure 10.12. By placing color scrollers or mixers on the PARs, they become quite versatile for creating fields of color. PARs are useful in all forms of performance. Because of the parallel distribution of the narrower beam spreads, they can be used to mimic the parallel rays of sunlight, or can be used to create strong highlights on performers from a backlight or sidelight angle. The author has even used PARs as low frontlight—the possibilities are limitless.

© CORBIS

FIGURE 10.12
PARs were popular-
ized by the concert
touring industry
because of their
durability and
light weight.

FLOODLIGHTS

Floodlights are non-focusable, broad distribution luminaires often used for lighting drops, providing broad areas of light, or for work light on stage. One type of floodlight is a striplight, so called because it consists of a line of lamps mounted into a channel strip with interconnected wiring providing for one, two, three, or four separate circuits. Striplights are generally specified based on their lamp type. Beyond choosing a specific lamp, striplights do not have a focusable optical system.

The PAR striplight, shown in Figure 10.13, uses the same type of PAR lamps as the PAR cans (PAR56 or PAR64 lamps) but mounts them in a channel. PAR56 strips can be quite effective for lighting a straight drop from both the top and bottom. PAR64 strips, which have a tendency to burn gel because the gel frames are much closer to the lamp in a striplight than when PAR lamps are used in the yoke-mounted PAR can, are best used only from overhead. PAR64 striplights can be quite effective for creating planes of downlight or backlight. Because they are wired for three or four circuits, they have some versatility, and are popular in repertory plots.

A T3 striplight uses double-ended tubular (T-type) lamps, usually of 300 or 500 watts. The lamp is placed in an asymmetrical reflector so that there is excellent vertical light distribution, as illustrated in Figure 10.14. The most popular

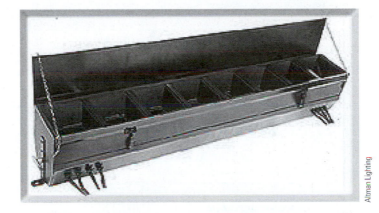

FIGURE 10.13
A typical PAR 64 striplight with hanging iron and optional flipper.

Altman Lighting

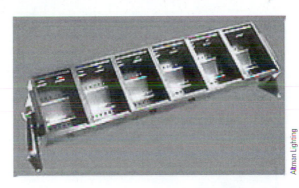

FIGURE 10.14
A T-3 striplight uses an asymmetrical reflector to provide good vertical light distribution.

Altman Lighting

form of this striplight, made by Altman Lighting, is marketed as a "Ground Cyc" so the term "Ground Cyc" has come to mean, in many markets, any type of T-3 striplight. As the term ground-cyc implies, these units are very useful as ground rows, although they can be hung from overhead electrics as well, for drop lighting.

The PAR38/R40/ER40 striplight uses small PAR lamps or reflector-type R- or ER-lamps. These lamps have a soft edge and are easy to blend. However, at only 300 watts and relatively low efficiency, the R40 striplight does not have a lot of "punch" on a drop. They are, however, used extensively in the repertory plot for the New York City Ballet, as shown in Figure 10.15.

For a small-size striplight, the MR-16 striplight is a good choice. The MR-16 strip uses the multi-faceted reflector-type lamp also used in many small slide projectors. This is a 12-volt lamp and so lamps are usually wired in series in a 3-circuit strip (see the Appendix on electricity), with 10 lamps per circuit. Burn-out indicators tell the electrician which lamp on the series circuit needs to be replaced should one go out. MR-16 strips can be lamped with a variety of

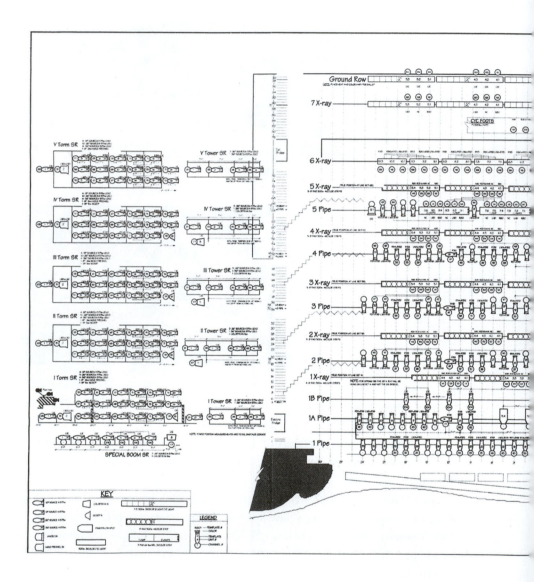

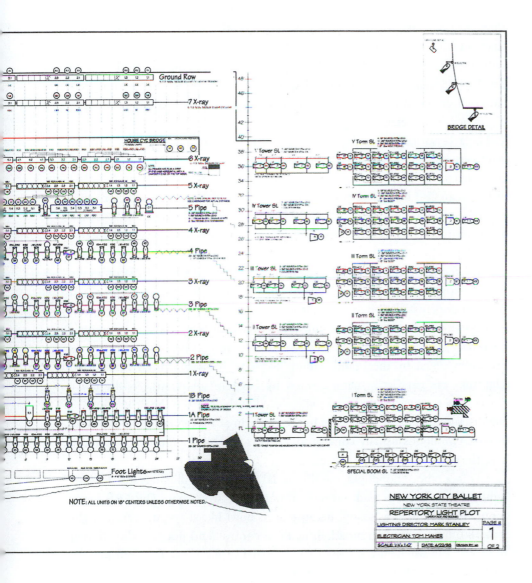

FIGURE 10.15
In his repertory light plot for the New York City Ballet, lighting designer Mark Stanley makes ample use of R40 300-watt striplights. (Used with permission of Mark Stanley.)

beam spreads such as the EYJ (wide flood), EYC (flood), or EYF (spot) lamp. MR-16 strips are very useful on small drops (16 feet or shorter) or whenever there is only a narrow space to fit lights between other elements, as they are less than 5 inches deep. When lamped with the EYF (spot) lamp, they emit light with a sparkle quality and so can be very useful for footlights (see the light plot for *Ain't Misbehavin'* depicted in Chapter 1, Figure 1.6). An even smaller version of a similar unit is the MR-11 striplight, which uses the MR-11 lamp, only 1⅜ inches in diameter.

The accessories for striplights include their gel frames as well as mounting hardware called "hangers." When used in a ground row application, they are mounted on triangular-shaped bases called "trunions." PAR56 and PAR64 strips—can also be accessorized with "flippers." Flippers are metal flaps that run the length of the strip and are used as a horizontal barn door. These can be quite useful for cutting unwanted light off of the playing area emitted by striplights lighting a drop further upstage. The location of the flippers on the unit (the downstage or upstage edge)—as well as the orientation of the lamp in the strip—should be indicated on the light plot, so the striplights can be prepared in advance of installation in the theatre.

A cyc flood, like the T-3 striplight, uses a tube-type lamp and an asymmetrical reflector to achieve good vertical light distribution. These types of fixtures are often called by the brand names "Sky-Cyc" (manufactured by Altman Lighting) or "Far-Cyc" (manufactured by Leviton/Colortran). As the latter name implies, they are designed to be placed fairly far from the drop. Usually, the distance from a drop is equal to the centering between lamps in the same circuit. Cyc floods usually come in one-, two-, three-, or four-lamp models. Like the striplights, they are lensless.

An older type of floodlight, the ellipsoidal reflector floodlight, is still used for lighting curved drops and, more commonly, for worklight. The ERF, commonly referred to as a "scoop" because of its bowl-like shape, distributes light in a 180° field. Although broad, difficult to control, and not very directional, the scoop can still be useful for very specialized applications. For example, the author has used them above the theatre's grid to cast a textured glow over the whole stage, as pictured in Figure 10.16.

AUTOMATED LIGHTS

Automated, or moving, lights can be powerful tools for the lighting designer. Able to change focus location, color, beam size and distribution, and gobo

Linda Essig

image at the touch of a button, automated lights can be used for flashy concert lighting effects, for subtle changes of atmosphere, color, or visual focus, and can save space in a crowded lighting rig by taking the place of "specials" that might otherwise be accomplished with a dozen or more fixed-focus luminaires. By utilizing a luminaire with beam control attributes such as programmable shutters, parts of the stage picture can be highlighted with great specificity—a doorway, a picture, or a telephone on a table can subtly draw attention when highlighted, and that visual focus can be maintained even as the scenery moves.

The first commercially viable automated lights were developed in the early 1980s by Vari-Lite Inc. for use in rock and roll touring, with some competition from the Morpheus Lights "Moto-Lite." In the 1990s, control protocol standardization enabled almost any lighting console to control automated lights to some degree without the need of an additional operator or specialized control system. This development made automated lights accessible to the "legitimate" theatre of drama, opera, and musicals.

FIGURE 10.16
In her design of *The Kitchen,* the author placed scoops above the theatre's grid to cast textured ambient light over the whole stage. Written and directed by Arnold Wesker; set design by Kathy Rathke.

Like the fixed-focus lights, automated lights may be spotlights or wash lights. There is even an automated striplight on the market (see Figure 10.17). Automated lights work on the principle of controlling various "attributes" of the luminaire either by addressing the attributes by name, such as "pan," "tilt," "gobo wheel," and the like or by assigning those attributes to channels of control in a traditional lighting console.

Among the spotlights, there are moving head luminaires and moving mirror luminaires, called "scanners" in Europe. The major portion of the moving mirror luminaire remains fixed and stationary while light is projected onto a small mirror at the front of the unit that can pan and tilt to move the beam image around the performance space. As development of these units progressed, more and more features have been added to them. Some have as many as eighteen attributes, requiring twenty control channels. In addition to pan and tilt attributes that control focus location, other attributes include gobo selection,

FIGURE 10.17
The Digital Light Curtain is an automated striplight.

gobo rotation, color wheel as well as color mixing, iris, and more. Moving mirror units are very durable, especially for touring situations, because most of the moving parts are within the unit. They have a large drawback, however. The pan and tilt limits on moving mirror units are, by necessity, less than 360° in each direction.

Moving head luminaires, on the other hand, may have almost 360° of tilt and over 360° of pan capability, making them very versatile. Both wash lights and spotlights are available in moving head units. The wash lights were the first to use cyan-yellow-magenta (CYM) subtractive color mixing to achieve a full spectrum of colors. Higher-end spotlights are starting to have that feature as well. Because wash lights are designed for applications where broad areas of light are required, this color mixing and changing capability is quite important. Unlike a color wheel or scroll of gel, it is possible to cross-fade between colors seamlessly.

If the only attribute requiring automation is color, then color scrollers or color mixers are a good option. As the name implies, a color scroller consists of a string of gel literally taped together to form a long scroll. The scroller device can fit in the gel frame holder slot of almost any type of light if the correct mounting plate is specified. A control signal sent to a power supply, and subsequently the scroller, tells the device where in the gel string to stop. At this time, color scrollers can hold between eight and thirty-two different colors.

A color mixer contains two or three scrolls. In the three-scroll version manufactured by Morpheus, each scroll is a gradient screen from clear to one of the subtractive primaries cyan, yellow, or magenta. Through subtractive color mixing, almost any color is available to the designer. The two-scroll version, manufactured by Wybron, consists of two gel strings specified to produce the greatest possible combination of colors through subtractive mixing of only two colors.

These color-changing devices can give the lighting design great flexibility, but like all equipment should be carefully chosen. What colors are needed on the color scroll? Will live changes be needed? In such a case, extra care must be taken to ensure that when a live change happens it goes from one desired color to another without passing through unwanted colors in between.

FOLLOW SPOTS

Follow spots are manually operated moving specials for highlighting lead performers as they move about the stage. Most are designed and manufactured to be follow spots, but for small low-budget situations, a follow spot can be as simple as an ERS with a drop-in iris and a follow handle. Commercially available follow spots have a lamp and lenses, an iris, a color-changing device called a "boomerang," horizontal shutters called "choppers" or "clappers" and some type of douser for mechanical dimming if, as in most follow spots, there is an HID source.

Follow spots are quite popular in lyric theatre (musicals and operas), but can be used in dramatic production as well. In these applications, the designer can establish an evocative stage picture and pull out the principles with follow spots. Many designers choose to have one color frame filled with a diffusion media so that the edge of the follow spot can easily switch between a hard edge and a soft edge. A hard-edged follow spot is very obvious to the audience and therefore a strong stylistic choice, conveying a theatrical or presentational design idea.

SPECIFYING THE RIGHT LUMINAIRE

With so much variety in the equipment available to a lighting designer, how can one make specific choices? First, one can use a series of simple questions to narrow down the choice to a family of instrument types, then use some simple charting, graphing, mathematics, or even intuition, to specify the right light from within that family.

Some questions to help narrow the choice of luminaires are as follows (possible answers are in italics):

▶ Is automation of color and/or location *absolutely* necessary? *Unless automation is really required, fixed focus units will be less costly to rent or buy and programming time will be significantly less than with automated lights.*

▶ Is precise beam control necessary to cut light off of scenery or out of the house? *If shutters will be required, ERSs are the logical choice; anytime really specific framing is required, shutters will be needed. If a pattern must be projected, ERSs are also necessary.*

▶ What quality and distribution is desirable for a given function? *If a soft-edged light is desirable, try a fresnel (unless shutters are needed). If the design requires a broad swath of light, a bank of PARs might work. If floodlighting a drop with sufficient space, a cyc flood could be a good choice.*

Once the type of instrument is chosen, some figuring is required to ensure that the right size of instrument—that is the unit with the optimal field angle for its purpose—is finally specified. Any one of the units discussed earlier can provide enough light on a single actor on a bare stage to enable to audience to see her or him. Usually, however, the actor is moving about with other actors in a performance space that is also illuminated to some degree. By using lighting instruments at the throw distances for which they were designed, a lighting designer can achieve adequate visibility.

There are a number of proposed methods of applying photometric information (including McCandless's 1931 method) to achieve uniform illumination from a given direction or purpose of light. When a lighting idea is implemented through the use of multiple lights focused at various points across the stage, those lights may be referred to as a "system." A simple and rather expeditious method for achieving uniform illumination from any direction is to chart field angle against a range of feasible throw distances for that particular spread.

The first step in this technique is to locate "focus points" or "modules" that are 6 to 8 feet from one another (one can stretch this to 10 feet if there is a very small inventory). This may be done by gridding the stage out into 6- to 8-foot squares, or plotting circles over the stage that are on 6- to 8-foot centers—as noted in Figure 10.18. Care should be taken to coordinate the placement of the modules with placement of furniture, platforms, stairs and the like so that,

FIGURE 10.18
The first step in choosing the appropriate beam spread is to plot the location of the stage modules at which the individual lights will be focused, as depicted here. Each "focus point" is no more than 8 feet from another.

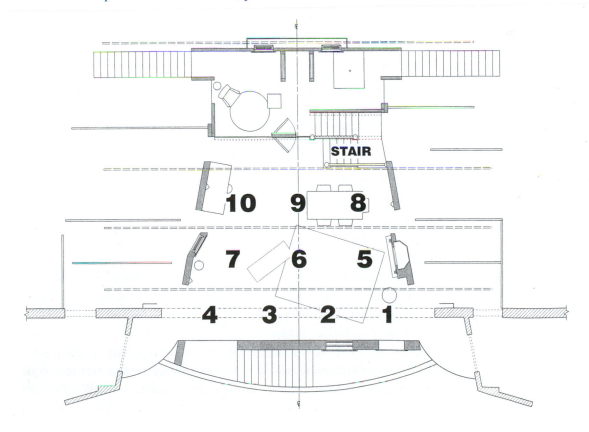

once focused, the hottest part of the individual lights is centered on these important staging areas, and can be controlled individually to enable the designer to achieve visual focus at those locations.

The designer's schematic diagrams can be broken down into functions such as main source, reflected light, tonality, fill, and so on. For each 8-foot module, the lighting position for each of these functions is already determined based on the desired angle and from there, the actual throw distance can be calculated. (Note that due to space limitations, it may be necessary to compromise on precise locations, but the designer should try to place each light in as close to its optimal position as possible.)

For commonly used ERSs, the following table can be used to estimate the appropriate beam spread:

THROW	SPECIFIED BY DEGREE	SPECIFIED BY LENS
<18 FEET	50°	$4^{1}/_{2} \times 6^{1}/_{2}$
15–25 FEET	40°–36°	6×9
25–35 FEET	30°–26°	6×12
35–50 FEET	20°–19°	6×16
50–65 FEET	12°–10°	6×22
>65 FEET	5°	10×12

This table can be expanded to include any type of lighting unit based on the photometric information furnished by the manufacturer. The minimum throw distance is where the diameter of the beam would be less than the size of the module at head height (the field diameter will be larger). The maximum throw is where the illuminance level falls off to below 50 footcandles for that throw.

Some designers and many students find it useful to have clear acetate overlays of various beam spreads in half-inch scale. These can be bought commercially or home-made at one-tenth the cost. To see the actual throw of the light when using an acetate overlay, look at a section along the center line of the beam of light. Computer programs such as Beamwright can also be used to compare the beam spreads of different types of light for their throw distances.

This modular technique is applicable to almost any direction of light across the entire stage, assuming that uniform illumination from that direction is the goal. As with any technique related to the art of stage design, this technique should be employed only as a guide, not as a rule. As discussed earlier, there are many more factors to visibility than mere illumination, such as contrast and adaptation.

One may very well end up with a field diameter of 15 feet to light an 8-foot module. This is necessary for two important reasons. First, the object being lit, the performer's face, is 5 to 6 feet above stage level, where the field diameter is narrower. More importantly, each light needs to blend seamlessly with the one focused at the next module so that as the actor walks across the stage, the light level on him or her does not vary dramatically—unless, of course, it is the intention of the design to do so. When focused, the fields of the lights are blended between their brighter central beams to create a uniform appearance from one module to the next.

If a set has a staircase or multiple levels, care should be taken to account for the change in elevation of the set. Although modules may be on 8-foot centers throughout the level portion of the set, an 8-foot run of stairs also means a significant change in elevation, thus requiring more than one light.

Another situation requiring adjustments to this modular technique is the use of direct sidelight, as one might use in dance. In such a case, the spread of light should be worked out in elevation so that for a mid-high side, for example, the light covers the full body of the dancer at near quarter line. This light may be the only sidelight needed as it will focus across the entire stage or, alternatively, a second light may be placed somewhat higher to carry the light across the far side of the stage, as shown in the elevation in Figure 10.19.

Often, specific illumination, rather than uniform illumination, is desirable. Many designers want to accent a given space or moment with a single luminaire focused in a specific way. In such instances, the designer should choose a light

FIGURE 10.19
Sidelight for dance may be chosen so that the light covers the full body of a dancer at the near quarter line of the stage. For head-highs, a second light of narrower beam spread may be placed above the first to punch up the far side of the stage.

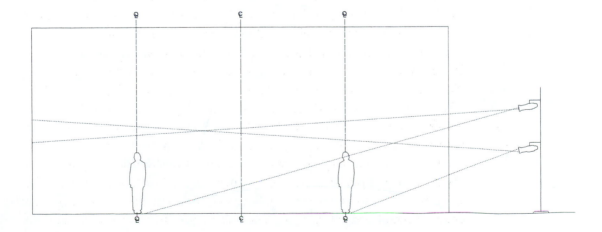

with a field angle that produces the desired size of light for a given throw. For units specified by field angle, this simple formula, the derivation of which is depicted in Figure 10.20, can be used to determine spread for a given distance of throw:

spread = 2 × tangent (field angle ÷ 2) × distance

**FOR ANY RIGHT TRIANGLE
THE TANGENT = OPPOSITE LEG/ADJACENT LEG**

**THE TANGENT OF ANGLE/2 = SPREAD/2 DIVIDED BY
THROW DISTANCE**

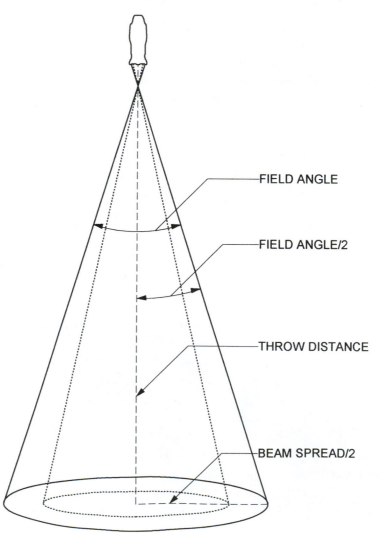

FIELD ANGLE

FIELD ANGLE/2

THROW DISTANCE

BEAM SPREAD/2

FIGURE 10.20
This diagram shows the derivation of the equation for beam spread: spread = 2 × tangent (field/2) × distance.

For PARs, because their beam shape is oblong, one needs to consider the beam and field angle for both the short and long axes of the instrument. Because the beam and field of PARs are so distinct, the designer should take both dimensions into account.

If all else fails, and both calculators and photometric data are unavailable, then the following shortcut table can be easily memorized and employed in making instrument choices while waiting for a plane, or meeting someone over morning coffee:

UNITS BY LENS	UNITS BY FIELD ANGLE	SPREAD PER FOOT OF THROW
4½ × 6½	50°	12":1'
6 × 9	36°	9":1'
6 × 12	26°	6":1'
6 × 16	19°	3":1'

A good way to train oneself to intuit appropriate beam spreads for a given distance is to focus lights for other designers and/or observe their focus sessions. Doing so will train one's eye to see the beam distribution of various types of lights and create a visual "library" of photometrics.

CHOOSING INSTRUMENTATION TO LIGHT SCENERY

Spotlights, wash lights, and flood lights, both fixed and automated, should be considered as options when deciding how to light the scenic space within or in front of which the performance happens. The scenery comprises a large proportion of the field of view. The amount of light and dark and the composition of color and texture on walls and/or a backdrop are all part of the cumulative vision.

A common scenic condition to light is a backdrop of natural muslin, or cyc (short for cyclorama). The cyc may be curved or straight. Although the wraparound effect of a curved cyc can be quite stunning, it is more difficult to light. The white cyc is a blank canvas for the lighting artist. In many plays, the backdrop may be designed to mimic sky; in dance or more abstract works, it may form a color field against which to see the dancers; in a concert it may be a screen for projections.

It is a good idea to take mental note of the sky under different conditions to create yet another visual image library from which to draw inspiration. When the sky is clear, it appears lightest at the horizon. Composing a cyc so it is lighter at the horizon pays off dramatically not only for naturalistic effect but because the brighter portion of the cyc will be down where the performers are, keeping visual focus in the active portion of the field.

Most of the striplights and cyc floods detailed earlier, when placed at an appropriate distance, can provide adequate illumination on a small-to-medium sized drop. However, in considering the composition of light on the drop, one can compose the light on it by lighting the drop from both top and bottom and using both flood lights and focusable lights. When striplights are placed on the ground or in a cyc pocket, they become a lighting "ground row." If one cannot use a ground row because of space limitations, it may be useful to hang two sets of striplights, one focused at the middle of the drop and one at the bottom, as shown in Figure 10.21, or to use cyc floods for overall coloration and PAR strips to punch up the bottom of the drop.

Curved backdrops are a bit trickier to light than straight drops, and instrumentation choices are more limited. To light into the curve, a round beam shape is a good choice. PAR strips should not be used to light a curved drop, as the oblong beam shapes cannot be blended as they wrap around the curve. T-3 strips can be used to light a curved drop if they are kept equidistant from the

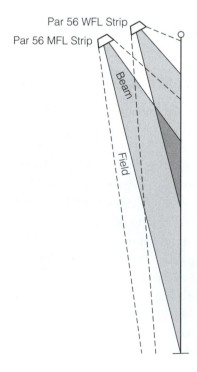

FIGURE 10.21
Two sets of PAR strips can be used to provide vertical illumination on a straight drop.

drop by placing them on a customized curved pipe downstage of the drop. Diffusion media will probably be required with T-3 strips to facilitate adequate blending. Because of their round beam shape and soft edge, fresnels in flood focus can sometimes be a good choice for lighting a curved drop, as can ERFs (scoops) if there is enough space for them. It is usually not a good idea to mix different unit types for the general floodlighting of a drop since the quality, intensity, and sometimes even color temperature might differ between units lighting the curved and straight sections of the drop.

If a backdrop is translucent (able to transmit light) the designer has more surfaces to compose. Although the drop may appear to be a two-dimensional plane, a greater sense of depth and atmosphere can be achieved by lighting front and back surfaces. Translucent drops are generally made from starched seamless muslin, rear projection screen, filled sharkstooth scrim, or another light-transmitting medium. If a transparent scrim is added in front of the translucency, it can add even more depth, as well as keep light from the downstage playing areas off of the backdrop.

Translucent drops may have different subject matter painted on the back and the front. For example, bare branches may be opaquely painted on the front of the drop, with leaves opaquely painted on the back. By lighting the front with cyc floods, one has a winter look, by lighting the front with leafy texture and the back with cyc floods so the leaves are visible, one can effect the transition from winter to summer. Such a drop is sometimes called a "transformation drop."

ERSs are also an excellent choice for adding texture to a blank backdrop or even to high set walls. In order to maintain visual focus, it is often necessary to break up large expanses of scenery with texture so the audience does not have the impression of blankness on the stage.

Scenery that is more three dimensional than a mere backdrop must also be considered in the overall composition of light and instrumentation choices. The designer may choose to use the same angles of light on the scenery as he or she is using on the actors, or to sculpt the scenery differently. As noted earlier, light that grazes textured surfaces from above, below, or the side accentuates the texture of a piece by creating highlights and shadows. Three-dimensional scenic form can be sculpted with light as well. To choose the appropriate instrumentation for such an application, one can go back to the original list of questions regarding beam control and light quality.

Key terms

BARN DOOR	GOBO
BARREL	GROUND ROW
BEAM ANGLE	HALATION
BIRDIE	HANGER
BOOMERANG	INKIES
CHOPPER	IRIS
COLOR MIXER	LEKO
COLOR SCROLLER	LUMINAIRE
COSINE DISTRIBUTION	MOVING HEAD LUMINAIRE
CROSS-FADE	MOVING MIRROR LUMINAIRE
CYC	PAR
CYC FLOOD	PEAK BEAM CANDLEPOWER
CYCLORAMA	PLANO-CONVEX LENSES
DONUT	SCANNER
DOUSER	SCOOP
DROP	SHARKSTOOTH SCRIM
ELLIPSOIDAL REFLECTOR FLOODLIGHT (ERF)	SHUTTER
	SPECIAL
ELLIPSOIDAL REFLECTOR SPOTLIGHT (ERS)	SPOTLIGHT
	STEP LENS
FIELD ANGLE	STRIPLIGHT
FIXED-FOCUS	SYSTEM
FLAT FIELD DISTRIBUTION	TILT
FLIPPER	TOP HAT
FLOOD LIGHT	TRANSFORMATION DROP
FOCUS POINTS	TRANSLUCENT
FOLLOW SPOT	TRUNION
FRESNEL	WASH LIGHT
FRESNEL LENS	WORKLIGHT
GATE	

11

ORGANIZATION
AND CONTROL

WITH instrumentation chosen, the lighting designer is almost ready to start drafting the final light plot. Before doing so, however, the lighting design intent needs to be organized so that the designer can keep track of all of the various functions and types of lighting units, and the colors chosen for them. There are many ways to organize the design information, but the "channel hookup," which, in its final form, is a required piece of the lighting designer's paperwork, provides a useful format for organizing a design based on lighting ideas or functionality.

This chapter explores the hookup format, introduces some philosophies of lighting control and the development of those philosophies and presents some methods for assessing control system needs. For the most up-to-date technical information on control technology, periodically check manufacturers' web sites, as this area of technology advances rapidly.

THE HOOKUP FORMAT

The hookup, in its final form, is the lighting designer's instructions to the electrician regarding how the stage lighting luminaires will be controlled by the lighting control system; it shows which lights are controlled together and by what channels (individual avenues of dimmer regulation). The hookup form itself is useful at this stage of the design process for organizing specific design details because it includes columnar information, in fairly standard order, about the channel, dimmer, position and unit number, instrument type and wattage, purpose, focus (focus point or stage area), color, and template for each individual lighting unit. Using channel hookup forms, such as those depicted in Figure 11.1, enables the designer to arrange the design according to the way lights function compositionally for the design, rather than by arbitrary groupings that have little to do with the ideas driving the design decisions.

The information that goes in the latter columns of the hookup form has already been determined by this point in the design process, at least in a preliminary fashion. The schematic diagrams lead the designer to specify the hanging position in the theatre—precise unit numbers will be determined at the final drafting stage; unit type and wattage can be determined based on the beam control and quality desired, as well as the throw distance; the purpose of light can be taken right from the notes on the schematic diagrams; the focus point was determined as part of the instrumentation specification process; and color and templates were specified at the design development/schematic diagram phase. The hookup form can be used to consolidate all of this information, a necessary step before final drafting begins (see Chapter 12).

At this stage, a lighting designer can decide the amount and type of control needed to implement the design. For example, does each light within a given function of light or system need to be controlled individually, or can some of these be grouped together? Because a large part of the cost of a lighting package is in the control system, economy of control could be important. The needs of the design in terms of specificity of control, desired effects, and user interface—particularly with regard to automated lights—will lead the designer toward an appropriate control system specification. In resident and academic theatre situations, one is usually confined to using an extant control system and the designer must adapt the design to meet the exigencies of that system by, perhaps, grouping lights together to stay within a fixed number of dimmers.

As an example of how the hookup form may be developed, let us return to *A Streetcar Named Desire*. To translate the needs of the first scene into a prelimi-

Show: **Hookup**   Page: ___ of ___
Designer: Date:
For: Theatre:

Channel	Dim	Position—No.	Type	Color	Focus	Notes

FIGURE 11.1
A channel hookup form, such as those depicted here, can be a useful tool for overall organization of design data.

Show Title

CHANNEL HOOKUP

Page 1
30 Jan 2004
Lighting Design by:
Assistant Lighting Designer

Theatre Name
Production Electrician:

Channel	Dim	Position	Unit#	Type & Wattage	Purpose	Focus	Color & Temp
(1)							
(2)							
(3)							
(4)							
(5)							
(6)							
(7)							
(8)							
(9)							
(10)							
(11)							
(12)							

nary hookup, one can list lighting functions, color, preliminary lighting positions, and unit types with preliminary channel numbers now added:

STREETCAR—PRELIMINARY HOOKUP

CHANNEL RANGE	POSITION	UNIT TYPE	PURPOSE/FOCUS	COLOR
1	SR booms	PAR 64 MFL	Sun through windows	L134
2–10	#1 Beam, #1 Electric	S4-26° or 36°	Sun support: apron, LR DSL/DSR/ML/MC/MR/doorway/sink area	R18
11–18	#2 Beam, #1 Beam	S4-26°	Skylight: apron, LR DSL/DSR/ML/MC/MR/doorway/sink area	R53
21–26	#4 Beam	S4-10°	Tonality BR L/C/R; LR L/C/R	L142
30	Practical electric	Practical		
31–38	#1 Elec/#2 Elec	S4-36°	Practical support: fapron, LR DSL/DSR/ML/MC/MR/doorway/sink area	L213
39	#1 Elec	S4-26°	Practical through portieres	L213

And so on, until each purpose of light in the schematic diagrams for the whole production is accounted for. The hookup may go through a number of iterations before completion, but eventually, the finished hookup will have even more detailed information: Precise channel numbers, the unit number at each position, individually noted purposes, and focus points. At this stage, however, a rough hookup is sufficient for keeping track of the entire design and assessing control system requirements.

FUNDAMENTALS OF THEATRICAL LIGHTING CONTROL

To be able to judge the advantages or disadvantages of a given control system, one obviously needs a basic understanding of control system technology and its capabilities. Lighting control technology changes and develops at a rapid pace. Recent trends in dimming and control give the lighting designer great flexibility in the control of lighting equipment. Lights can be controlled individually or in groups, complex cue sequences can be accomplished with the touch of a button, automation and special effects can be controlled from the same console as the regular lighting, and new products for dimming and/or control seem to hit the market almost monthly.

A control system usually consists of the control console, known as the "front end" of the system, and the dimmers, sometimes called the "back end." Figure 11.2 illustrates the relationship between these components and the lights themselves. In order for the console to control the luminaires, the lights are first plugged into circuits. Circuits may be in permanent raceways as in most resident theatres, such as in Figure 11.3, or be run through individual or multi-circuit cables. The circuits are then either hard-wired directly into dimmers, as in a permanent installation, or "hard patched" (plugged in) to the back of the dimmer rack, as they are for the touring production depicted in Figure 11.4. The dimmers are controlled by the control console through a digital cable. It is the dimmers that alter the electricity to the lamp, causing its intensity to change. Power to the dimmers is supplied by the building's electric power distribution system (see the appendix). In obsolete control systems, the front and back ends are one and the same, operated mechanically rather than electronically.

Most contemporary control consoles are memory consoles. That is, computers with hardware and software interfaces designed specifically for controlling theatrical lighting. In such systems, a control channel controls each dimmer. The

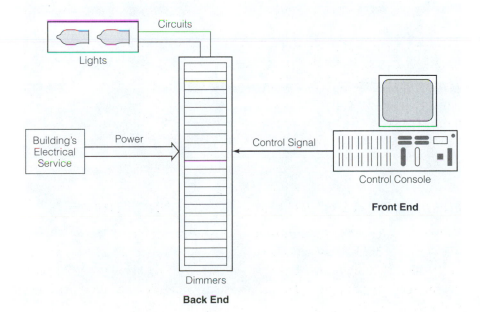

FIGURE 11.2
A simple riser diagram of a theatrical control system showing the relationship between control console, dimmers, and building power.

FIGURE 11.3
Raceways such as those depicted here house the wiring of permanent circuits.

FIGURE 11.4
Temporary cables run into the back of touring dimmer racks on *Thoroughly Modern Millie— National Tour.*

channel is the electronic "handle" for the dimmer. Control channels may control more than one dimmer, but a dimmer can only be controlled by one channel, unless it is a specific kind of "multiplexed" dimmer that enables two circuits to be hard patched into the same dimmer but controlled individually. To assign a dimmer to a control channel, one "soft patches" the dimmers to the channels. Analogous to the hardware-to-hardware action of hard patching circuits to dimmers, soft patching uses the software within the control console to place a dimmer or, if standardized control protocols are used, a moving light attribute under the control of a specific channel.

There are three basic philosophies governing the way contemporary control consoles "remember" cues: tracking (also called "last action"), highest-takes-precedence, or hybrid. There is a historical context behind the development of these philosophies. The first electric lighting control systems were mechanical resistance dimmers. Resistance dimmers increase or decrease the resistance on a circuit, thereby causing the light to dim when resistance is high or play at its fullest intensity when the dimmer is not adding any resistance to the circuit. Figure 11.5 shows an old resistance dimmer pack. To operate resistance dimmers, a person literally had to move a large mechanical handle to change the intensity of light. Once brought to a specific level *the light would stay at that level until the handle was moved again*. In other words, a light would track through a show at a level until its dimmer handle was moved. This is background to the development of tracking style consoles such as the Strand Light Pallette and 500 series, and the ETC Obsession.

Resistance dimmers were usually quite large, both physically and in terms of their load, sometimes having a 6000W or 7200W capacity. Resistance dimmers need to be loaded to capacity to operate. This meant that during the period when

FIGURE 11.5
An old resistance dimmer rack containing eight dimmers.

Linda Essig

resistance dimmers were prevalent, lighting was designed in broad strokes, rather than specific units. Resistance dimmers sometimes were used to control smaller dimmer packs, however, known as auxiliary boards or preset boards. Four-, 6-, or 8-plate auxiliary packs could be controlled by one 6kW dimmer. Individual levels could be set ahead of time or "pre-set" and then brought up together by using the main resistance dimmer as a master.

Once electronic dimming became more common in the 1960s, analog electronic preset consoles were developed. Unlike resistance boards, electronic preset consoles are still in use today when manual control is desired, as might be the case in a small live music venue or school. A preset board consists of one or more banks of sliders that have a one-to-one correspondence with the dimmers; channel slider 1 controls dimmer 1, channel slider 2 controls dimmer 2, and so on. Slider controls are operated manually and are calibrated from 0 to 10, with 10 representing full intensity. Because these boards come equipped with two or more banks of sliders, each equipped with master sliders, entire cues can be "preset" on a bank of sliders without that cue appearing on stage until its master slider is activated. If two banks of sliders are activated simultaneously, the dimmer reads the highest level being sent down the control wiring so as to avoid levels above 100% that would blow out the lamps. Hence the term "highest-takes-precedence." Figure 11.6 depicts a forty-eight channel, two-scene preset console.

The number of channels on a two-scene preset is dependent upon the number of dimmers available, physical space available for the console, the operator's ability to operate the console, and cost. Like the dimmer packs themselves, preset consoles are usually available in multiples of twelve channels (12, 24, 36, 48, and 96). Some preset consoles have additional features such as bump buttons at each fader or even some memory capability. Such consoles are known as "memory-assisted preset consoles." Such consoles may have the ability to record an entire cue into a slider or to do some soft patching, or both. Thus, a 48-channel, two-scene preset console can be programmed with ninety-six preset cues that can then be executed with the individual sliders.

Computer control consoles are the most prevalent type of console. All can store cue data, the soft patch, fade times, system information, and so on. Their capacities in these areas vary from manufacturer to manufacturer.

While the designer is understandably concerned with the control console's ca-

FIGURE 11.6
A two-scene preset console.

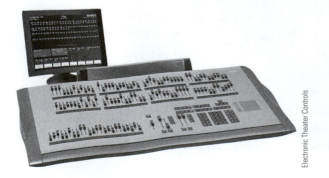

Electronic Theater Controls

pabilities, it is the dimmers that carry the actual electrical load of the luminaires. Dimmers have a maximum load capacity, usually indicated in watts. Some common dimmer capacities are 1200W (1.2kW), 2400W (2.4kW), and 5000W (5kW). Knowing the dimmer capacity is important to developing the channel hookup. If, for example, a small theatre has forty-eight dimmers of 3000W each, there can be no more than forty-eight dimmable channels of control, each having no more than 3000W of lighting load plugged into them at any one time—even if the control console offers more channel capacity.

Control console criteria

If one is fortunate enough to be able to select a control system for a production or a performance space, there are a number of factors to consider. At the very least, the control console must have enough memory capacity for the necessary number of channels and cues. The preliminary hookup discussed earlier can provide a good estimate of the number of required channels. A careful reading of the script or libretto, as well as attending rehearsals in the rehearsal hall, will enable the designer to develop a cuing scheme and from there estimate the required cue capacity.

The control philosophies discussed earlier are another major factor in making control console decisions. Many designers of lighting for dramatic performance and musical theatre prefer a tracking-style console. In a tracking-style console, the console essentially remembers when a channel is told to change its level. Otherwise, that channel "tracks" at the same level. This control philosophy is useful in theatre where the event runs in the same sequence each time. If the designer records all the cues and then decides, for example, that the level of a practical is too bright, the new level can be recorded in the first cue in which it comes up and that new level then tracks through the entire show.

Highest-takes-precedence (HTP) consoles grew out of the preset console idea. In an HTP console, the entire cue with all of its channel readings is recorded as a kind of snapshot and then the console electronically cross-fades from one complete look to another. This type of console is popular for use in architectural and entertainment venues and in TV studios, as well as for theatrical productions.

Although the results may look the same when cues are played back in performance, the syntax of keystrokes between different types of consoles, or from one manufacturer's product to another, differs. Designers in training should experience both major control philosophies to assess which interface works best for their style of cuing.

To accommodate the prevalence of automated lights and accessories, hybrid consoles have been developed. These consoles contain a specialized software interface to control moving light attributes. They also combine features of both tracking- and HTP-style consoles. For example, a hybrid console automatically tracks the levels of position attributes but looks at level and color attributes in an HTP fashion. Hybrid consoles also have some capacity to control fixed-focus lights, although the interface that does that may be different than the other two types of consoles. Hence, on large productions, designers often opt to have separate consoles for fixed-focus and automated lights.

Consoles commonly can operate in different modes, such as program mode, playback mode, or backup mode. One feature to look for is the ability to operate in both playback mode and program mode simultaneously. This allows the designer to make programming changes while the technical rehearsals are running. Most consoles have this ability. Some consoles have built in backup systems. In some consoles, this is a completely redundant system, but in others it is merely the ability to operate twelve cues manually. If backup is likely to be needed, for example in an area with significant electrical disturbances, or when there is a lot of money at stake, as in a commercial production, redundant backup is probably needed.

The layout of the monitor screen is a relatively minor factor in choosing a console but is part of the user interface and so a designer may have preferences with regard to the information in front of him or her at the tech table. Understanding that information and being able to make efficient use of it is important to both the smooth operation of the console and a pleasant technical rehearsal experience. Many consoles can display at least two types of information simultaneously, usually the channel screen (or screens) and a cue list. Figure 11.7 shows a typical monitor screen displaying channel information in "stage" mode (some consoles refer to this as "live" mode), as well as a partial cue list on the bottom right and fader playback information on the bottom left.

Effects packages and their interfaces are additional factors that distinguish one console from another. Specialized effects software allows the designer to program light chase effects that may be as simple as an A-B-C marquee chase, or complex subroutines, if the console has that capability. If such effects are crucial to the design, the specifier should consider the number of available steps in a sequence, the types of sequences available (positive, negative, bounce, ripple, and so on), the ability to program the time of and between each step, the ease of programming, and the way in which the effects cues link to the regular cues during playback.

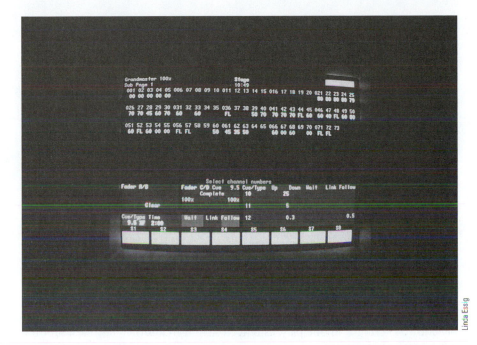

FIGURE 11.7
The monitors
of a highest-
takes-precedence
console.

In some instances, manual submasters may be a desirable console option so that certain lights can be controlled manually. Or, some consoles enable a chase effect to be loaded into a submaster and played back manually.

If possible, a designer should specify a control system based solely on the user interface they prefer, the needs of the channel hookup, and the cuing scheme for the show. There are, however, external factors to consider as well. The theatre building has a fixed amount of power in it. Its load capacity determines the maximum number of dimmers that can be used. The control system, both front and back ends, is often the single most expensive item in the lighting budget. Often, bids for the cost of a production's lighting package are not based on the number of luminaires but rather on the number of dimmers and any automation package. Money, therefore, is another parameter in control system specification.

REFINING THE CHANNEL HOOKUP

More often than not, designers must fit their hookup needs into an extant control system. In resident and academic theatres, for example, there may be a fixed number of circuits hard-wired on a dimmer-per-circuit basis into 96 or 192 dimmers (dimmers often come in racks of 96). The design of the hookup—the channel assignments—and in a sense the lighting as a whole, is affected by the parameters of the control system. The details of the preliminary hookup may need to be prioritized. For example, if the first iteration of the hookup indicates that the reflected light, which provides for visibility at both downstage left and midstage left modules of the stage are in separate channels, is it possible to control these two instruments together in the same channel and always have them operating together? If, in rehearsal, one sees that these two parts of the stage are always used simultaneously—that they never need to be controlled separately—then the luminaires can be controlled by the same channel, and, if the electrician decides it is necessary, the same dimmer as well.

Another way of thinking about the channel hookup, the control system, and the design as a whole is to consider what directions and colors of light may have more than one purpose in different scenes. For example, can the practical support for the night scene be used as fill light in the day scene? If color choices are made carefully, this type of economy in design can be achieved.

In designing for repertory situations, whether for dance or dramatic performance, this kind of thinking is essential. The sidelight from stage left may function as sunlight in one play, as reflected light in another, and as sculptural form-giving light in the dance program that plays in the theatre on Monday nights. Although one may design a channel hookup for a rep plot based on location and direction of light, one should still consider how those various directions function conceptually within the design of the individual events that play within that repertory.

Once control system parameters have been assessed (in resident theatre) or determined (in a rental situation), specific channel numbers can be assigned to the lists of purposes and positions on the preliminary hookup. It is useful to group together channel numbers that will be used together. In other words, lights used in scene 1 might be sequential in the hookup, as would the lights in scene 2, and so on. Or, the hookup may be organized based on a more general direction and function of light, as many of the luminaires will be used in more than one scene. Another consideration when finalizing these numbers and the overall hookup organization is how the cues will be built in the theatre. The former approach may be useful in a multi-scene play with specific discrete locations, and the latter approach more appropriate in dance repertory. Some designers even try to organize their hookup so that it makes sense on the computer screen, with blocks of 20 or 25 channels. Doing so enables the designer to visualize the relationship between channels when looking at the monitor.

With channel numbers, instrument types, and locations determined on this preliminary hookup, the designer can now turn his or her attention to drafting the final light plot and section.

KEY TERMS

BUMP BUTTONS

CHANNEL

CHASE

CIRCUIT

CROSS-FADES

CUE

DIMMER

FADER

HARD-PATCHED

HARD-WIRED

HIGHEST-TAKES-PRECEDENCE (HTP)

HOOKUP

HYBRID CONSOLES

PRACTICAL

PRESET

PRESET CONSOLES

RACEWAYS

RESISTANCE DIMMERS

SLIDERS

SUBMASTERS

TRACKING

12

DRAFTING THE FINISHED PLOT AND SECTION

THE finished light plot and section are the shop drawings of the lighting design. That is, they are the drawings that convey the design intent to the electricians who will hang, circuit, and focus the lights to implement the design. These drawings, although potentially complex and time consuming to produce, are *not* the design. The design is the formation and visualization of the design ideas, the development of the schematic diagrams and rough hookup, and eventually the light cues. Yet, drafting the finished plot and section is a critical step in communicating the design to those who will execute it.

Generally produced in ½" = 1'0" scale (unless a very large venue necessitates a smaller scale), the light plot shows the layout of all of the lighting units at every position, whether drawing with paper and pencil or using a computer drafting program. The plot may be one page or many pages depending on the size and complexity of the show. To a novice, drafting a light plot and section may seem a daunting task, but it need not be. The light plot appears at first to be a plan view looking down from above the level of the lights. Actually, the plot is a composite view because it will incorporate all hanging information including elevations of booms and ladders, set-mounted equipment, and other lighting information.

This chapter takes a step-by-step approach to turning a preliminary hookup into the finished draft and completed final hookup. Before the drafting can be completed, the designer must determine specific placement of each lighting instrument on each hanging position and understand common drafting conventions.

FINALIZING LUMINAIRE PLACEMENT AT EACH POSITION

Before committing a line to the final plot, the units must be appropriately located along each position. A paperwork tool that will help with this step is the instrument schedule. An instrument schedule contains the same information as a channel hookup, but instead of sorting that information by channel number, the information is sorted by position. If using a spreadsheet or database management program for the hookup, the software should be able to sort the information by hanging position. If working out things roughly on paper, then it is necessary to make a list of all of the lights, their channel numbers, and purposes for each given position. This may be done on individual sheets of paper for each position, to help keep track of the information. An example of the instrument schedule form is depicted in Figure 12.1.

The rough plot can be done either by placing a piece of tracing paper over the ground plan with the lighting positions indicated, indicating lighting positions on an extra copy of that plan, or by laying out positions on individual pieces of paper for each position. If the latter, draw the pipe in ¼" scale onto the paper and mark it clearly with the center line. The center line will be the datum line for measuring distances to stage left (SL or L) and stage right (SR or R). Each horizontal position, front-of-house, or onstage electric, should be marked with tick marks at 18-inch centers, as most of the units discussed in Chapter 10 are designed to hang on 18-inch centers (automated lights usually take up a bit more space and should be placed accordingly). Vertical positions such as box booms or booms should be marked off with 2-foot centers to allow for enough space between side arms.

Now, the designer can lay out the units on the positions with the appropriate spacing. As this is a rough plot rather than a finished one, an "X" to mark each luminaire location and a channel number to keep track of what it is should be sufficient at this layout stage. The first units to be placed should be those that have a critical focus, such as a downlight directly over a specific point on stage,

AIN'T MISBEHAVIN' | INSTRUMENT SCHEDULE |

Page 1
06 Aug 2003
LD: LINDA ESSIG
ALDS: D. GALLAGHER, B. THRASHER
HEAD ELECTRICIAN: DOUG VANCE

SKYLIGHT OPERA THEATRE
BROADWAY THEATRE CENTER
MILWAUKEE WI

#1 Electric

U#	Chn	Dim	Type & Wattage	Purpose	Focus	Color	Template
1	(27)		S4-36 575w	SL Front	UL	G 328	
2	(50)		6x12 750w	Shadow - blue	Stair	R67	
3	(30)		S4-36 575w	SL Front	Stair	G 328	
4	(1)		S4-26 575w	Downlight	DL	C/C	
4	(11)		Scroller	Scroller	DL	see note	
5	(28)		S4-36 575w	SL Front	UC	G 328	
6	(149)		6x12 750w	Sconce texture	Wall R	L107	GAM 857
7	(155)		6x12 750w	Chaise spl	Chaise	G970	
8	(2)		S4-26 575w	Downlight	DC	C/C	
8	(12)		Scroller	Scroller	DC	see note	
9	(29)		S4-36 575w	SL Front	UR	G 328	
10	(37)		S4-36 575w	SR Front	UL	G 970	
11	(2)		S4-26 575w	Downlight	DC	C/C	
11	(12)		Scroller	Scroller	DC	see note	
12	(38)		S4-36 575w	SR Front	UC	G 970	
13	(3)		S4-26 575w	Downlight	DR	C/C	
13	(13)		Scroller	Scroller	DR	see note	
14	(147)		8" FRESNEL 1kw	Sconce support DS	DR	L151	
15	(40)		S4-36 575w	SR Front	Stair	G 970	
15A	(60)		6x12 750w	Shadow - yellow	Stair	G 460	
16	(39)		S4-36 575w	SR Front	UR	G 970	

or a light that may be obstructed by scenery if not placed in the exact right position. Once these critical lights are placed, the rest of the luminaires can be placed according to the design notes made on the elevation and section views of the set.

The designer may find that he or she cannot fit all of the necessary lights on a given position. It may be necessary to add a lighting position. If this is not feasible, then the lighting designer needs to prioritize the design decisions and possibly make some cuts. Designers often find themselves making compromises on angles of light so as to make the design fit into the theatre. Having clear ideas about the piece and what is most important for the design makes such compromises possible and not random.

The same process is repeated for every position, including booms, ladders, and set mounts until all of the lighting purposes and luminaires indicated in the preliminary hookup are accounted for on the rough plot. Final drafting can begin once this preliminary step of laying out units is completed. Figure 12.2 shows part of the rough plot for *Ain't Misbehavin'*. Luminaires are indicated only with X's, and a channel number guides the draftsperson back to the hookup where information about unit type, wattage, and color can be found.

FIGURE 12.1

An instrument schedule is used to organize lighting design information by position and unit number.

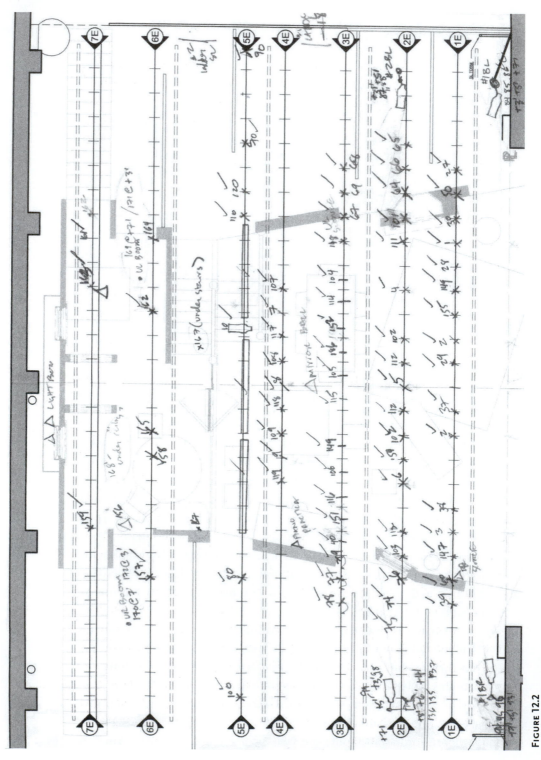

FIGURE 12.2

On the rough plot for *Ain't Misbehavin'*, the location of luminaires on each position is indicated with an X and the channel number. Many designers find it helpful to color-code their rough plot, using different colors for each unit type.

DRAFTING CONVENTIONS

Theatrical drafting relies on numerous conventions so that an electrician in Seattle, for example, can read and understand a light plot from a designer in Florida. For light plots, these conventions generally entail the layout of the plot, use of symbols, numbering of positions and units on them, line weight, and scale.

The layout of the light plots is usually oriented so downstage is toward the bottom of the page, with the center line of the stage running vertically up the paper. The title block, which contains important information about the production and the designer, should be at the lower right hand corner or along the right hand margin so that when the plot is folded or rolled, the title block can be easily viewed. Positions upstage of the proscenium arch in a proscenium theatre should be drafted to scale in their actual location, but the location from the stage to front-of-house positions, if permanently located in the theatre, can be telescoped to save paper and eliminate empty white space on the drawing. In thrust and arena stages, the permanent grid or catwalks should be drawn in their actual positions.

The draftsperson uses a variety of line weights to help clarify the drawing. The author advocates using four line weights: The heaviest for the theatre architecture; the second heaviest for the luminaires and lighting positions; the third for text, center line, and plaster line; and the lightest for the scenery. Following this hierarchy of line weights makes it appear as if the lights are hanging above the scenery (which, for the most part, they are) and situated within the theatre walls.

The luminaires themselves are indicated by lighting symbols. Each different unit type is drafted using a different symbol. In other words, a 26° ERS and a 36° ERS have similar but slightly different symbols, a 6-inch (6") fresnel is indicated by a symbol resembling the shape of a fresnel, and so on. The United States Institute for Theatre Technology (USITT) has recommended certain generic symbols be used for certain types of stage lighting luminaires. Their recommendation, a draft of which is seen in Figure 12.3, is a useful guideline, but does not necessarily meet the needs of every design. The author advocates using simple symbols such as these if drafting by hand but using symbols that are detailed to look like and actually take up as much space as the luminaires they represent if it is possible to do so with a computer drafting program. When drawn onto their positions, the luminaires should be oriented in the way they will be hung: pointing either upstage, downstage, stage left, or right (parallel or perpendicular to the hanging position). The electrician does not need to know the aiming angle to hang the lights, and drawing lighting units pointing every which way eventually leads the light plot to appear cluttered and confused.

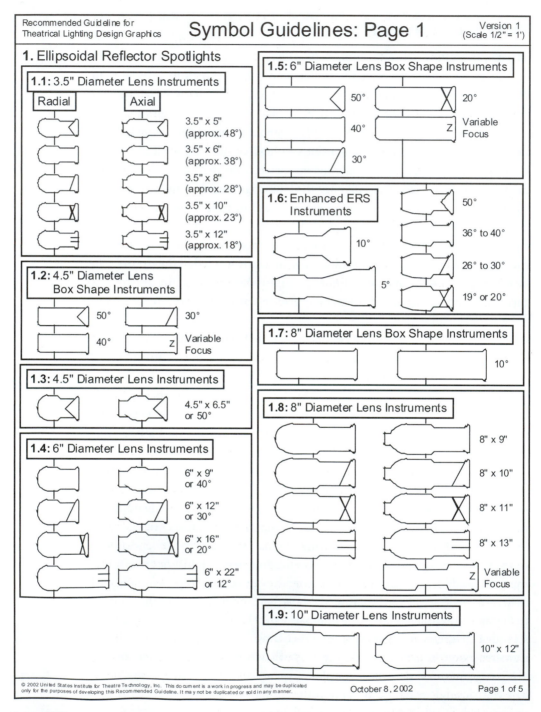

FIGURE 12.3
USITT's draft standard for lighting symbols. The final adopted version is not yet available. (© 2002 United States Institute for Theater Technology, Inc. Used with permission.)

Opinions vary as to how much information should be included within and adjacent to the luminaire symbols. At minimum, the unit number is required and is usually placed within the symbol's outline. Information helpful to the electrician such as color number and channel number are included by most designers as well, with additional space for the electrician to add dimmer numbers once those are known. However, the drawing should never look cluttered or become unreadable, as might happen if too much information is included.

The numbering convention for luminaires is to number units from stage left to stage right consecutively at each position. This facilitates the work of the electrician as he or she hangs the lights at the load-in and checks them while standing on stage prior to each performance. Note again that the lights are numbered at each position, starting with unit number 1. Thus, the farthest stage left luminaire on each electric or cove, whether on stage or front-of-house, is unit number 1. If positions run downstage to upstage, the lights are usually numbered in that direction as well, when upstage of a proscenium arch. Units downstage of the proscenium arch may be numbered downstage to upstage or away from the arch, as in the example plot from the Broadway production of *Chicago* shown in Figure 12.4. One should always number units in a consistent manner. On vertical positions such as box booms, booms, torms, and ladders, luminaires are numbered from top to bottom.

When numbering multi-circuit luminaires, they are usually designated by letters rather than numbers, with the circuits numbered. For example, a pipe with four PAR56 three-circuit striplights on it would be drawn as shown in Figure 12.5.

In any case, one must include a key to these symbols both for reference and because symbols often vary from plot to plot or designer to designer. The key should include every symbol used in the plot and an explanation of what it represents in terms of both unit type and wattage. A legend explaining what the various numbers in and around the symbols mean should also be included, as in the key and legend depicted in Figure 12.6. The unit number at each position is usually indicated inside the unit, with color number in front where the gel frame is located, and channel and dimmer numbers indicated at the back of each symbol, often within a circular or hexagonal frame.

Lighting positions follow the same numbering conventions of stage left to stage right and downstage to upstage. For example, the #1 Electric is the most downstage overhead position, usually located just upstage of the set line. Booms are likewise numbered from downstage to upstage, usually with a differentiation between stage left and stage right booms.

Vertical positions such as box booms, booms, and ladders should be indicated in both a plan view at their actual locations and elevation view, as shown in

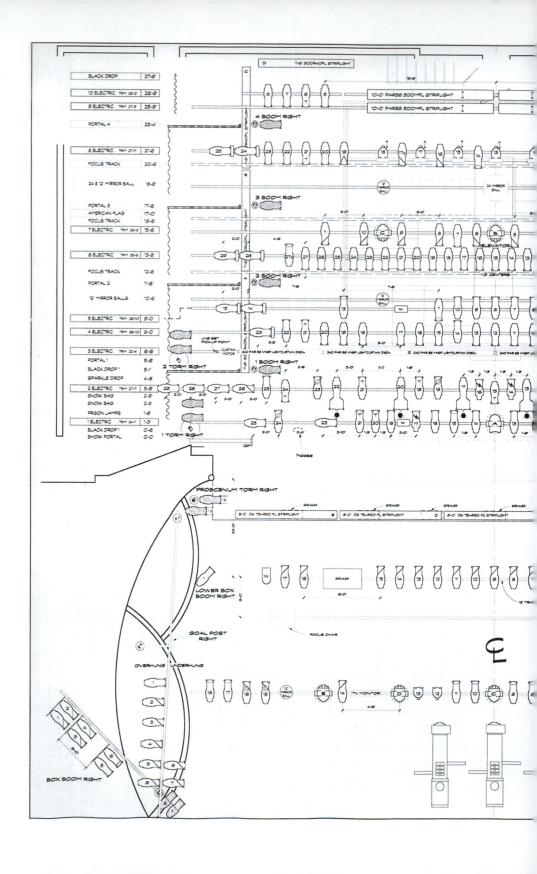

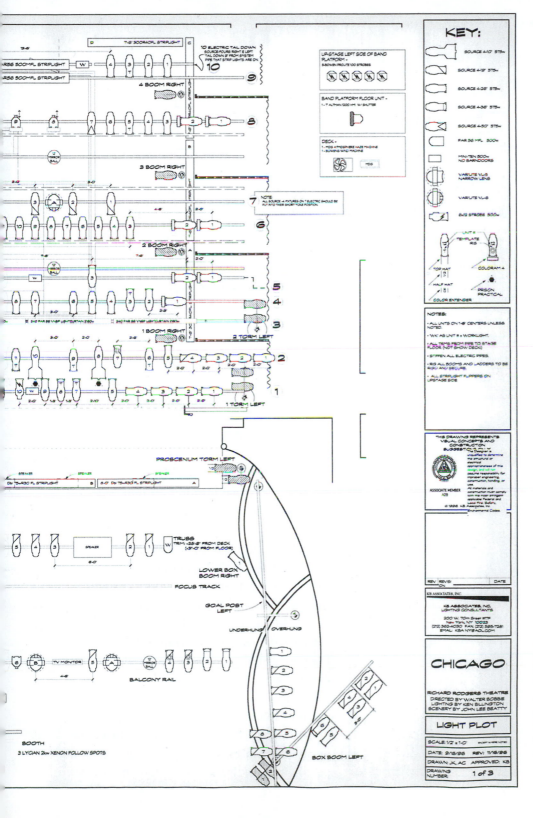

FIGURE 12.4
The first page of Ken Billington's light plot for the Broadway production of *Chicago*. (Used with permission of Ken Billington.)

FIGURE 12.5
When drafting
multi-circuit units
such as striplights,
one usually letters
the luminaire and
numbers each
circuit within
the luminaire.

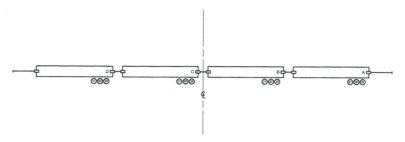

Figure 12.7. The plan view should be crosshatched or shaded to indicate its placement on the ground and drawn in its actual location, if possible. On smaller drawings the boom elevation can be adjacent to the plan view, shown as if exploding from it, with the lighting units appearing to be pointing toward the stage. On larger plots, such as for *Chicago,* the boom and ladder elevations are drawn on a separate page. When drawing vertical positions, the draftsperson dimensions from the stage floor to the side arm, because this is the dimension the electrician needs to know to execute the design. Boom or ladder elevations that repeat, as they might in a repertory plot, do not need to be drafted repeatedly. Rather, one can label an elevation "#1 Boom SL and #1 Boom SR." The plan view, indicating the actual position on both sides of the stage with dimensions to center line and plaster line, does need to be drawn, however.

Each position should be accompanied by a clear label that includes not only the name of the position but also an inventory of lights at that position and the trim height (if applicable). Although trim heights will also be indicated on the section, and equipment totals on the shop order, it is very helpful to the electrician to have this information right on the light plot when the show is hung so that he or she needs to consult only one piece of paperwork.

A hanging schedule should be included for any theatre that rigs scenery and lighting on a per-show basis, that is, all proscenium theatres

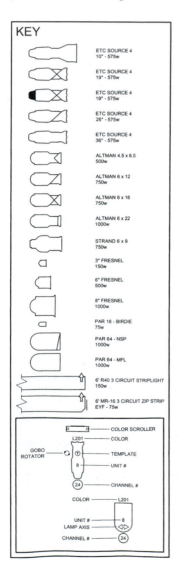

FIGURE 12.6
This sample key and legend shows the unit type and wattage for each symbol, as well as a legend explaining the labeling of each.

and many thrust theatres. The hanging schedule, such as that depicted in Figure 12.8, lists everything that hangs above the stage with its lineset number, distance from plaster line, and trim height noted. Everything that is rigged overhead, electrics, masking, drops, other pieces of flying scenery, signage and the like all need to be indicated on the hanging schedule.

One last section of the plot is the notes section. Some general notes one usually includes on the light plot are the following:

▶ Units hang on 18-inch centers except where noted
▶ Trim heights measure from stage floor to pipe and are approximate; final trim heights to be determined in the theatre
▶ Boom heights measure from boom base to side arm
▶ See hookup for template numbers
▶ All gel frames to be painted flat black

The conventions of the lighting section are very similar to those of the plot in terms of page layout and line weights. This drawing should include a hanging schedule along the top of the drawing (if applicable) and dimensions from the stage floor to the pipes. Electrics that fly in and out ("work") in the course of the performance should be indicated in both their playing position and storage position in the flies. A title block and key to symbols are as important on the section as on the plot. Figure 12.9 shows these conventions employed in the lighting section for *Chicago*.

#2 BOOM SR

2 - ETC SOURCE 4 36° 575w
3 - 6" FRESNEL 1kw

Boom hieghts measure from stage floor to side arm.

FIGURE 12.7
When drafting vertical positions such as booms, ladders, and box booms, one should indicate the position in plan view (crosshatched or shaded), as well as in elevation.

DESCRIPTION	TRIM HEIGHT	DISTANCE FROM 00'-00"	LINE SET
NO. 5 BORDER	20'-06"	26'-10"	24A
NO. 7 ELECTRIC	25'-00"	25'-10"	24
HANGING BULB ELECTRIC	18'-00"	25'-05"	23
RP STORAGE	GRID	23'-00"	22
NO. 6 ELECTRIC	23'-00"	22'-01"	21
NO. 5 LEG	00'-00"	21'-06"	20
NO. 4 BORDER	20'-06"	20'-09"	19
NO. 4 LEG	00'-00"	19'-05"	18
SCRIM WALL	00'-00"	18'-06"	17
NO. 3 LEG	00'-00"	17'-02"	16
NO. 5 ELECTRIC	23'-00"	16'-05"	15
NO. 3 BORDER	20'-06"	15'-00"	14A
NO. 4 ELECTRIC	28'-00"	14'-00"	14
	GRID	13'-03"	13
	GRID	12'-06"	12
MIRROR BALL	25'-00"	11'-09"	11
	GRID	11'-00"	10A
NO. 3 ELECTRIC	24'-06"	10'-03"	10
NO. 2 LEG	00'-00"	09'-06"	09
NO. 2 BORDER	21'-00"	08'-09"	08
	GRID	08'-00"	07
	GRID	07'-03"	06
NO. 2 ELECTRIC	28'-06"	06'-06"	05
NO. 1 LEG	00'-00"	04'-11"	04
NO. 1 ELECTRIC	24'-06"	03'-04"	03
NO. 1 BORDER	20'-00"	02'-02"	02
MAIN CURTAIN	GRID	01'-05"	01
DESCRIPTION	TRIM HEIGHT	DISTANCE FROM 00'-00"	LINE SET

FIGURE 12.8
A sample hanging schedule showing all of the scenery, masking, and lighting positions hanging over the stage.

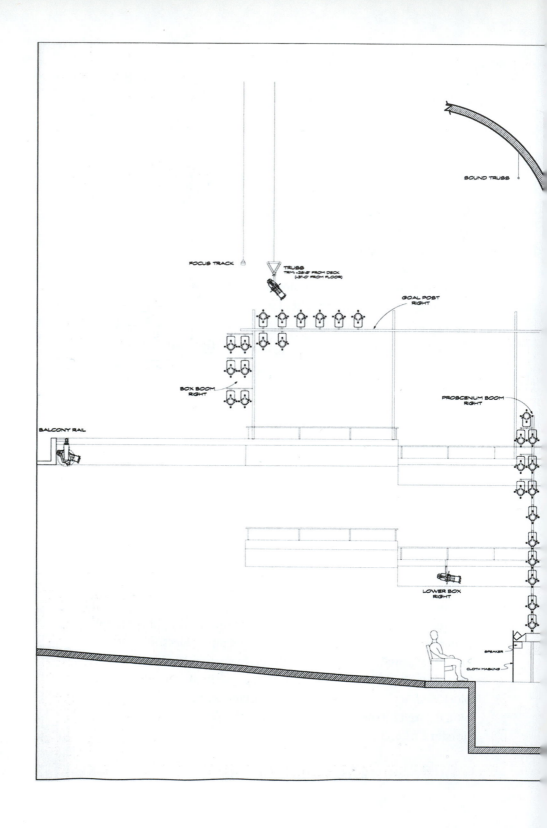

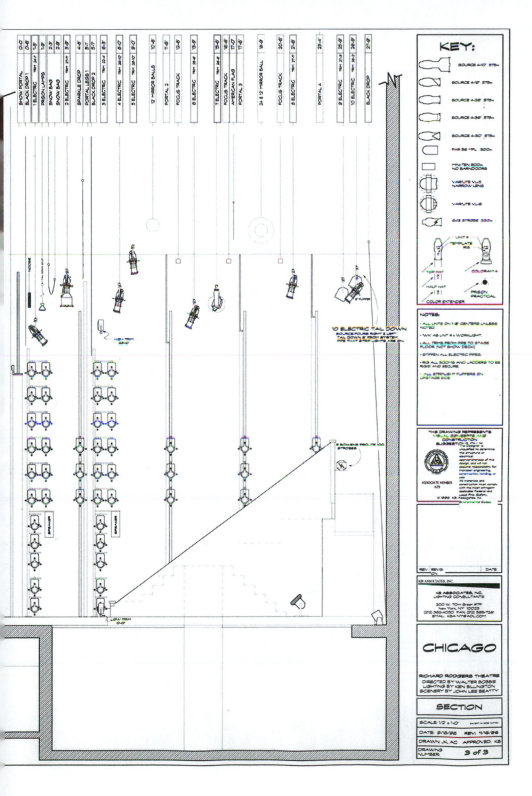

FIGURE 12.9
The lighting section for *Chicago* as designed by Ken Billington. (Used with permission of Ken Billington.)

HAND DRAFTING

The conventions of drafting are often best learned by hand so they become "muscle memory." A light plot drafted by hand may even have more style and finesse than one drafted using computer-aided drawing, but the information on a hand-drafted plot and a CAD-drafted plot should not differ—only the medium is different. If all of the layout work is done ahead of time, as described earlier, the final drafting need not be an onerous task. One should gather drafting supplies such as those shown in Figure 12.10 (and listed here) and have them handy before beginning:

- ▶ T-square, parallel rule, or drafting machine on an appropriately surfaced drawing board
- ▶ Transparentized vellum drafting paper
- ▶ Scale ruler
- ▶ Lighting symbol template in $\frac{1}{2}$" = 1' scale
- ▶ Circle and square template ("little buddy" or "common shapes")
- ▶ Large and small 30°/60° and 45° triangles
- ▶ Adjustable angle triangle
- ▶ 2H and 4H drafting pencils or lead holders
- ▶ Lead pointer (or pencil sharpener if using pencils)
- ▶ Eraser ("Mars Plastic" works well) and erasing shield
- ▶ Pad of notepaper
- ▶ Pounce powder and dusting brush

FIGURE 12.10
Some of the drafting supplies one needs if drafting by hand are the following: scale ruler, 30°/60° triangle, 45° triangle, erasing shield, drafting brush, lettering guide, eraser, lead pointer, drafting template, lead holders, drafting dots, and parallel rule.

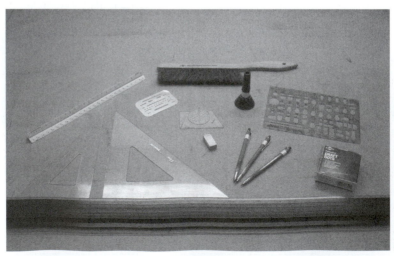

Linda Essig

With the rough layout already done, the first step of final drafting is to lay a clean piece of drafting paper (most light plots are at least 30 inches × 42 inches) over the plan of the set. Draft the center line, proscenium arch (if applicable), and stage edge first, tracing them directly from the set designer's plan or a plan of the theatre. Next, lay out each hanging position with a light line, construction line, or non-photo blue pencil. Be sure that in the overall layout of the page, there is room for the on-stage positions as well as for front-of-house positions, elevations of booms, key to symbols, and title block. Most draftspeople prefer to allocate space for these important parts of the drawing early on. If the whole theatre space cannot be accommodated on a single, reasonably sized sheet, then it is fairly common to place front-of-house positions on a separate page from on-stage positions.

Next, draw the luminaires in a dark and distinct line weight. The 2H lead is useful for the theatre architecture and lighting symbols, with the harder 4H lead left for text and scenery. Individual preferences in lead density vary. Once the luminaire symbols are drawn on, the position itself can be drawn between the units, in the same line weight. A single line is sufficient to represent the pipe, although some prefer a double line. This line should be seen only *between* the units, not within them, so the lights look like they are hanging on the pipes and so that the space inside the symbol's outline can accommodate the unit numbers and, if applicable, template or iris symbols. For clarity, the ends of each position should be articulated with a tick mark. However, recall that all dimensioning will be done from center line and either plaster line, set line, or stage edge.

After each position is completed, add the unit numbers (stage left to stage right, downstage to upstage, top to bottom). These are the final unit numbers and need to be transferred to the hookup form to complete that piece of paperwork once the plot is finished.

Other text and labeling can be done next, including position labels, the hanging schedule, and notes. When drafting by hand, the neatness of the lettering is very important. Draftspeople-in-training should spend time practicing different lettering styles until they become facile enough to print both neatly and quickly. Always use guidelines when printing on the drafting so that the text is oriented precisely horizontally (or, in some cases, vertically). Practicing one's lettering also leads to better pencil control and so can improve overall rendering skill. Dimensioning can also be done along with the other text.

Drawing the set is usually the last step in hand drafting, because it is drawn in the lightest line weight. Because the lights should appear to float above the set, the set should be indicated only between the lights, not through them. Figure 12.11 depicts a hand-drafted plot for a small flexible space.

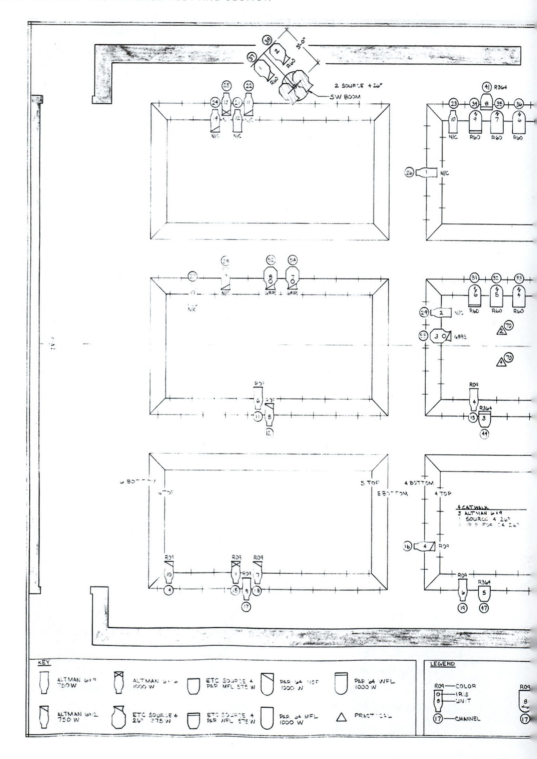

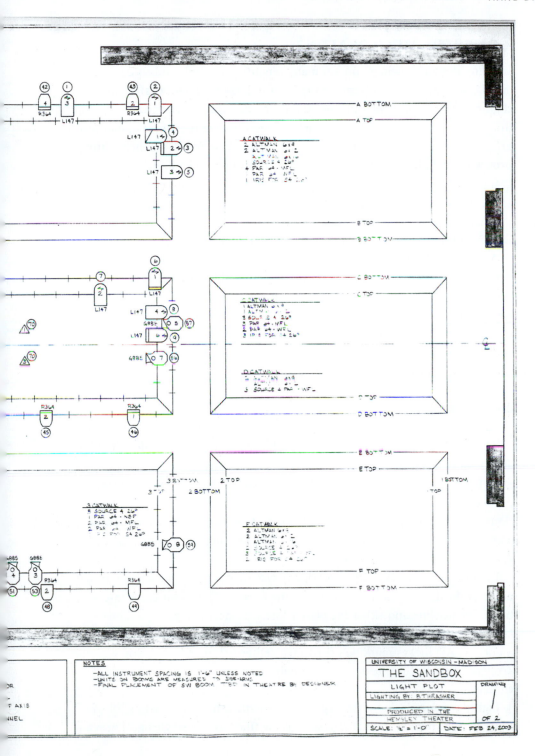

FIGURE 12.11
This hand-drafted example for a flexible space communicates design information as clearly as one drawn using CAD. (Used with permission of Brandon Thasher.)

COMPUTER-AIDED DRAFTING

Lighting design drawings contain many repetitive symbols and so computer-aided drafting (CAD) tools can be very useful. The process for drafting may be slightly different, but the outcome should be the same: a clear, concise shop drawing for the electricians executing the design. Two of the most popular programs for theatrical drafting are AutoCAD and VectorWorks. Other drafting programs include WYSIWYG, an integrated moving light visualization program, or Soft Plot, a drafting and paperwork organization program. ArchiCAD and TurboCAD are also used by some. One of the great advantages of working in CAD for those designers who work in the same venue repeatedly is that the drawing of the theatre space can be used as a template for all future drawings.

AutoCAD (ACAD) is used throughout the world by architects and engineers. It has a fairly open architecture, which enables intermediate and advanced users to customize the program somewhat. Many professional theatres use AutoCAD for their theatre plans and the program is popular in academic training programs because the manufacturer (AutoDesk) offers deep educational discounts. When drawing in this program, one does so in "model space." That is, the draftsperson draws in actual size and tells the program the appropriate scale when the drawings are plotted. (The light plot in Figure 1.6 was drafted using AutoCAD.)

To begin an ACAD plot, one needs to set up the drawing units, type styles, and layers. These elements can be recorded into a drawing template. Thinking ahead about layer management is a very important step in the ACAD process. Each layer can hold a different type of information that can be displayed and plotted in discreet colors and line types. Some common layers are lights, positions, theatre, sightlines, center line, text, and set (for multi-set shows, each scene or act can be on a different layer). While drafting one can turn on or off various layers to manage views.

Because ACAD works with a coordinate system, it is a good idea to set the 0,0 point of the drawing at the 0,0 point of the theatre. This point is the intersection of center line and either the plaster line, set line, or stage edge. Thus, one can use the running dimensions on the program's status bar to get measurements. ACAD makes marking off 18-inch center tick marks very easy with its array or offset feature. Text is easily editable and the program includes a spell checker.

Lighting symbols and other repeated elements can be inserted as "blocks." Blocks can be pieces of a drawing, such as the title block, a single lighting symbol, or an entire drawing such as the set plan. Once a symbol library is built (some are available commercially), the symbols can be used over and over again. Blocks can also be set up to have "attributes" such as unit number, color, wattage, and so on. Those attributes can then be downloaded into a database manager such as Access or FileMaker.

In drafting a light plot in ACAD, one usually works in only two dimensions (although ACAD has extensive 3-D capabilities) with vector-based lines rather than solid objects. Therefore, once all is drafted, one has to go in and erase some unwanted lines from within the lighting instruments. If one is often working in the same space, it is well worth the time, however, to draw a three dimensional model of the theatre because then AutoCAD can be used to check the throw and beam spread of lights and even sightlines from a given seat in the house.

VectorWorks, and its add-on module VectorWorks Spotlight, are very popular with professional lighting and set designers. Originally called "MiniCad," VectorWorks began as a Macintosh-only, object-based program and so was picked up early on by many designers who were Mac users. (The program is now available for both Mac and PC platforms.) Despite its name, VectorWorks is an object-based program. Thus, many people find it easier to get started right away with drafting, without having to do any of the customization and setup ACAD might require.

With VectorWorks, one is drawing as if on paper. Initial setup therefore involves setting paper size and scale. Like many graphics programs, the Vector-Works interface consists of a series of palettes for 2-D and 3-D drawing. The Spotlight module includes a stage lighting palette, which enables the draftsperson to insert lighting objects. It also includes some handy features such as automatic unit numbering. The light plot and section for *Chicago* in Figures 12.4 and 12.9 were drafted using VectorWorks.

VectorWorks data can be downloaded into the stage lighting database management program Lightwright. Lightwright (originally called ALD PRO) is the first and most widely used lighting data program in the United States. Most of the channel hookups, instrument schedules, and related paperwork in this book were generated in Lightwright. Lightwright can sort lighting information, count color by sheet or individual cut piece, calculate dimmer loads, and send information back into VectorWorks.

There are numerous other programs for drafting and paperwork management. Some control system manufacturers are currently developing products that integrate control software with design paperwork. ETC's Emphasis system, for example, merges Cast Lighting's WYSIWYG software with their popular

Rendering furnished courtesy of Prelite Studios, LLC

FIGURE 12.12
This rendering by Tom Thompson of Justin Collie's design for a Korn concert tour was produced using Cast Lighting's WYSIWYG software.

Expression console. WYSIWYG is a rendering, drafting, and paperwork management program that is of particular use in the concert lighting field as it enables the designer to visualize and record moving light presets in advance of entering the venue. Figure 12.12 shows a WYSIWYG rendering for a rock concert.

Software development is often driven by the needs of the larger entertainment market including theme parks and television, rather than by the needs of the theatre. Theatre professionals, however, can make good use of the tools available to them to make implementation of their design ideas both possible and more efficient.

KEY TERMS

CENTER LINE

DATUM LINE

FLIES

HANGING SCHEDULE

INSTRUMENT SCHEDULE

SECTION

LIGHT PLOT

LINE SET

MULTI-CIRCUIT LUMINAIRES

SECTION

SET LINE

SHOP DRAWING

SHOP ORDER

TRIM HEIGHT

UNITED STATES INSTITUTE FOR
    THEATRE TECHNOLOGY (USITT)

13

EXECUTION OF
THE DESIGN

WITH the light plot, section, and final hookup complete, the production phase begins—the design is almost ready to be executed in the theatre. An important collaborator joins the process at this juncture, if not before: the production electrician. On large productions, there may be an assistant lighting designer also, to assist the designer in the creation and revision of the design and production paperwork in the studio as well as the execution of the design in the theatre.

THE SHOP ORDER, BID PROCESS, AND LIGHTING SHOP

After the design drawings are complete, but long before the load-in, the lighting designer or assistant must produce a shop order or equipment list. On a commercial production, or other large production where the lighting package will be rented, the shop order is the official bid specification for the show and so must include everything needed to implement the design. In a resident theatre situation, the shop order may be a simple listing of equipment but should also be included with the design drawings, as it will help the electrician to pull and prepare the show from the stock inventory.

The shop order may be a listing of equipment by position, or may be a summary equipment list. The designer should be as specific as possible about the make and model of equipment he or she wants for the show. Because each position on the plot was accompanied by an inventory at that position, it is fairly simple to produce a shop order of either sort as a "take-off" from the plot and associated design paperwork. A generic shop order entry for #1 Electric might be as follows:

#1 Electric:

- ▶ 14—19° Source Four ERS 575w/115v, C-clamps, color frames, template holder, safety cable
- ▶ 3—36° Source Four ERS 575w/115v, C-clamps, safety cables
- ▶ 3—Wybron Color Ram II color scroller for Source Four 36°, clamp, safety cable
- ▶ 1—42' 1.5" pipe with stiffeners
- ▶ 1—Fireproof border, as needed
- ▶ Cables, jumpers, control wiring as per production electrician

As seen in the last line, it is the production electrician who determines the needed cable lengths and perishables order (gel, templates and other expendables). On the bid documents for *Thoroughly Modern Millie—National Tour* (Figures 13.1 and 13.2), designer Don Holder writes:

FIGURE 13.1
Although the lighting designer includes cables in the bid documents for a show, he or she leaves it to the production electrician to determine actual quantities. (Used with permission of Donald Holder.)

CABLE:

- ✓ Actual length and quantity to be determined by Production Electrician
- ✓ All positions to be fed by 6 circuit multi-cable with quantities and lengths to be determined by the Production Electrician.
- ✓ Supply cabling for multiplexed units as per Production Electrician
- ✓ Rental package must include:
  - • Twofers
    Smart Twofers for Multiplexed Units.
  - • Jumpers
  - • Cable

CONTROL:

1   **ETC Obsession II 3000 Lighting console** with most current stable software version.

2   Color VGA Monitors.

> provide keyboard
>
> provide MIDI AND SMPTE Input/Output Enabled
>
> provide ETC-NET Full Remote Node
>
> provide FULL REDUNDANT BACK UP
>
> provide Operators Manual

1   Hand Held Remote Focus Unit with 200′ feet of control cable.

Voltage Regulators, Control Interface, Control Cable, UPS, Opto-Splitters as per Production Electrician.

✓ ETC Obsession II to trigger the Grand MA Board via MIDI Show Control.

✓ Provide all required hardware and accessories to allow Grand MA Board to be slaved to Obsession II.

1   **MA Lighting- Grand MA Lighting Console** with most current software version FOR TECH ONLY-June 27, 2003-July 30, 2003.

2   **MA Lighting- Grand MA LIGHT Lighting Consoles** with most current software version to be used for normal show operation after Opening (Second Console to be used as full running back up).

1   15″ Color VGA Monitor.

1   17″ Color VGA Monitor.

> provide Alphanumeric Keyboard
>
> provide Kensington Turbo Mouse Trackball
>
> provide 4-port DMX backup switch

Voltage Regulators, Control Interface, Control Cable, UPS, Opto-Splitters as per Production Electrician.

✓ Grand MA LIGHT will control all moving lights.

✓ Second Grand MA LIGHT to act as full running back up.

✓ Supply all necessary interface and cables to comprise a full system as per Production Electrician.

DIMMERS:

✓ As part of this bid include costs for all disconnects, power and data distribution, and hardware required for a fully operational system.

✓ All dimmers must be ETC Sensor racks with most current software version

✓ Racks will be configured for multi-plexing

✓ Racks must accept six (6) circuit socapex multi-cable

✓ The quantity of dimmers will be specified by the production electrician. The following is only the designer's estimate

4   ETC Sensor Racks of 96 x 2.4kw

4   Howard Eaton 100w 12v Radio Controlled DMX Dimmers—Provide Batteries and Chargers.

FIGURE 13.2
The control system and everything designer Don Holder wants on his design table in the theatre are indicated in this section of his shop order for *Thoroughly Modern Millie— National Tour.* (Used with permission of Donald Holder.)

On a commercial production, the entire control system and even all the accessories the designer wants on the tech table need to be ordered, as indicated in Figure 13.2, another portion of the shop order for *Thoroughly Modern Millie—National Tour.*

FIGURE 13.2
(continued)

TECH TABLE:
- ✓ For Production period only – Load In through Opening night
- ✓ Items listed under tech table will be returned after opening.
- ✓ Remote Obsession, Grand MA and Monitors as per Production Electrician.
- ✓ Computers will be returned 1 week after opening.

10   High Intensity Long Neck 18" "Little-Lites" with weighted base
4   4'x 8' Plywood Tables with Masonite Tops, Black contact paper and legs.
5   14" (small for unobstructed view of the stage) VGA Video Monitors for ETC Obsession II (these are Designer Monitors)
       ETC NET Remote Nodes as per Production Electrician.

Conventional Lighting Paperwork Kit:

2   PENTIUM III 800 MHz Computer Systems; 256 MB of RAM; 6GB Hard Drive; 56K Fax/Modem; Extended Keyboard; 2 button Mouse with roller wheel; 3 1/2" Floppy disk drive; 40x CD-RW Drive; IOMEGA 250 ZIP Drive; Mini-Tower Case; <u>(1)-17" Monitor with 4MB Video Ram, (1)-19" Monitor with 4MB Video Ram</u>; Ethernet capability; network card.

Moving Light Tracker Kit:

1   PENTIUM III 800 MHz Computer Systems; 256 MB of RAM; 6GB Hard Drive; 56K Fax/Modem; Extended Keyboard; 2 button Mouse with roller wheel; 3 1/2" Floppy disk drive; 40x CD-RW Drive; IOMEGA 250 ZIP Drive; Mini-Tower Case; <u>(1)-21" Monitor with 4MB Video Ram</u>; Ethernet capability; network card.
- ✓ Supply necessary equipment to network all computers with Ethernet connection

Software: All computer(s) must have the following software installed

       Windows XP operating system
       Microsoft Office XP small business
       Vectorworks Version 9.5
       FileMaker Pro Version 5
       LightWright Version 3s
       Adobe Photoshop Version 5
       America OnLine Version 8
       Obsession OffLine (same version as console) with Virtual PC software

Printer.
1   - Macintosh and DOS/Windows Compatible Hewlett Packard Network Laser Printer w/cables, cartridges; 500 page sheet feeder; 10'-0" IBM parallel printer cable; built-in HP JetDirect 600N Print server card for Ethernet.
1   - 10/100 5 port Etherfast Workgroup Switch, w/ appropriate network cards and cables
- ✓ Supply all necessary Cables to connect printer and components to PC's

Communication:

4   - Motorola Radius GP300 or better w/ clips and overnight charger (for use by design team to communicate with electricians)

The bid documents for a show begin not with the equipment but with important information about the date the package is needed, the producers' and general manager's contact information, as well as that of the designer and production electrician. Because bid documents are legal specifications, the front matter of the document, which can run to ten pages or more, also usually includes clauses indemnifying the designer from any errors or omissions regarding the structural and engineering integrity of the design. It also outlines the responsibilities of the rental shop with regard to testing and packaging the equipment for rental. Other general notes might include things like "All luminaires to be UL approved," "All lumniaires and accessories to be painted flat black," and "No substitutions to be made without the express written consent of the lighting designer."

The general manager sends the bid documents to one or more rental shops to get package pricing. The price is usually based on the production period plus an initial weekly rental period, plus additional weeks at a lower price per week. Once the bid is accepted by the producers, the preparatory period can begin in the shop. The production electrician is provided with space in the shop to prep the show and the shop generates a "pull list" that converts the designer's shop order to a format compatible with their inventory system.

The electrician lays out the units as if they were on the pipes, tests them, labels them by unit number, and prepares the cables that will run from the units to multi-circuit cable, and eventually the dimmers. For complex shows, mock-ups may be necessary in the shop to test effects, moving light capabilities, or the like.

In a resident theatre situation, the lighting "package" is usually pulled from an existing inventory. Ideally, there is enough time between productions in the theatre to allow for the units to be cleaned and prepped, instead of going from one show directly to another. This is not always the case, of course. The electrics staff prepares the color and template orders from the designer's paperwork in advance of loading into the theatre.

In addition to prepping the perishables, the resident theatre electrician may need to determine a circuiting plan for a given show, to figure out which lights will be plugged to which circuits/dimmers in the theatre.

ELECTRICITY AND CIRCUITING

To develop a circuit plot, the electrician must have an understanding of electrical principles and quantities, outlined in greater depth in the Appendix. Generally, an electrical circuit exists when there is a flow of free electrons. For stage lighting, a circuit usually consists of a power source, a switch (the dimmer), a load that offers electrical resistance (the luminaire), and conductors (the cables that go between the different parts of the system). Multiple dimmers serve to distribute electricity in appropriate quantities to the lamps and other electrical devices.

There are four electrical quantities of concern to the stage electrician: voltage, current, wattage, and resistance. *Voltage* is the potential electrical difference or electromotive force across two points. If this potential difference exists and there is a conductor present to carry free electrons, then electrical current will flow between the two points. The potential difference is measured in volts and the current, the flow of the electricity itself, is measured in amperes, or amps, for short. While *current* can be thought of as the amount of electricity flowing through a circuit, the *wattage* is a measurement of the power consumed to perform work, such as light production. *Resistance* is necessary to impede the infinite, unrestricted flow of electrons. Resistance is measured in *ohms* and is provided by the lamp, as well as, to some small degree, by the cables.

These quantities are related as follows:

watts = volts × amps
amps = volts / ohms

The circuit breakers found on stage lighting dimmers are safety devices required to protect the conductors in a circuit from carrying more current than they safely can and for which they are rated. If the current in a circuit exceeds the capacity of the breaker, either because too many watts are on the circuit or some other circuit malfunction, then the circuit breaker will "trip," switching it off.

The electrician considers the capacities of circuits, dimmers, and the building electrical distribution in designing the circuiting plan for a production. For each position on the stage, the electrician must determine the quantity of circuits needed to complete the path between each dimmer and its load (the lamp or other device) and from where in the theatre those circuits will originate.

Although in many cases each circuit will be able to go to its own dimmer, the electrician may begin the circuiting plan by determining which lights on a given position can be controlled by the same dimmer, and therefore have only one circuit run to them with a "twofer" breakout to the individual units. The electrician must decide where the dimmers will be located and then can determine how much cable is needed. In a commercial production such as *Thoroughly Modern Millie—National Tour,* dimmers are in portable racks, as shown in Figure 11.4, and temporary cables are brought in to create circuits that go from the lighting positions to the portable racks. In a resident theatre, circuits are often permanent and wired directly to individual dimmers. Figure 13.3

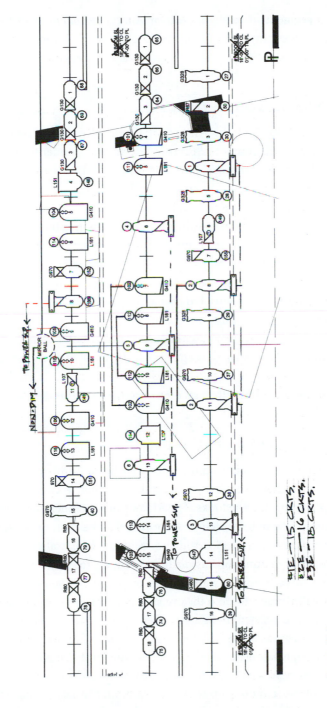

FIGURE 13.3

A segment of the light plot for *Ain't Misbehavin'* with the electrician's notes as to the number of circuits needed at each position and the direction of control wiring.

shows a segment of the light plot for *Ain't Misbehavin'* with the electrician's notes as to the number of circuits needed at each position and the direction of control wiring.

LOADING IN TO THE THEATRE

Stage electrics load in to the theatre first, before any scenic elements, while the deck is clear of obstructions. A crew of electricians, under the production electrician's leadership, hangs all of the lighting and special effects equipment and cables them according to the circuiting plan. Color and templates are put into the units, as well as any peripheral devices such as color scrollers or gobo rotators, along with their control cables. In a theatre with a fly system, each position is tested or "flashed out" while on deck and problems solved while the position is still easily accessible.

Unless the circuits are permanently wired into a dimmer-per-circuit configuration, the electrician must hardpatch the circuits into the dimmers before the dimmers are softpatched to their control channels. If multi-cables have been used for the circuits, then patching is a simple matter of plugging the multi-cable into the appropriate receptacle on the back of the dimmer rack. Some older theatres may have a patch panel where, as the name implies, circuits are plugged into receptacles that are then wired to the dimmers.

THE ASSISTANT LIGHTING DESIGNER

The assistant or associate lighting designer has a number of important functions on a large production, enabling the designer to concentrate on creating and refining the lighting looks. The ALD's primary function is to be an archival secretary for the lighting design, recording the position, focus, and intensity of the lights throughout the load-in and technical rehearsal period. The ALD has numerous other functions as well, which may range from attending design meetings in the designer's absence to organizing expense reports. The ALD may be called upon to do a theatre survey in advance of design development phase, and the assistant designer is often expected to execute the final drafting.

Many designers work with the same assistant for years, essentially making them a design associate. The level of responsibility an ALD holds on a given production, beyond the basics of record-keeping, is determined by the designer and his or her relationship with the assistant. On large productions, such as commerical musicals, there may be two, three, or even four assistants, each per-

Linda Essig

forming discrete tasks such as tracking moving lights or follow spots, and updating paperwork and tracking cues. Figure 13.4 depicts lighting designer Don Holder with two associate lighting designers, an assistant lighting designer, and a moving light tracker at the production tables of *Thoroughly Modern Millie—National Tour*.

FOCUSING THE SHOW

In preparing to focus the show, the designer and assistant designer review the light plot, instrument schedule, and channel hookup. The designer may consult his or her preliminary notes regarding where each specific light should be focused on the stage. Regardless of whether a production is designed with seventy lights or seven hundred, the designer should know the purpose of each light and therefore the location, or focus point, at which the light is to be focused. The instrument schedule, with its listing of each unit by hanging position, is a useful tool for review of each individual unit.

In addition to the rehearsals the designer may have seen earlier in the process, it is imperative that the designer sees a run-through of the show before the focus session. Attendance at the run-through gives the designer important information about the show's blocking. The designer can see, even in the rehearsal hall, the areas of the stage that are used at specific moments and how the performers move about it. The performers' actions in relation to physical elements such as windows and doors can be observed. If the design includes many lights used for specific effect or precise control, then the designer needs to see where on the stage to focus these lights at this rehearsal.

The assistant lighting designer prepares for the focus call by preparing the focus charts. Focus charts are a record-keeping format on which the ALD will be able to record the specific focus of each light on stage. The focus chart format is similar to the instrument schedule format in that it lists equipment by position, with additional space to write in the focus information. Notes can be made on these forms (such as those depicted in Figure 13.5 from the Broadway production of *Footloose*), as to where the designer stands while focusing each light, where shutter cuts are taken, the position of the barrel, and so on. In academic theatres where the show has a short run, focus charts may not be necessary, but in the commercial theatre when the run is open-ended, focus charts are a crucial part of the paperwork package turned over to the stage manager for the maintenance of the show.

The master electrician is organizing the focus crew at this time and the means by which the crew will reach each of the lighting positions. For overhead electrics, access will be by a ladder or a "personnel lift," such as that shown in Figure 13.6. It is critical that people who use the ladders and personnel lifts are adequately trained regarding the safety procedures for their specific apparatus. If a ladder is used, additional crew members should be positioned on the ground to prevent the ladder from shifting. Lifts should always be operated with outriggers installed, which prevent the lift from tipping over. Recently manufactured OSHA-approved lifts (OSHA is the Occupational Safety and Health Administration) contain a locking safety device such that the lift cannot be operated if the outriggers are not appropriately installed and leveled.

If there are scenic obstructions, or the trim heights of the electrics are too high to allow for safe access from the ground, it may be necessary to use a focus track to reach all of the lighting positions. A focus track is a traveler track with a boatswain's chair hung from it, such as that depicted in Figure 13.7. From a focus track, the lighting positions are within reach of the focus electrician. The electrician must wear fall protection rigged to a fall arrest system. If such rigging is necessary, it is more economical to place a focus track between two electrics, so that it may service both. Focus tracks should only be used by crew members experienced in the rigging and operation of such devices.

Access to front-of-house positions varies from theatre to theatre. Ladders may be placed in boxes to reach the box booms or a ladder may be integrated within the box boom; positions like ceiling coves can usually be reached from the positions themselves; in some cases a focus track may be necessary to reach a front-of-house truss.

Meanwhile, the electricians prepare for the focus session by gathering the tools they will need, such as an adjustable wrench and heat resistant gloves. Additionally, an electrician should have a screwdriver handy for fine tuning

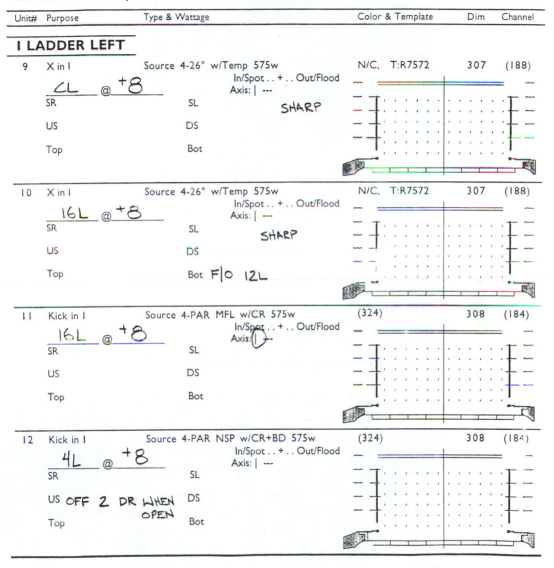

FIGURE 13.5

This page from the focus charts for *Footloose* shows focus information for four of the lights on the #1 Ladder SL. (Used with permission of Ken Billington.)

FIGURE 13.6
A personnel lift is used to access lights on overhead electrics.

Linda Essig

FIGURE 13.7
A focus track is an efficient way for the focus electrician to reach instruments from an aerial position. Focus tracks are particularly useful over a raked stage or a complex set where access by personnel lift would not be possible.

Linda Essig

the alignment of units if needed, a test light in case any electrical problems are encountered, and a pin spreader for connectors that are not making good contact.

Before the actual focusing begins, the master electrician and his or her crew should check that all the lights are in good working order. The electrician completes a dimmer check or a channel check to ensure that every light comes on, is appropriately patched, and correctly gelled and templated (if applicable). Problems can and should be diagnosed or troubleshot at this point and fixed before focusing. Alternatively, the production electrician may assign a small part of the crew to troubleshoot and repair minor problems during the focus session.

The designer and master electrician should confer regarding the focusing procedure. Rather than starting with channel 1 and working forward in the channel hookup, units will be focused in order across a position. In other words, the focusing starts with a unit at one end of a position and proceeds across the entire position, unit by unit. The designer should be mindful that the electricians may be working many feet over the stage level and their safety is important. The focus session will proceed efficiently and safely if done in an orderly fashion.

Many designers and electricians prefer to focus front-of-house positions first and then move to the onstage positions working their way upstage as they go. Some designers like to have electricians at various positions throughout the theatre so that when one electrician must pause to re-position himself or herself, another can focus a unit at a different position. In situations where the design is fairly symmetrical, as it may be in a design for dance, the designer may focus only half of the lights, and rely on the design assistant and his or her notes to complete the focus on the other side of the stage. Ideally, the scenery is completely loaded in before the focus session begins. Unfortunately, this is not always the case and focusing must occur where it can and when it can, with units that focus on specific set pieces put off until the end of the session.

FOCUSING EACH LIGHT

The actual action of focusing begins with an electrician in place at a specific position. The designer or assistant designer calls up the channel number of the first unit and reminds the designer of that unit's function in the design, and the designer stands at the appropriate location on the stage. For an example, refer to the focus chart for the Broadway production of *Footloose* in Figure 13.5. The assistant called up channel 188 and told the designer the light was for, "crosslight in 1." The designer, Ken Billington, stood in the appropriate place on the stage: in this instance on center line, 8 feet upstage of portal line.

The electrician points the light at the designer so that the hot center of the light is aimed at the designer's head. Although ellipsoidal reflector spotlights have a fairly even beam distribution, the beam does tend to be brightest or "hottest" at the center, and this hot spot is the guide for proper placement of the unit. The designer generally stands with his or her back to the light, and watches for the shadow of his or her head to be centered in the beam of light. If a designer is shorter than the average height of the cast, he or she will probably have the electricians focus the hot spots of the luminaires just above the head, rather than directly on it. When the light is properly positioned, the designer, either vocally or through hand signals, tells the electrician to "lock" the unit, meaning tighten the yoke of the unit and side handles so that the unit stays in the desired position. The next step is to adjust the beam edge (for ERSs), beam spread (for fresnels), or beam axis (for PARs). To adjust the beam edge of an ERS, the designer may say "soften it" or "run the barrel." The electrician responds by adjusting the lens train of the unit, thereby changing the relationship between the lens assembly and the reflector. Moving the lens train forward generally softens the edge although this may vary from unit to unit. For #1 Ladder Left unit #9 on *Footloose*, a sharp beam edge was preferred by the designer and executed by the focus electrician.

In addition to the precise placement of light from individual units on the stage, another consideration during the focus session is the way in which light from one unit blends with light from another unit to create seamless coverage of the stage from a given direction. Areas of darkness on the stage are wonderfully dramatic, but only if intentional. By using the modular system described in Chapter 10 as a guide during the focus, one can assure adequate blending between units. When the initial design "modules" were developed, it was with the understanding that there would be one unit per module from a given direction as needed. (For low angles of light, fewer units are required because the low light may cover more than one module.) Now that the focus session has begun, the designer stands in the center of each of those modules when focusing the specific light. Rather than bring shutters in to frame the module, shutters are left open, so that light blends from one unit to the next. Figure 13.8 shows the way the beam and field can be overlapped to create this uniformity of illumination.

After the beam edge adjustments are made and the barrel secured, shutter cuts are taken. Decisions on where shutter cuts are taken depend on what the designer intends for the light to do. For many of the units in *Footloose*, for example, shutter cuts were taken to control light spilling onto the footlights downstage, or onto the rear or side walls.

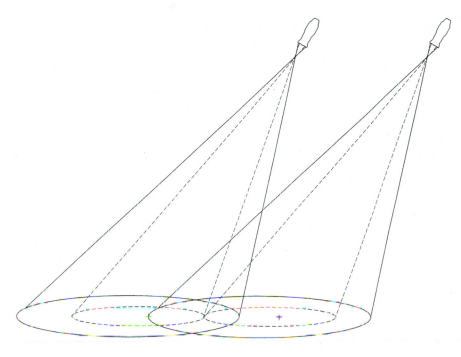

FIGURE 13.8
When focusing, the designer overlaps the beam of one light with the field of one focused at an adjacent module to assure seamless blending of light across the stage.

Often, a sharp shutter cut across a piece of scenery looks artificial and should be avoided. Early in the design process, one should consider where such shutter cuts can be "buried." In a design that has fairly realistic scenery with walls and molding, shutter cuts can often be buried in architectural elements of the set, such as the tops of doorframes, picture rails, or the molding over a fireplace.

Fresnels can vary between a tight spot and a wide flood, an adjustment that can be made during the focus session. Often a designer starts with a fresnel in spot position because it is easier to see the hot center of the beam, and have the electrician aim the fresnel at the correct location. The unit can then be "flooded out" if desired after the pan and tilt (horizontal and vertical movement axes) adjustments are locked in place.

For PARs, the only element that can be adjusted, aside from the pan and tilt of the lamp holder or "can" itself, is the axis of the PAR lamp inside the can. With newer units one rotates the lens to change the axis of the beam. For #1 Ladder Left unit #11 on *Footloose*, a Source Four PAR MFL, the focus chart indicates a vertical beam axis. Although the axis adjustments can happen during the focus session, it is more efficient to pre-set the axis of the lamp in the shop or when the unit is initially hung, as it is sometimes difficult to adjust without dismantling the unit. Therefore, the axis of the lamp should be noted initially on the light plot.

The focus session can progress most efficiently if the designer and the focus electricians can establish a focus rhythm. One way the designer can help to do this is to address the variables of each light in the same order. For example, this focus order might involve saying:

1. Hot spot on me
2. Lock it
3. Run the barrel out (or in)
4. Top cut to the chair rail
5. Bottom cut out of the house
6. Side in to here
7. Other side open

If the designer addresses each instrument in the same way with the shutter cuts in the same order, the electricians can anticipate what the designer needs and the focus session will run efficiently and therefore more quickly.

Focusing the box boom position can occasionally be tricky because of the box boom's potentially oblique angle to the stage. This oblique angle distorts the beam image and thus it may be difficult to take shutter cuts parallel to the stage edge (see Figure 13.9). The rotating shutters on ETC Source Four and Altman Shakespeare fixtures have alleviated this problem, but one may still need to take compound cuts (two shutters combined for one function) to cut light off of scenery.

FIGURE 13.9
Box booms can sometimes be both difficult to access and difficult to focus.

Linda Essig

Keeping accurate records of where each light is focused and its shutter cuts or beam axis is one of the assistant lighting designer's most important functions. The stage manager and electrician use such records to maintain the show throughout the run or to re-create the lighting design if a production is touring. The records are kept on the focus chart forms discussed earlier.

Immediately before the focus session begins, the designer or assistant lighting designer marks a grid on the stage, usually by laying down two pieces of webbing along center line and set line (or wherever the upstage/downstage datum line is located). This webbing, called a "focus tape" is marked off in 1- or 2-foot increments measuring left and right from center line and up or down stage from the other line, thus creating two axes of a measured grid. When the designer stands at a specific location on the stage, the assistant can then record that precise location on the focus chart by writing, for example, "6'L, +3'." Such a designation means the designer was standing 6 feet stage left of center, and 3 feet upstage of the set line.

Shutter cuts are recorded on the focus chart as well, most commonly with either a picture of the beam with shutter cuts noted or verbally with notations for the upstage, downstage, stage left, and stage right cuts. These are some customary abbreviations for such notations:

- ▶ OOH—out of house. Usually a downstage cut, this means that light is cut out of the audience area.
- ▶ OOP—off of portal (or proscenium). Light is cut off of the right or left portal legs.
- ▶ HH—head high. Shutter cuts are often taken a comfortable distance above the designer's head as he or she stands at the focus point. The notation "HH + 2'" would be an appropriate way to record such a cut.

The focus chart also includes information about beam edge, beam size, or beam axis, depending on the unit type. In the course of the production process, units may be refocused and adjusted. On a production where focus charts are necessary, such changes should be kept up to date on the focus charts so that there is always an accurate record of the show.

OTHER DUTIES OF THE ELECTRICS STAFF

The electrics staff is larger during the load-in period than during the actual run of the production. The electricians are responsible not only for the stage lighting, but for setting up the stage manager's cue lights and running lights. In some theatres, depending on the jurisdiction of the various departments under contract to the theatre or the production, the electricians may be responsible for setting up sound and communications (headset) equipment as well. Many of these tasks can be accomplished during the set load-in, prior to the focus session.

The electrics staff works toward electrifying scenic elements during and after the set load-in. This may be as simple as wiring stage practicals to the more complicated job of wiring automated equipment, providing retractable cables for moving scenery, and rigging special atmospheric effects such as smoke or haze, and even rain and water effects.

THEATRICAL CREWS AND UNIONS

When working in professional theatres, whether commercial or not-for-profit, one is likely to come across members of a number of theatrical trade unions, or be a member oneself. Two of the most important unions are the International Alliance of Theatrical Stage Employees, or IATSE, and Actors Equity Association, AEA or just "Equity." The IATSE has a national "local," #829, called United Scenic Artists Association, representing lighting designers, set designers, costume designers, scenic artists, sound designers, and allied craftspeople. Other IATSE locals are based on location and represent stage technicians. Equity represents both professional actors and stage managers. Other performers' unions are AGVA (American Guild of Variety Artists, representing primarily dancers), AGMA (American Guild of Musical Artists), SAG (Screen Actors Guild), and AFTRA (American Federation of Television and Radio Artists, representing commercial and recording artists).

Because union contracts for the stage hands and the actors will affect the scheduling of rehearsals, including technical rehearsals, the lighting designer should be familiar with the IATSE agreements governing the production staff as well as the Equity agreement governing the performers. For example, the designer may want to come in early in the day to work with the electrician on writing cues, but the electrician's contract requires an "eight-hour overnight," so there must be eight hours between the end of rehearsal one night and the next morning's call—a very reasonable kind of regulation. (Actors' contracts usually call for a twelve-hour overnight.) Another example is the lighting designer who wants to take pictures at a dress rehearsal to record their work, but must, through the stage manager, give the actors twenty-four-hour notice and right of refusal before doing so. The production stage manager (or production manager in a resident theatre) is usually the team member most familiar with the ins and outs of the specific contracts on a production, so he or she should be consulted if there is a question.

Technicians are generally paid an hourly rate with overtime paid for working more than five hours without a meal break or more than a given number of hours on a performance day. Focus touch-ups requested by the designer can become expensive if not efficiently planned for in advance to make the best use of the time provided by the agreement with the theatre or the producer.

Resident theatres, even those without an IATSE contract for their staff, also have schedule guidelines under which work calls and rehearsals must be conducted. The designer, assistant designer, and electrician should work toward clear and effective communication so that what little time exists between load-in and opening can be used most efficiently and artistically.

Although constrained by budgets, scheduling, and space, the artists and technicians who collaborate on creating a performance must never lose sight of their artistic goals. Robert Edmond Jones, a noted scenographer and theatre theorist, said it best when he wrote of the relationship between design and execution in his 1941 work *The Dramatic Imagination*:

> There are no arbitrary rules. There is only a goal and a promise. We have the mechanism with which to create this ideal, exalted, dramatic light in the theatre. Whether we can do so or not is a matter of temperament as well as technique. The secret lies in our perception of light in the theatre as something alive.
>
> Does this mean we are to carry images of poetry and vision and high passion in our minds while we are shouting out orders to electricians on ladders in light-rehearsals?
>
> Yes, that is what it means.

KEY TERMS

AMPERES OR AMPS	PERISHABLES
CIRCUIT	PERSONNEL LIFT
CIRCUIT PLOT	PRODUCTION ELECTRICIAN
CONDUCTOR	PULL LIST
CUE LIGHT	RESISTANCE
FOCUS CHARTS	RUNNING LIGHT
FOCUS TAPE	SET LINE
FOCUS TRACK	SHOP ORDER
HARDPATCH	SOFTPATCH
LOAD-IN	TRAVELER
MULTI-CABLE	TWOFER
OHMS	WATTS
	WATTAGE

14
CUING

WITH the lights hung and focused in the theatre, the time has finally come to bring the lighting design ideas to realization by composing the actual lighting looks in the theatre. Unlike the set and costume designers who can see their designs in their respective shops prior to seeing them on stage, nobody sees the actual lighting design until quite late in the production process. Although a significant phase of the lighting design was completed with the light plot, in a sense, the lighting designer's job actually *begins* at the cue-writing stage. Everything that came before is just preparation for that moment in the dark theatre when the lighting designer brings up the first lights to compose the first cue.

Designer/director communication is very important at this point in the collaborative process, as is adequate preparation. The necessities of cuing include a cue synopsis, cheat sheet, and the control system itself. The most important tools, however, are the lighting designer's own eyes, as well as his or her sense of space, composition, proportion, and the ability to apply the technological equipment available in a calm and efficient manner, in service to the art of the performance.

WHAT IS A LIGHT CUE?

The term "light cue" has a two-fold definition: A light cue is the state of the lighting at a particular moment, as well as the designated place in a performance for a light change to occur. So, a cue is both the change of light and what the lighting composition changes to. A cue may be subtle, imperceptibly shifting focus from one part of the stage to another over several minutes. Or, cues can be blatant and loud, bumping from color to color synchronously with music or movement.

As with all of the other steps in the design process, the cuing process requires active choice-making and clear direction based on the point of view toward a work and its style. The lighting designer must make choices regarding the following four attributes of light cues:

▶ Why the cue is needed (i.e., its function in the overall design of the production)

▶ What the cue *is* (i.e., what lights are used to create the composition on stage and how does the lighting look relate to the looks that precede and follow it)

▶ Where in the performance the cue happens (i.e., its placement in text, music, or action)

▶ How long the change takes (i.e., the duration of the cue)

The first of these attributes, the function of the cue, must be addressed before the other three attributes can be determined and subsequently implemented. Some possible functions of light cues are to shift visual focus, support motivated action (such as Blanche lighting a candle in *A Streetcar Named Desire*), establish relationships in time such as flashbacks, indicate spatial proximity or distance, indicate causality or relationships, shift emotional atmosphere of a scene, punctuate changes in music or rhythm, and more. As with other choices, the choice to make the lights change should be based on an idea—an idea about why the lights should change. Otherwise, one is faced with a design full of dancing, moving, changing lights with no meaning. As one reads the material, one can find moments in the script where there is change. Before placing a light cue there, the designer should determine, perhaps with the aid of the director, whether the change that occurs is a change of action that will be undertaken by the performers or a change of environment manifested by the lighting.

Developing a cuing scheme can begin quite early in the design process. It may even begin with the first or second readings of the material and research into or knowledge of the style and genre of a particular piece. Although it is not necessary to stay within the conventions of specific styles and genres, some theatrical performance styles do have cuing conventions associated with them. For example, in musical comedy, there are conventional ways of cuing a musical number that might include the following:

- ▶ Picking up the performer in a follow spot with the downbeat of the musical introduction
- ▶ Changing color with a key change
- ▶ Building to a climax with the musical build near the end
- ▶ Bumping down on the button of the music
- ▶ Restoring the look of the book scene on the peak of the audience applause

For a straight play, such as *Proof,* one might consider a cuing scheme that changes the light each time we go in or out of a scene with the dead father. Or, one might choose to develop a scheme whereby those changes begin to evolve and grow more pronounced and obvious as the play progresses.

One should conceive of and plan the cues in advance of writing them, perhaps even in advance of designing the light plot. It is after attending rehearsals prior to the cue setting or level setting session that the lighting designer can make the specific decisions about the placement and duration of cues aligned with their purpose in the overall design. In other words, the designer *knows what each cue should look like before going into the theatre.* Some designers *start* their process by considering the cues—the way light will move throughout the event. Others wait until they can see the way the production is progressing in the rehearsal hall. Doing both, preconceiving the cues and observing the rehearsal, may be the best way to design the cues organically to best suit the performance.

PREPARING TO WRITE CUES

It is critical that the lighting designer meet with the director to discuss the placement and function of the light cues prior to the first technical rehearsals. Individual director/designer relationships are unique. This meeting might be quite short and generally focus on the conventions the cues are meant to establish; these conventions might include the establishment of the reality of a place or the transitions in and out of musical numbers. Depending on the production, however, the content of this director/designer meeting could be quite specific. It is not uncommon in the opera world, for example, for a director and designer to go through the opera's score page by page discussing every cue, its placement down to the beat in a measure, and its function. Figure 14.1 shows

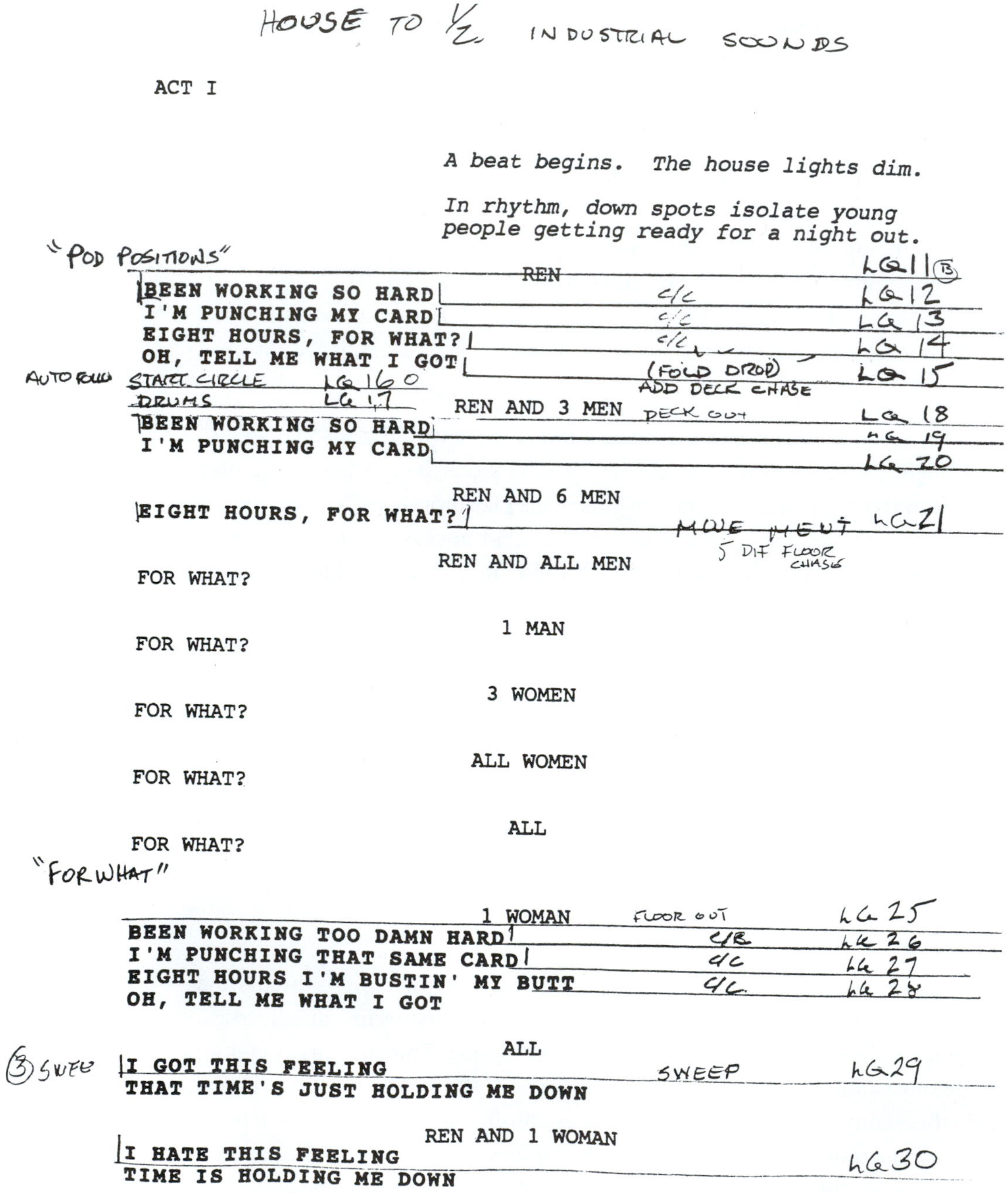

HOUSE TO ½ INDUSTRIAL SOUNDS (handwritten)

ACT I

A beat begins. The house lights dim.

In rhythm, down spots isolate young
people getting ready for a night out.

"POD POSITIONS" (handwritten)

	REN		LG 11 Ⓑ
BEEN WORKING SO HARD		c/c	LG 12
I'M PUNCHING MY CARD		c/c	LG 13
EIGHT HOURS, FOR WHAT?		c/c	LG 14
OH, TELL ME WHAT I GOT		(FOLD DROP)	LG 15

AUTO FOLLOW START CIRCLE LG 16 0 (handwritten)
DRUMS LG 17 (handwritten) ADD DECK CHASE (handwritten)

	REN AND 3 MEN	DECK OUT	LG 18
BEEN WORKING SO HARD			LG 19
I'M PUNCHING MY CARD			LG 20

EIGHT HOURS, FOR WHAT? REN AND 6 MEN MOVEMENT LG 21 (handwritten)
5 DIF FLOOR CHASE (handwritten)

FOR WHAT? REN AND ALL MEN

FOR WHAT? 1 MAN

FOR WHAT? 3 WOMEN

FOR WHAT? ALL WOMEN

FOR WHAT? ALL

"FOR WHAT" (handwritten)

	1 WOMAN	FLOOR OUT	LG 25
BEEN WORKING TOO DAMN HARD		c/B	LG 26
I'M PUNCHING THAT SAME CARD		c/c	LG 27
EIGHT HOURS I'M BUSTIN' MY BUTT		c/c	LG 28
OH, TELL ME WHAT I GOT			

Ⓑ SWEEP (handwritten)

	ALL		
I GOT THIS FEELING		SWEEP	LG 29
THAT TIME'S JUST HOLDING ME DOWN			

	REN AND 1 WOMAN		
I HATE THIS FEELING			LG 30
TIME IS HOLDING ME DOWN			

FIGURE 14.1
One page from Ken Billington's book for *Footloose* indicating placement of the first twenty cues of the opening number.
(Used with permission of Ken Billington.)

the second page from Ken Billington's *Footloose* production book indicating the placement and function of a sequence of cues.

Once placement is roughly determined, many designers consolidate the cue information into a cue synopsis. The cue synopsis is a listing of every cue in a show. It includes notes on the cue number, its count (duration), its placement in the script or blocking, and its function, as illustrated in Figure 14.2, a page from the cue synopsis for *Ain't Misbehavin'*. Some designers prefer to keep this information in the form of notes in their script and refer only to the script throughout the tech rehearsal process. It is worth noting, however, that the cue synopsis

CUE	COUNT	ON	FOR
Q1	5	SM ready	Preset
Q2	5	SM ready	House to1/2
Q2.5	4	ready	House and preset out
AIN'T MISBEHAVIN'			
Q3	3	Cynthia in place	Victrola, windows, hanging bulb
Q4	4	music	start build of step, room
Q5	6	antic transfer to Mr Tate	build room
Q6	6	1,5,1 "OOHs"	build piano area
Q7	2	1,6,1 antic piano	up on steps/room
Q7.2	12	auto follow	lose rooms above
Q8	4	2,5,3 "you"	build into jack horner
Q9	3	5,2,1 antic "like jack horner" repeat	build (use foots)
Q10	4/8	7,last "you. . .^"	return to "realism"
LOOKIN' GOOD			
Q11	4	9, downbeat of "looking good"	in-1 focus for train formation
TAINT NOBODY'S BUSINESS			
Q12	0	14,last /antic downbeat of "T'aint"	bump chg for "taint nobody's biz"
Q13	6	16,1,1 "there aint'"	add choral focus near table
Q14	3	18,6,1 for "I_____"	build
Q15	4/6	nobody's biz peak applause	restore room - more sunsetty
HONEYSUCKLE ROSE			
Q16	6	20,7,2 Una's vocal entrance	change/ pink downs
Q17	3	23,1,1 "Rose"	focus DR with downlight
Q18	4/8	23, 'last'/Una cross down steps	restore room
SQUEEZE ME			
Q19	4	"just like^ you did before	focus at chaise/add steps
Q20	6	25,7,1 "^Just Like you did"	build back special
Q21	8	25,10,1 "^I just get so you know"	pull in even more
Q22	8/4 d1	C. X US	build into handful of keys
HANDFUL OF KEYS			
Q23	3	32,1,first/"yeah yeah now ^that's enough'	build DS
Q24	3	36, last "handful of keys"	change
Q24.5	0	m. 79 "^ Bang those."	foots up
Q25	3	43,1,2 piano break/crescendo	build bax
Q26	4	peak applause	restore room/duskier

FIGURE 14.2
Part of the cue synopsis for *Ain't Misbehavin'*.

FIGURE 14.2
(continued)

FINALE			
Q150	4	165, last	add blue bax for 2 sleepy people
Q151	0	on kiss	bump change for scat
Q151.1	auto	preset scrollers	
Q152	2	173, last	color chg to magenta for "I cant"
Q152.1	auto	preset scrollers	
Q153	3	175, antic "be sure its true"	color change (scroll to pink)
Q153.1	auto	preset scrollers	
Q154	4	177, 1,2 "true"	build color from downs
Q155	8	182,1,1 'Sin . . ."	build bax
Q156	4	182, last	change to honeysuckle color
Q157	3	185, 2,2	build
Q157	5/3	backlight chase	
Q158	4	189, 1,4 last "pow pow"	build fronts and sides
Q158.1			downlight chase
Q159	3	192, 1,2 "wah wah" hold	build
Q160	3	192, 1, 4 last hold	last build
Q160.1			scroller chase
Q161	0	button	bump out fronts
Q162	2	peak applause	fronts restore
Q163	3/4	into tableau DL	focus on group DL
Q164	1	antic Mr Tate	focus at piano
Q165	3	"do one"	restore Q162
Q166	0	button	bump blackout
Q167	2	ready	restore
Q170	5	as exit	post set
Q171	5	clear	house up

is a very useful piece of paperwork for the stage manager. The stage manager often places cues in his or her calling script from this cue synopsis. In any case, the designer, or the design assistant, should note the placement of the cues in the script, and clearly communicate that placement to the stage manager.

In order to facilitate the making of the cues, the lighting designer develops a cheat sheet. Different from the schematic diagrams used to develop the lighting compositions prior to drafting the light plot, the cheat sheet is a summary of lighting design information in a consolidated form for use during the technical rehearsals. The cheat sheet may be in the form of a list organized either by channel numbers and purposes (which might be in the same order as the hookup), or in an order more conducive to the way in which the show will be cued. Figure 14.3 shows Ken Billington's sidelight cheat sheet from *Footloose*, showing channel numbers, the plane of the stage where the lights are focused, and whether the lights are making a near (N), center (C), or far (F) shot. The right-hand column indicates channels that light various set pieces. Cheat sheets may also be in the form of a map of the stage showing where all the channels are focused, as in Figure 14.4, or a combination of these styles. For some shows, especially those with distinct scene locations, it may be necessary to produce a series of maps in order to incorporate all of the necessary design information. The cheat sheets are essentially a quick reference guide for the cuing process.

FOOTLOOSE   RICHARD ROGERS
                                             10/98

SIDES	LEFT					WALLS	
101	(71) X DS	161	121	(72) X DS	301	271 RAIL	R.83
102	I FAR		122	I FAR	302	272 RAIL L	353
103	CTR		123	CTR		273 RAIL C	354
104	NEAR		124	NEAR		274 RAIL R	355
105	DIAG F		125	DIAG F	303	275 RAIL (T)	G.714
106	C		126	C		277 X TO L	R.80
107	N		127	N		274 X TO R.	
108	II F		128	II F	304	276 BEAM FROM L	
109	C		129	C		278 " R	
110	N		130	N		221 DOORS L	
111	III F		131	III F	305	222 DOORS R	
112	C		132	C		227 CLOUDS STORM	203
113	N		133	N		228 CLOUDS	202
114	IV F		134	IV F	306	229 MOTORS	
115	C		135	C		27 DOOR DL	
116	N		136	N		218 DOOR DR	
117	V		137	V	307	**PORTAL**	
118	VI		138	VI		289 R	137
181	KICK DS	34	211	X IN I FAR	302	290 L	
182	I	322	212	" C		289 TOP	
183	DIAG	323	213	" NEAR			
184	II	324	**BORGER BLAST**				
185	III	325	468	B 1		**SHOW DROPS**	
186	IV	326	469	2		219 LOGO INTERMISSION	N/C
187	V	327	470	3		220 LOGO OPEN	N/C
119	TEMP DIAG	N/C	471	4		225 (T)	G.540
188	II		472	U		226 WASH	203
189	III · IV		473	R		**KITCHEN**	
190	V		474	G		201 WINDOW	N/C
120	SHIN US	203	475	E		202 "	161
139	SHIN US	308	476	R		203 "	R.79
140	SHIN DS	308	477	L		**COUNTRY WESTERN**	
285	US IN I	327	478	A		US	486-487-488-489
			479	S		DS	482-485-484-483
			480	T			
			481	OUTLINE			

FIGURE 14.3
Ken Billington's cheat sheet for *Footloose* takes the form of a composite list of lighting elements. (Used with permission of Ken Billington.)

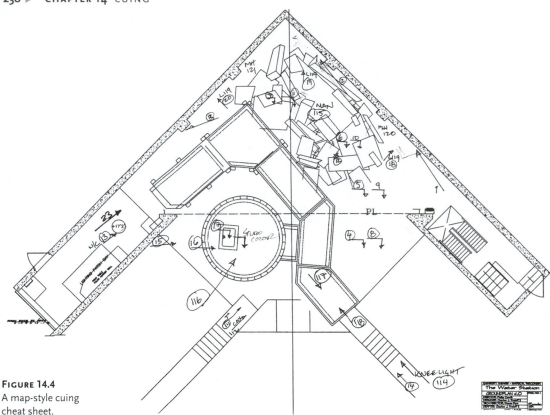

FIGURE 14.4
A map-style cuing
cheat sheet.

WRITING THE LIGHT CUES

Ideally, the lighting designer has an opportunity to write and record light cues during a level setting session before the actors walk on stage for their first technical rehearsal. In academic theatres, this cue writing time is almost always built in; in resident professional theatres it usually is not, although the efficient designer may be able to carve some time out of a focus session if it finishes early. A designer of a commercial musical can most likely negotiate some dark time in which to write cues; in opera and dance, a special lighting rehearsal is scheduled during which the lighting designer works directly with the director or choreographer to build the cues.

There may be a scheduled dry tech. A dry tech is a technical rehearsal involving all departments except the actors and costumes (sound, lights, scenery, projections, and the rest). On large musicals, a dry tech is often necessary as lighting and scenery movement must be coordinated safely before the performers arrive on stage.

Sitting in the darkened theatre before that initial cue writing session is a bit like the painter standing before an empty canvas. What will that first brush stroke be? Knowledge of what the lighting environment should look like is very important at this juncture. Sketches, storyboards, and notes taken at rehearsal are invaluable. Decide first what the most important light(s) in the composition are (the main source) and bring those up to full intensity, or an intensity appropriate for that moment in the event. Balance the composition around that level, adjusting for appropriate visibility and visual focus. If the initial level setting takes place without the actors present, one should have somebody (a production assistant or an electrician) "walk the stage" so that there is a realistic impression of how the lighting will appear on the actors' faces as they move about the playing space.

Perhaps a reference to the initial schematic diagrams, storyboards, and sketches is useful at this juncture. What lights were originally intended for use in this cue? Are they functioning as expected? What is the blocking for this moment as it was observed in the rehearsal hall? A good designer keeps his or her eyes open to unexpected results. Furthermore, a good designer sees the whole stage picture, not just the small part where the actor is standing. What is the overall focus of that stage picture? How does the lighting on the background relate to the lighting of the playing space? Is there a stray shutter cut hitting an overhead border and causing a visual distraction? All details of the stage picture must be addressed.

A common error in building cues is to concentrate solely on the way the people look, cuing in the background later. Equally common is a designer who spends 95% of his or her cuing time composing the setting, while paying too little attention to the way light plays on the performers, especially their faces. Remember that the background, whether it is a cyclorama, abstract scenery, or even a black void, is the visual context for the foreground. The entire stage should be composed as a whole.

USING THE CONTROL SYSTEM

In recording the cues, one should take full advantage of the control system's capabilities. Chapter 11 introduced the principles of control technology, and the basic options available in the front end of a control system. Most computer lighting consoles, whether they are of the tracking, highest-takes-precedence, or hybrid variety, offer numerous features designed to make cue writing more effective. Among these features are the following:

▶ *Split Counts:* This feature enables the upfade of a cue to operate at a rate independent of the downfade of the cue. Therefore, lights may come up at a faster rate than they go down—a very useful feature if lights are changing to accommodate stage movement. Most consoles also enable a delay to be recorded on to one side or the other of the cue so that the up and down fades can start operating at different times.

▶ *Parts:* The "Part" function allows the cue to be split into six or eight parts, each operating at a different rate. Therefore, channels 2–5 might be rising to a given level in 6 seconds while channels 6–10 and 12 rise at a different rate, and other channels move at yet another rate. This feature can provide extremely fluid movement of light.

▶ *Groups:* Groups are used not to fine-tune the operation of a cue but rather to speed up the cue writing process itself. Groups are particularly useful when there are large clusters of channels operating together. A cluster of channels can be recorded at full intensity or at proportional levels as a "group" (much as one records a cue) and then can be called up later in the cue writing process as if it were a channel. Once the group is active, the channels within the group can be adjusted individually.

▶ *Focus Points* or *Preset Focus:* This feature is found on hybrid consoles. It enables the designer to record moving light attribute information into building blocks that can then be used in writing actual cues. If using moving lights, the lighting designer should take the time at the beginning of the cuing process to write as many focus points as he or she will need.

▶ *Live* (or *Stage*) and *Blind* (or *Preview*) displays: By displaying a cue in "Blind" or "Preview," changes can be made to a cue without affecting the readings of the channels currently playing on stage. These levels are displayed in the "Live" or "Stage" display.

One should ensure that as the cue setting session progresses, data is recorded onto disk regularly and frequently so that cue data is not lost. A hard copy of the cues can be printed each day as well, assuring that all the hard work of the lighting designer will not be lost through either operator error or an electronic glitch.

THE TECHNICAL REHEARSALS

The technical rehearsals are the lighting designer's moments in the spotlight. Many people enter the technical rehearsal period with a feeling of dread about the long hours involved and the proximity to opening night. For the lighting designer, however, the technical rehearsal period is that most exciting time when all the design elements fuse (hopefully) with the acting and words of the play, the movement of the dance, or lyricism of the music.

Technical rehearsals are facilitated by the stage manager who provides the scheduling framework within which the other members of the production team can do their work. The stage manager is also the person who controls how the rehearsals and performances are run, calling cues for lights, sound, scenery, and actor entrances.

The goals of each particular rehearsal period should be established before-hand—for example, will the ensemble attempt to run the piece from start to finish with as little stopping as possible or will the rehearsal be going from cue to cue, skipping text where there are no light changes, sound cues, or moving scenery? Often, the first tech is in the latter form, or cue-to-cue, which enables the purely technical challenges to be solved early. As the technical rehearsal process progresses, the focus of the rehearsals usually shifts back to the per-formers and their performances and less time will be taken by technical pauses.

The lighting designer works very closely with the director during the techni-cal rehearsals; therefore, clear communication with the director is crucial. Hopefully, the director will make his or her comments and concerns known to the lighting designer early in the technical rehearsal process, enabling the de-signer to adjust and fine-tune from there. Unfortunately, many director/light-ing designer teams find themselves unable to communicate about lighting until the technical rehearsals begin, which is already late in the production process. Clear communication *about the play* and the director's and designer's intent and visual ideas for it early in the design process helps to prevent unpleasant surprises in the theatre.

The lighting designer must also communicate clearly with the other design-ers during the technical rehearsals, since this is the first time the three designers see all of the visual elements come together. Are the colors of the set appearing as desired and expected under stage lights? Is there a distractingly bright, white apron on the maid's costume? When the design team has worked within a well-defined and consistent visual and conceptual framework from the outset, these kinds of questions, if they arise at all, can be addressed quickly. However, if communication has been poor, it might be too late to adjust the color of the set or a costume. Lighting is perceived, not always correctly, as being the easiest vi-sual element to change, and the design may have to be compromised. Early communication and agreement about stylistic, color, and other imagistic choices saves time and money in the theatre. If the director has seen sketches or other forms of pictorial representation of the lighting, which is often so hard to describe in words, the entire production can benefit.

Changes to more than just dimmer readings often have to be made during the technical rehearsal and perhaps even the preview period. On productions of new plays, for example, a script change might trickle through the production team to become a major color change or the relighting of an entire musical number. Changes in blocking may mean refocusing a number of lights during a work call. At this juncture, with opening night looming near, it is important that the lighting designer maintain both a positive, collaborative attitude and an efficient manner so that changes can be both accommodated and embraced.

Once the production opens, the lighting designer or assistant lighting designer (ALD) turns over copies of all lighting records to the stage manager so he or she can accurately maintain the show. Some theatres or producers also expect archival copies of the show records, although the design itself remains the intellectual property of the designer. A designer may want to fine-tune and adjust cues throughout the run of a show, but once it opens, the design process is complete.

Key terms

ASSISTANT LIGHTING DESIGNER	DRY TECH
CHEAT SHEET	FOCUS POINT
CUE	LEVEL SETTING SESSION
CUE SYNOPSIS	SPLIT COUNTS
CUE-TO-CUE	STAGE MANAGER
CUING SCHEME	TECHNICAL REHEARSAL
DIRECTOR	UPFADE
DOWNFADE	

15

LIGHTING DESIGN INTO THE FUTURE

IN 1968, when Stanley Kubrick envisioned the future à la 2001, he included a space station, long-range space travel, and a very controlling computer named "Hal." Although the space station is still under construction, much of Kubrick's vision has come to fruition in the form of computers that control our cars, our buildings, and our stage lighting. I have been first an observer and then a participant in the world of theatrical lighting design since the 1970s and so have witnessed this digital revolution first hand. I am not a prognosticator, but I can identify a few trends in stage lighting that will surely affect us in the future.

The digitization and gizmoization of lighting will undoubtedly continue. Automated lighting—exciting, but somewhat in the periphery when the first edition of this book was written—is considered standard equipment now. The next step in this area seems to be both greater resolution and complexity of images. Automated image projectors are starting to make an impact. These are more than just slide projectors on pan and tilt yokes. Rather, research and development seems to be heading toward adding full digital projection capabilities to sophisticated automated lights.

Energy efficient HID sources, although not yet as commonly used now as I had predicted they would be in the first edition of this book, are continuing to grow in popularity. This is in large part because of the prevalence of automated luminaires that have HID sources.

In terms of light sources, undoubtedly one of the most exciting recent developments, and one that is likely to have a significant impact on stage lighting, is the development of LED luminaires. "Superbright" LEDs can be found in a number of small flood light fixtures and striplights, as well as in linear tubing that can be used to create scenic effects and accents. These luminaires are often designed with white, red, green, and blue lamps for almost infinite color mixing.

As microchip technology enables the production of smaller and smaller devices, we may see more handheld devices for controlling stage light, giving lighting designers greater creative flexibility, and the technical staff on which they depend greater efficiency.

One of the most important developments in stage lighting in the 1980s was the standardization of the DMX512 control protocol that, as of this writing, is still used for most console-to-dimmer communication. However, engineers and developers have been working on the "next new thing"—advanced control network, or ACN—which may have a similar effect on the connectivity not just of lighting devices, but on the greater integration of lighting control with other stage systems such as sound and scenic control as well.

Computer visualization, which seemed on the verge of revolutionizing theatrical lighting design process, has instead been supplanted recently by fiber optic systems for pre-visualization and even pre-cuing on a scenic model. Nevertheless, computer visualization continues to grow in popularity in the touring industry where there is never enough cuing time and the subtle composing of light may not be as important as the bold graphic statements a designer can make with automated luminaires.

What does all of this mean for the performance lighting designer? More tools, more paintbrushes, more flexibility, and the need for more seamless interface between the designer and the technology, so that the technology can continue be used to create stage images in service to design *ideas*.

APPENDIX:
PRINCIPLES OF ELECTRICITY

A lamp requires electricity to incandesce, fluoresce, or sustain an arc to produce light. Electricity is the result of activity on the atomic and sub-atomic level as electrons from positively charged atoms move toward negatively charged atoms. Electrical current is the flow of these free electrons through a conductor such as copper wire.

ELECTRICAL QUANTITIES AND DIRECT AND ALTERNATING CURRENT

For theatrical use, electrical current, indicated by "I" in equations, is produced most commonly by batteries and generators. Batteries may provide the small amounts of electricity needed for flashlights used backstage, but it is the utility company's generators that provide the electricity for a building's electrical service.

Because a battery consists of terminals that remain consistently negative or positive over time, the current generated by a battery flows consistently through a circuit in one direction. A circuit powered by a battery is called a direct current (DC) circuit because of this one-way flow of electrons. Direct current circuits are the simplest type of circuits and, as such, are useful for examining various electrical terms and quantities.

In a DC circuit, in order for the electrical flow to exist, there must be a battery, a conductor between the two terminals of the battery, and a load that provides some resistance ("Ω" or "R") to that flow. Without such resistance, all of the electrons would flow immediately and almost instantaneously from one terminal to the other in a short circuit. For the circuit pictured in Figure A.1, an incandescent lamp provides the necessary resistance on the circuit.

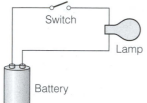

FIGURE A.1
This simple DC circuit consists of a battery, switch, lamp, and conductors.

Even the conductors can cause some resistance on a circuit. A thin copper wire offers more resistance than a thick one, creating more current. Therefore, wires vary in the amount of current they can carry by their size and type of insulation. (See the "Grounding and Circuit Protection" section that follows.)

Because there is a difference in the charge between the two terminals of a battery, the potential exists for the flow of electrons. This "potential difference" or "electromotive force" (EMF) is the voltage (V) across the circuit and is measured in volts. The current (flow) itself is measured in amperes or amps.

These three quantities, current, resistance, and voltage, are related to one another such that

$$\text{resistance} = \text{voltage/current or } R = V/I$$

A fourth quantity, power, measured in watts (W), is also important: Power is the rate at which energy is consumed to perform work. For stage lighting, that work is the lighting of a lamp within a luminaire. Power is related mathematically to current and voltage as well such that

$$\text{power} = (\text{current}^2)\,\text{resistance. Or, } W = I^2R = IV. \text{ Inversely, } I = W/V$$

This last equation is used often by the theatrical electrician to calculate the current in a circuit when the load, measured in watts, and the voltage, which is a constant, is known.

As mentioned previously, building electrical service is provided by generators rather than by batteries. A transformer in the building converts high voltage electricity generated by the power company to the standard 120/208V service of commercial buildings. In such service, electricity flows sinusoidally in alternating directions and so is called alternating current (AC). Voltage, too, varies sinusoidally. In AC circuits, because the current and voltage are always changing, one is actually referring to average, or "root-mean-square" (RMS) current and RMS voltage, rather than the consistent current and voltage of a DC circuit.

BUILDING ELECTRICAL DISTRIBUTION AND PHASING

Most commercial buildings, including theatres, are wired with what is called a "wye" configuration. In such a configuration, three lines or "legs" of electricity are brought in. The sine wave of electricity in each leg is 120 degrees out of phase from the others. If the current on all three legs is balanced, then theoretically there is no current carried along the neutral leg which completes the circuit back to the building transformer. The potential difference (that is, voltage) between any one leg and the neutral is 120V and between any two legs is 208V. In residential electrical service, it is worth noting, only two legs are brought into a house, each 180 degrees out of phase with the other. Therefore, in residential service, the potential difference across two hot legs is 240V, which is needed to power appliances such as clothes dryers and some air conditioners.

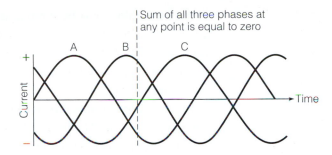

FIGURE A.2
The waveforms of all three electrical phases.

When dimmers are hooked up to a building's electrical service, all three legs are used. One third of the dimmers are wired to each leg and, according to National Electrical Code regulations, each has its own neutral as well. Because current exists when there is voltage and a complete circuit, it is important to balance the loads on the three phases to avoid harmonic noise from the lighting system. Problems may occur if, for example, all of the dimmers carrying front-of-house loads are wired to the same phase. If all of those lights go out at once, leaving current in only two legs, an unbalanced load results. Thus, significant current is carried by the neutral wire and the potential for hum and distortion in other systems exists. When the electricians install dimmers in the theatre, they should do so in such a way that the load at each hanging position is spread across all three phases of electricity. This minimizes the chances of creating unbalanced loads. See Figure A.2.

GROUNDING AND CIRCUIT PROTECTION

Between the building transformer and the dimmers is a distribution box. This box generally contains five terminal lugs within it: three for the "hot legs," one for the neutral, and one for the ground. The ground wire provides an extra path for electricity in the event of a short circuit. When a short circuit occurs, electricity tries to find the path of least resistance back to the beginning of the circuit. Without the ground wire, that path of least resistance might be through the body of an electrician. Grounding provides an extra modicum of safety when working with and around electricity.

Safeguards are further provided by circuit breakers. The distribution box is equipped with one large circuit breaker which shuts off power to the dimmers in the event that one of the feeds carries more than its rated load. At this point in the wiring, this could be as much as 400 or 600 amps per leg. This special disconnect breaker is often referred to as the "company switch." Each individual dimmer is also protected by a circuit breaker. The breaker is designed to trip if it senses that the circuit is carrying more than its rated load, thus switching off the circuit.

Breakers trip not only if there is a short circuit, but also if a circuit is loaded beyond its capacity. The load capacity of a circuit is based on the type of conductors and connectors that make up the circuit. If a conductor carries more than the current for which it is rated, heat is produced, which can melt insulation and eventually result in fire. Circuit breakers shut down the circuit before this can occur. The National Fire Protection Agency (NFPA) publishes the National Electrical Code (NEC), which lists the ratings of various sizes and types of conductors. A portion of this code governing some types of stage cables is shown in Figure A.3.

The circuits in most theatres are rated at either 20 amperes (20A) or 15 amperes (15A). If the voltage is known to be 120V, and the maximum current is 15A, then, using the formula noted earlier, the maximum load is 1800 watts (1800W) (watts = volts × amps). Plugging two 1000W PAR64s into this circuit will cause the circuit breaker that protects the circuit (either on the faceplate of the dimmer or at a patch panel) to trip and cut off the electricity to the lamp. Additionally, many electricians "de-rate" their circuits to 80% of maximum load to account for the voltage drop that occurs over the length of a cable run. In such an instance, the maximum load on the 15-amp circuit would be 1440W.

CONNECTORS AND WIRING

The bundles of temporary rubber ("Type SO" or "Type SJO") cables one often sees backstage each contain three conductors. As noted above, there must be a "hot" and a "neutral" to complete an AC circuit. Additionally, in all contemporary theatres, as mandated by the National Electrical Code, there is a ground wire. In the United States, the insulation on these three conductors is of standardized color: the hot is black (although hot lines may also be blue or red when it is necessary to differentiate between the three hot legs in the service); the neutral is always white; and the ground is always green. There are different insulation color standards in Europe.

The connectors on the ends of the cables have three terminals, one for each of these three conductors. These also have a standard configuration depending on the type of connector. For stage pin or "2 pin + ground" connectors (see Figure

Size	Thermoset Type TS	Thermoset Types C, E, EO, PD, S, SJ, SJO, SJOO, SO, SOO, SP-1, SP-2, SP-3, SRD, SV, SVO, SVOO		Types AFS, AFSJ, HPD,
AWG	Thermoplastic Types TPT, TST	Thermoplastic Types ET, ETLB, ETT, SE, SEO, SJE, SJEO, SJT, SJTO, SJTOO, SPE-1, SPE-2, SPE-3, SPT-1, SPT-2, SPT-3, ST, SRDE, SRDT, STO, STOO, SVE, SVEO, SVT, SVTO, SVTOO		HPN, HS, HSJ, HSJO, HSO
		A[†]	B[†]	
27*	0.5	. . .	. . .	. . .
20	. . .	5**	7**	. . .
18	. . .	7	10	10
17	. . .	. . .	12	. . .
16	. . .	10	13	15
15	. . .	. . .	. . .	17
14	. . .	15	18	20
12	. . .	20	25	30
10	. . .	25	30	35
8	. . .	35	40	. . .
6	. . .	45	55	. . .
4	. . .	60	70	. . .
2	. . .	80	95	. . .

Allowable Ampacity for Flexible Cords and Cables Based on Ambient Temperature of 30°C (86°F)

* Tinsel cord

** Elevator cables only

[†] The allowable currents under subheading **A** apply to 3-conductor cords and other multiconductor cords connected to utilization equipment so that only 3 conductors are current-carrying. The allowable currents under subheading **B** apply to 2-conductor cords and other multiconductor cords connected to utilization equipment so that only 2 conductors are current-carrying.

(FPN): It is intended that this table be used in conjunction with applicable end-use product standards to ensure selection of the proper size and type.

FIGURE A.3

The National Electrical Code (NEC) lists the allowable ampacities for various sizes and types of conductors including type S, SJ, and SJO, commonly used in theatres. (Reprinted with permission from NFPA 70–2002 National Electric Code®, copyright ©2001, National Fire Protection Association, Quincy, MA 02269. This reprinted material is not the complete and official position of the NFPA on referenced subject, which is represented only by the standard in its entirety.)

A.4) most commonly used in the professional theatre, the ground wire always goes on the center terminal, the neutral on the terminal closest to it, and the hot on the terminal farther away. For other types of connectors such as "twist lock" or "straight blade" (the type in your house) connectors, the screw terminals are usually color coded thus: green for ground, silver for neutral, and brass for hot.

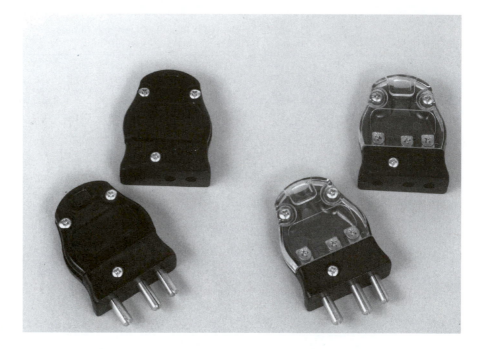

VOLTAGE, TRANSFORMERS, AND SERIES AND PARALLEL CIRCUITS

Electrical devices, including lamps, have a "design voltage." This is the voltage at which the device is meant to operate. For most stage and studio lamps, this design voltage is 120 volts (120V). Some lamps, however, are designed to run on a higher or lower voltage. The HID lamps in some follow spots and automated fixtures are designed to run on 208V, which can be provided by running a circuit with two hot legs to the lamp. Other lamps are designed to run on 6V, 12V, or 24V. To enable dimmer multiplexing, ETC developed a 77V lamp for their Source Four fixtures. If lamps are operated at higher than their design voltage, lamp life will be severely reduced, if the lamp does not fail immediately. Running an incandescent lamp at lower than the design voltage will cause a loss of light, but exponentially increase lamp life.

One way to alter the voltage across a circuit is to put a step down transformer in the circuit. This device will, as its name implies, change the 120V electricity to a lesser voltage. Transformers are generally designed to go from 120V to 12V or 6V. Less common are 24V transformers, but they are also available.

Another way to provide the correct voltage to these low-voltage lamps is to wire them in such a way that they *share* the electricity, dividing it into equal

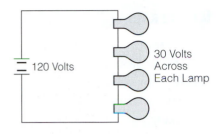

FIGURE A.5
A typical series circuit configuration.

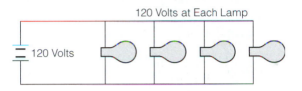

FIGURE A.6
A typical parallel circuit configuration.

parts. Such a wiring technique is called *series wiring*. In a series circuit as in Figure A.5, all of the devices are in a single line. If ten 12V lamps (such as those in MR-16 striplights) are wired in series, then the potential difference across each lamp is 12V.

Line voltage devices (devices whose design voltage is the normal voltage provided on a circuit, that is 120V) are generally wired in a parallel circuit configuration. In such a circuit, devices are wired in such a way that line voltage is available to every device, as shown in Figure A.6. Note, however, that the total wattage of all of the devices on the circuit cannot exceed the maximum rated load.

SAFETY

Electricity is a powerful force for performing work; it can also cause great harm in the form of electrocution or fire. Insulation, ground wires, and circuit breakers can protect workers from the free flow of electrons. Never try to bypass safety devices such as circuit breakers in order to raise the curtain on a performance. If a circuit breaker continually trips, for example, all components of a circuit must be tested thoroughly before one assumes the problem is with the breaker itself. Safety should always be of primary concern when working with and around electricity.

KEY TERMS

ALTERNATING CURRENT (AC)

AMPERES OR AMPS

CIRCUIT BREAKER

COMPANY SWITCH

CURRENT

ELECTROMOTIVE FORCE (EMF)

DESIGN VOLTAGE

DIRECT CURRENT (DC)

GROUND

HOT LEG

INSULATION

NEUTRAL LEG

PARALLEL CIRCUIT

PIN CONNECTOR

POWER

RESISTANCE

SERIES CIRCUIT

SHORT CIRCUIT

STAGE PIN

STEP DOWN TRANSFORMER

TWIST LOCK

VOLTAGE

VOLTS

GLOSSARY

additive mixing—production of colored light by mixing the light output of two or more separately controlled and individually colored light sources.

aiming angle—the angle at which a luminaire is pointed or focused.

alternating current (AC)—flow of electrons in alternating positive and negative directions, often sinusoidally.

amperes or amps—the unit of measurement of electrical current.

amplitude—the height of a sinusoidal wave form.

Appia, Adolphe—Swiss scenographer and theatre theorist [1862–1928].

apron—forestage; that part of the stage that extends downstage of the proscenium, usually in a proscenium or modified thrust theatre.

arena stage—a performance space in which audience seating is on all four sides of a central playing area.

assistant lighting designer—a person who assists the lighting designer with drafting, paperwork, and information management.

automated lights—luminaires that can pan and tilt remotely and may be able to alter color, beam spread, or other variables.

backdrop—a scenic element, usually fabric, hung behind the performance space to create a background.

backlight—light originating from upstage and focused downstage; often used to separate the figure from the background.

balcony rail—a front of house lighting position on the face of a balcony, usually found in proscenium theatres.

barn door—an accessory for fresnel luminaires that can be used as an external shutter.

barrel—that part of an ellipsoidal reflector spotlight that houses the lenses.

batten—a pipe hung horizontally from a line set or the grid; also, the horizontal wooden member of a scenic flat in traditional flat construction.

beam—that part of the light output of a spotlight from the center outward to 50% of peak candlepower. Also, sometimes used as the name for a fixed front of house lighting position.

beam angle—the angle between edges of beam as defined above.

beam spread—the degree to which light is disbursed over a given distance.

Billington, Ken—American lighting designer [c.1946–]

birdie—colloquial term for an MR16 theatrical luminaire.

black body locus—on the C.I.E. chromaticity diagram, the line along which a blackbody radiator incandesces at different color temperatures.

black body radiator—the standard source used in measurement of color temperature.

black light—ultraviolet light used in conjunction with phosphorescent materials for special effects.

blocking—the movement and placement of actors on the stage, as determined by the director of the production.

book scene—in a musical, a scene of dialogue and text rather than singing.

boom—a vertical lighting position that sits on a base or flange on the floor, often placed to the sides of the stage for side light.

boom base—a metal casting, plate, or flange into which a pipe is installed to form a boom.

boomerang—the manual color changing device found in most follow spots.

border—horizontal masking curtains hung over the stage to mask electrics or scenic elements further upstage.

box booms—front of house vertical lighting positions usually located high and to the side of the stage.

brightness—luminous intensity.

bump buttons—programmable momentary switches on a control console.

candelas—the unit of measurement of luminous intensity.

candlepower—luminous intensity, measured in candelas.

catwalk—walkable lighting positions, usually permanent, that also serve as access to lighting positions.

C-clamp—a luminaire accessory, also called a pipe clamp, used to hang a theatrical luminaire on a lighting position from its yoke.

center line—the imaginary line running downstage-upstage through the center of the proscenium arch, used as a datum line for stage measurements.

channel—the electronic or mechanical "handle" by which a dimmer, and therefore a lamp's intensity, or a moving light attribute, is controlled.

channel hookup—the paperwork format that lists which lights at which positions are controlled by which channels and/or dimmers, their purpose, type, and color.

chase—a type of lighting effect in which lights or lighting attributes are controlled in a cuing loop.

cheat sheet—a summary of the lighting design used at technical rehearsals so that the lighting designer can efficiently access channel information.

chopper—a horizontal shuttering device in a follow spot.

choreographer—the production team member responsible for making dances.

chromaticity—color saturation.

CIE chromaticity diagram—a graphical document that describes light color on *xyz* axes.

ciliary muscle—a part of the eye that controls the curvature of the lens and therefore accommodation (the ability to shift focus from near objects to far).

circuit—the pathway by which electricity travels from its distribution source (often a dimmer) to the luminaire or other electrical device.

circuit breaker—a device that provides over-current protection to electrical devices.

circuit plot—a plan that indicates how electrical ciruits are to be run to each lighting position and subseqently each luminaire.

circuit raceway—a metal channel enclosing electrical wiring with flush-mounted receptacles or pig tails into which luminaires and other electrical devices are plugged.

cold cathode—a lamp type consisting of a glass tube containing an inert gas such as neon, xenon, or krypton to maintain an electrical arc; commonly referred to as "neon light."

color—the hue of a light; also, the gel media used to selectively transmit light to produce colored light.

color key—a diagram indicating colors of light in relation to each other for one module, usually used in designs for uniform illumination.

color mixer—an automated lighting accessory that uses subtractive mixing of two or three color scrolls or fins to produce multiple colors.

color rendering index—a measurement of light color that predicts the ability of a light source to render color accurately.

color scroller—an automated lighting accessory consisting of a gel string between two drums enabling remote color changing.

color temperature—the measurement in Kelvins of the "warmness" or "coolness" of a white light source.

color wheel—a lighting accessory consisting of a round disk with multiple openings for gel, mounted on a fixed or variable speed motor.

colorimetry—color measurement.

compact fluorescent—a lamp type consisting of a fluorescent tube that has been bent in on itself to form a twin, triple, or quad configuration.

company switch—an electrical distribution disconnect box for portable stage dimmers.

composition—an amalgamation of parts to make a whole.

conductor—a material, such as copper wire, capable of carrying electrical current.

cones—a type of cell on the retina in the human eye responsible for color vision and detail discrimination.

contrast—the relationship between two or more values, colors, textures, and so on.

correlated color temperature—a measurement in degrees Kelvin that equates the color of a discharge lamp to that of a standard source.

cosine distribution—the distribution of light across the beam of a spotlight in which light falls off from peak beam candlepower in a cosine-shaped curve.

counterweight—in a rigging system, the balance to the weight of the line set and whatever lighting or scenic equipment is hanging from it.

cove—a front of house lighting position found in the ceiling of some theatres.

cross-fade—a type of light cue in which some lights rise in intensity as others are decreased.

cue—a light change or the impetus in the script or blocking for that light change.

cue light—a light controlled by the stage manager to signal standby and execution of cues such as actor entrances or fly rail cues.

cue synopsis—a listing of each cue, its duration, placement, and purpose.

cue-to-cue—a type of technical rehearsal in which only those sections of the performance that contain technical cues are rehearsed.

cuing scheme—the overall plan or idea driving the placement and type of light cues.

current—the flow of free electrons through a conductor.

curtain warmer—a light placed at front of house focused on the act curtain to give it an inviting glow.

cut sheet—a page from a manufacturer's catalog.

cyc (cyclorama)—a backdrop of neutral color extending across the width of the stage.

cyc flood—a luminaire designed for vertical illumination of a backdrop, usually having an asymmetrical reflector.

dance tower—a vertical lighting position, usually placed in the wings, consisting of a box truss within which lights are hung.

data sheet—manufacturer's information about a luminaire.

datum line—a line from which measurements are taken, in theatre usually center line and either set line or plaster line.

desaturation—the phenomenon of a color appearing to fade due to retinal fatigue.

dichroic filter—a glass color filter with microscopically thin refractive coatings for very precise spectral transmission.

diffuse—spread out, soft.

diffusion media—a filter that scatters light so as to cause it to appear softer and/or wider in distribution.

dimmer—the electronic or mechanical device that alters the electricity (usually the current) in a circuit to change the intensity of light.

direct current (DC)—electricity, as from a battery, that flows in one direction from positive to negative.

directional frost, or silk—a type of diffusion medium that spreads light predominantly along one axis.

director—the production team member responsible for the overall mise-en-scène, including blocking and overall visual design.

distribution—the shape of light output.

donut—an accessory used in front of the lens of an ellipsoidal reflector spotlight to sharpen the image projected by a template pattern.

douser—in follow spots, automated lights, or other luminaires with discharge sources, a device that drops in front of the lamp to cut light output.

downfade—a type of light cue in which intensities are decreased.

downlight—light originating from directly overhead; also called toplight.

dramaturg—a production team member whose responsibilities include literary research and assisting the director with text interpretation.

drop—a scenic element, usually fabric, plain or with subject matter painted on it, hung as a backdrop, mid stage curtain, or act curtain; see also cyc and backdrop.

dry tech—a type of technical rehearsal at which technical elements are rehearsed without the actors present.

effects charts—an alternate name for a color key or magic sheet.

electrics—lighting positions hanging overhead, usually parallel to the stage, having variable trim height.

electromagnetic energy—the spectrum of energy of which visible light is a small part.

electromagnetic spectrum—the range of electromagnetic energy extending from induction heating through visible light to cosmic rays and beyond.

electromotive force (EMF)—voltage or potential difference.

elevation—a scalable front view.

ellipsoidal reflector floodlight (ERF)—an unlensed luminaire consisting of a lamp in a large bowl-like reflector, also called a "scoop."

ellipsoidal reflector spotlight (ERS)—a common type of theatrical luminaire consisting of a lamp, ellipsoidal reflector, and two plano-convex or compound lenses or one step lens.

energy—the capacity to perform work; usable power.

fader—a manual or virtual means for rasing or lowering a channel or group of channels.

Feder, Abe—pioneering American lighting designer [1910–1997].

field angle—the included angle between which the light output of a spotlight goes from the center outward to 10% of peak candlepower.

filament—that part of an incandescent lamp that glows to produce light.

fill light—a compositional function of stage light, usually from a frontal direction, that illuminates the shadows or shade created by the main source of light.

filters—gel media.

filtration—selective transmission; the means by which colored light is achieved on stage.

fixed-focus—pertaining to a luminaire that is locked in position, as opposed to a moving or automated light.

flange—a mounting plate for a stage luminaire or a small boom.

flat field distribution—a colloquial, although inaccurate, term for cosine distribution.

flexible space—a theatre type in which the audience and playing areas can be changed to serve individual production needs.

flies—colloquial term for the overhead stage rigging in a proscenium theatre.

flipper—an optional accessory for a striplight that functions as a barn door or flag to cut light from unwanted areas of the stage.

flood light—a luminaire, usually open-faced, with a broad beam distribution and little controllability.

fluorescent—a type of light source in which phosphors emit light in the presence of an arc of ultraviolet energy.

focus—to point or aim luminaires; the alignment of lamp, reflector, and lens to project a specific pattern or beam quality; the area in the visual field that most draws attention.

focus charts—the forms on which a designer or assistant records all luminaire focus information.

focus point—a pre-recorded group of moving light attributes that can be used as building blocks for cues.

focus tape—webbing or other material marked off in regular units for use in keeping records of focus information on the focus charts.

focus track—a traveler track from which a seat can be suspended so that a focus electrician can have access to overhead lighting positions.

follow spot—a usually large and intense lighting unit that can be moved manually to follow performers on the stage.

footcandles—a unit of measurement of illuminance (incident light).

footlight—a stage light placed on the downstage edge of the stage to provide low front light or to light a performer's feet and legs.

fovea—the area on the retina of the eye on which the cones are most densely concentrated.

French scenes—scenes demarcated by the entrances or exits of an actor.

frequency—the number of times per second a waveform repeats.

fresnel—a type of stage lighting luminaire consisting of a lamp, spherical section reflector, and Fresnel lens.

Fresnel lens—a type of step lens originally designed for use in lighthouses.

front-of-house—in proscenium and thrust theatres, that area of the space that is downstage of the proscenium arch; the audience area.

gate—The location within an ERS of the second focal point of the reflector at which gobo patterns and other accessories can be projected sharply.

gel—polyester film color filters.

gel media—color filters.

genre—a movement or style in dramatic literature or presentation.

gesture—communication through nonverbal action; as used here, the means by which light can create meaning.

gobo—template pattern.

Gordon Craig, Edward—British designer and theorist [1872–1966] who, early in his career, worked with Sir Henry Irving.

ground—in an electrical installation, the conductor that, for reasons of safety, can return electricity to earth.

ground row—a row of instruments or striplights placed on the deck in front of or behind a cyc and used to light it; also, the scenic masking to conceal these lights.

Guthrie, Tyrone—producer and director [1900–1971] who championed the resident theatre movement and the development of thrust stages in the United States.

halation—the ambient light beyond the field of an ERS caused by internal reflection in the barrel and lenses.

halogen incandescent—a type of lamp, usually with a compact filament, that contains an inert halogen gas to increase filament life.

hanger—the hanging accessory for a striplight.

hanging schedule—a listing of all elements that hang over the stage from the theatre's rigging system.

hardpatch—to physically plug circuit cables into dimmers.

hard-wired—connected via permanent wiring, as circuits are connected to dimmers in a dimmer-per-circuit configuration.

head block—the leading pulley in a counterweight rigging system.

header—the horizontal element of a portal.

head-high—a location on a boom for sidelight that is between 6' and 8' off of the deck.

high intensity discharge (HID)—a type of light source featuring an enclosed electrical arc.

highest-takes-precedence (HTP)—a control system philosophy, also called a preset philosophy.

highlight—an area of high brightness, often on a figure or other three-dimensional element; to draw visual focus to.

hookup—a listing of the design based on channel of control (channel hookup) or dimmer (dimmer hookup), showing which lights are controlled by which channels and/or dimmers, their location, type, purpose, and colors.

horizontal sightlines—cross-stage sightlines, those affecting the location of sidelight positions such as booms.

hot leg—the conductor that carries current from the building electrical system to the dimmer rack.

hue—color name.

hybrid consoles—control consoles that combine features of HTP consoles and tracking consoles with moving light capabilities.

illuminance—incident light, measured in lux (metric) or footcandles (U.S.).

incandescent—a type of light source in which a wire coil, usually tungsten, offers electrical resistance on a circuit causing it to glow.

incident light—the light hitting a surface; illuminance.

inkies—common colloquial term for 3" fresnels.

instrument schedule—a listing of all of the lights in a production, sorted by hanging position and unit number.

insulation—the nonconducting material enclosing current-carrying wire.

intensity—brightness; candlepower; the level to which a dimmer is adjusted to alter the electrical flow to a light.

inverse square law—the relationship of intensity and distance to incident light such that illuminance = (candelas/distance^2) × cos (angle of incidence).

iris—a feature of follow spots or an accessory for ERSs that enables circular framing of the beam of light.

Irving, Sir Henry—British actor/manager [1838–1905] who sponsored numerous advances in stagecraft and lighting.

Kelvin—the unit of measurement of color temperature.

ladders—a type of lighting position consisting of two vertical members and horizontal "rungs" from which lighting instruments are hung from pipe clamps.

legs—vertical masking curtains, usually hung to the side of the stage to define the wings.

leko—a generic slang term for an ellipsoidal reflector spotlight, derived from the trade name "Strand Lekolite."

lens—an optical device that uses refraction to disperse or focus light.

light—visually evaluated radiant energy.

light emitting diode (LED)—a type of light source that uses solid state circuits to produce light.

light plot—the lighting designer's drafted plan indicating the location of all of the lighting and special effects equipment for a production.

lighting designer—the production team member responsible for developing the look of the lighting, specifying the type and placement of lighting instruments, and creating lighting compositions in the theatre.

line set—a set of pulleys and a head-block from which three to seven lines suspend a batten.

load-in—the production period during which the lights and then the scenery are installed in the performance space.

luminaire—an entire fixture assembly including the instrument, lamp, and mounting device.

luminance—brightness, measured in candelas per unit area.

luminous flux—the total light output from a lamp, measured in lumens, also called the time rate flow of light.

lux—the metric measurement of illuminance.

magic sheets—schematic diagrams of the lighting compositions.

masking—scenic devices positioned to conceal performers backstage, lighting positions, or other scenery.

McCandless, Stanley—twentieth-century teacher of architecture and lighting design at Yale Unviersity [1897–1967].

mise-en-scène—overall directing scheme including placement of performers and scenery.

modified thrust—a type of performance space in which the audience surrounds a portion of the stage area on three sides with additional playing space upstage of a proscenium arch.

motivated light—a compositional function of light that supports the idea of a source of light rooted in reality.

motivating light source—a reality-based compositional function of light that provides a reason for light to be present, e.g., sunlight, a table lamp, and the like.

moving head luminaire—a type of automated light that pans and tilts on a rotating yoke.

moving mirror luminaire—a type of automated light that remains in a fixed position but includes a mirror that pans and tilts to reflect the emitted light to the desired stage location.

multi-cable—stage cable that includes multiple conductors for mulitple circuits, usually six.

multi-circuit luminaires—lighting instruments such as strip lights and some cyc floods that include multiple lamps wired in multiple circuits for color variety.

Munsell, Albert Henry—American color theorist [1858–1918] who developed a three-dimensional model of color that includes hue, value, and chroma.

music director—the production team member responsible for leading the orchestra and refining the cast's singing.

nanometers—a small unit of measurement, 1×10^{-9} meters, used to describe wavelengths of light.

neutral density filter—a filter that decreases the intensity of light output from a luminaire without changing its color, used alone or in conjunction with a color filter.

neutral leg—the conductor that carries current from the dimming system back to the electrical distribution system.

object color—the pigmented finish color of objects.

ohms—the unit of electrical resistance.

optic nerve—the pathway of neuro-transmission between the eye and the brain.

pan—horizontal movement.

par—parabolic anodized reflector lamp type or the luminaire in which one is used.

parallel circuit—a type of circuit in which the line voltage is delivered to each load on the circuit.

peak beam candlepower—maximum intensity, usually at the center of the beam from a spotlight.

perishables—those items on a production, such as gel filters and templates, which are not expected to last indefinitely and may need to be replaced during the course of the run.

personnel lift—a device consisting of a platform on a telescoping stem for accessing overhead lighting equipment and scenery.

phosphor coating—the material on the inside of the bulb wall of a fluorescent lamp that emits light when excited by ultraviolet radiation.

photometrics—the measurement of light.

photons—particles of light energy.

pin connector—a commonly used type of electrical plug consisting of two pins for the load wire and a third pin for the ground, also called 2P + G.

plan view—in drafting, the top view of the stage, usually a horizontal section through a plane 4 feet above stage level.

plano-convex lens—a lens consisting of one flat side and one outwardly curved side, used in pairs in ellipsoidal reflector spotlights.

plaster line—the horizontal datum line in a proscenium theatre, located on a plane along the upstage side of the proscenium arch.

point of view—in relation to lighting conceptualization, the ideational stance toward the material being designed.

portal—a scenic element consisting of vertical elements and a horizontal header, often used to frame the stage.

power—the energy consumed to perform work measured in watts.

practical—a stage property that is electrified, as a table lamp, sconce, chandelier, or the like.

preset—to manually set sliders in advance of cue execution; the set arrangement of sliders to form a cue; to record moving light attributes in advance of cue execution.

preset consoles—a lighting control system in which cues are set on banks of sliders, also called scenes, having master sliders that can be used to execute cross fades between cues.

primary colors—a set of hues from which a maximum number of other hues can be derived; in light the most commonly used primary sets are red-green-blue for additive mixing or cyan-magenta-yellow for subtractive mixing.

production electrician—the production team member directly repsonsible for executing the lighting design and any other electrified production elements.

projection designer—the production team member responsible for designing the look of and specifying the equipment for achieving projected effects.

proscenium—a permanent architectural archway framing the stage and separating the stage area from the audience area.

pull list—paperwork generated by a rental shop to enable the staff to integrate the lighting designer's shop order with the shop's inventory system.

quality of light—hardness or softness of light, often related to or the result of the distribution of light and/or its color.

raceways—enclosed channels containing electrical wiring that terminate in load circuit receptacles located along their length.

radiosity—luminance caused by inter-reflection and the computer-rendering algorithm that accounts for such inter-reflection.

ray-tracing—a computer-rendering algorithm that tracks individual beams of light from a source to target.

reference white—in a given lighting composition, that color that the audience will read as white.

reflected light—a compositional function of light designed to mimic light that in reality would be reflected from surfaces.

reflector—the device in a luminaire that controls and/or distributes light via reflection.

refraction—the bending of light as it passes from a medium of one density into a medium of another, used in the design of lenses for optical control.

rendering—a sketch, painting, or computer visualization of the look of the lighting.

research—external material, visual or otherwise, used by the lighting designer to aid in design process and/or implementation.

resistance—impediment to the flow of electrons.

resistance dimmers—devices, now obsolete, that increased resistance on a circuit in order to decrease light output from a lamp or lamps.

retina—the part of the eye where the receptor cells rods and cones are located.

rods—the receptor cells in the human eye responsible for black and white night vision and peripheral vision.

Rosenthal, Jean—American lighting designer [1912–1969], often called the mother of modern lighting design.

running light—a dim light placed backstage used to illuminate backstage walkways or work areas, not meant to be seen by the audience.

Sabbatini, Nicola—Italian architect, scenographer, and lighting innovator [1574–1654] of the Renaissance period.

scale model—a three-dimensional representation of scenery, built to accurate scale.

scanner—European term for a moving mirror automated luminaire.

scene breakdown—a listing of all of the individual scenes in a theatrical work, their locations, physical needs, and other elements of importance.

schematic diagram—graphic description of a lighting composition indicating direction, compositional purpose, and color of light.

scoop—theatrical slang for an ellipsoidal reflector floodlight.

scrim—an open weave scenic material that, depending on its weave, when grazed with light may appear opaque but will be transparent when objects behind it are illuminated.

section view—a vertical cutaway view of the stage, usually drawn along center line and indicating all elements beyond that line.

series circuit—a type of circuit in which line voltage is shared equally by load devices, thereby reducing the voltage across each load.

set line—the downstage-most edge of the scenery, usually at the show portal, that may be used as a datum line for upstage/downstage measurements.

set-mounted—a condition in which a lighting instrument is affixed directly to scenery.

shade—in color theory, a hue plus black; in a composition, that side of the figure that is away from the main source of light.

sharkstooth scrim—a type of scrim characterized by a rectangular weave, commonly used for bleed-through effects.

sheaves—the pulleys in a counterweight rigging system.

shop drawing—technical drawing from which design elements can be directly executed.

shop order—a listing, by position or in summary, of all of the lighting equipment for a production.

short circuit—a circuit that has no resistance and therefore infinite flow of electrons.

shutter—a device within an ellipsoidal reflector spotlight used to shape the beam edge with straight lines.

side arm—a mounting accessory for hanging lights on vertical positions, such as booms.

sidelight—a direction of light emanating from the side of the actor.

sightline—an imaginary line from an extreme seat to and beyond a scenic obstruction behind or above which lighting or scenery cannot be seen from that seat.

silk—a type of diffusion medium striated to spread light predominantly along one axis, also known as directional frost.

skylight—a compositional purpose of light meant to represent ambient light from the sky.

sliders—manual faders on a control console.

snoots—an accessory, similar to a top hat, used to reduce halation.

sodium vapor lamps—a type of enclosed arc light source in which the arc is sustained by sodium gas.

softpatch—to assign dimmers to channels of control, or the listing of those assignments.

special—a compositional purpose of light used to highlight a specific location on the stage.

spectral distribution—the amount of each discrete wavelength of light in a given light source.

split counts—a light cue timing in which the duration of the upfade portion of the cue differs from the duration of the downfade portion.

spotlight—a type of luminaire characterized by a well-defined, symmetrical, conical beam.

stage manager—the production team member responsible for coordination of all production elements during rehearsals and performances, including calling light cues and maintaining the overall quality of the production.

stage pin—see pin connector.

step-down transformer—a device for proportionally decreasing line voltage to provide the appropriate design voltage to the lamp or other device.

step lens—a variation on a plano-convex lens in which the flat side is cut away in sections to reduce lens weight.

storyboard—a method of lighting visualization in which one or more properties of light are tracked on a scene-by-scene basis throughout the show.

straight play—a dramatic play, as opposed to a musical.

striplight—a luminaire consisting of multiple lamps mounted in a channel, usually with three or four circuits.

strobe light—a luminaire for flashing effects.

style—the manner in which meaning is conveyed.

submasters—on a control console, sliders programmed to manually control a channel, group of channels, or effect.

support—a compositional purpose of light that extends the idea of the motivated light across the playing space.

system—a group of lights serving the same compositional purpose across the playing space.

table base—a mounting device for a luminaire that enables a unit to be placed on the stage floor, deck, or table.

technical rehearsal—a type of rehearsal that incorporates all scenic, lighting, and sound elements.

texture—in light, mottling of the beam in a regular or irregular pattern or shape, usually created by projecting a template pattern (gobo).

throw distance—the distance light travels from the luminaire to a location on the stage, usually at head height.

thrust stage—a type of performance space characterized by audience seating on three sides of the playing area.

thumbnail sketch—a small quick drawing that evokes design intent.

tilt—vertical movement.

tint—a hue plus white; in light, a pale color.

tonality—a compositional function of light, the intent of which is to provide an overall hue to the shadow areas of the stage.

tone—a hue plus gray.

top hat—an optional accessory for an ERS used to reduce halation.

toplight—also called downlight, light originating from directly over the head of the performer.

torm—a vertical lighting position permanently mounted on the upstage side of the proscenium arch.

tracking—a control console philosophy in which a channel remains at a recorded level until directed to change.

transformation drop—a type of translucent drop painted with subject matter on the back that is not seen until the drop is backlit.

translucent—able to transmit light but not be seen through, as starched muslin or rear-projection screen.

traveler—a scenic curtain that moves horizontally.

trim height—the height above the stage floor at which an electric pipe or scenic element is hung.

trunion—a deck mounting device for a striplight, usually triangular in shape.

twist lock—a type of electrical connector.

twofer—a wiring device that enables two male connectors to be plugged into one cable.

ultraviolet radiation—electro-magnetic energy just beyond the blue end of the visible spectrum.

United States Institute for Theatre Technology (USITT)—a professional organization "dedicated to the professional development of men and women who are an integral part of the performing arts community."

upfade—a type of light cue in which channels increase in intensity.

uplight—light emitted from below horizontal so that light emanates in an upward direction.

value—brightness; position on the gray scale.

visibility—the ability to see.

visible spectrum—that part of the electro-magnetic spectrum that can be evaluated by the human visual system.

visual acuity—the ability to distinguish detail.

visual size—the size of an object as it appears to the viewer, as opposed to absolute or object size.

voltage—the measurement of electro-motive force or potential difference.

volt—the unit of measurement of voltage.

vom—short for vomitory, a downstage exit from a thrust stage, usually to an area below the audience seating.

wash light—a type of luminaire characterized by a soft-edged beam, often used in multiple groupings to provide broad swaths of light on the stage.

wash—a broad swath of usually colored light across the stage.

wattage—electrical power, measured in watts.

wavelength—the length of a single cycle of a sinusoidal wave, used in the measurement of the color properties of light.

wings—areas to the offstage sides of a stage, often defined by legs.

worklight—a function of light designed to provide adequate illumination for work to be done on stage, not to be used for performance.

CREDITS

Figure 3.21   Wybron, Inc., Colorado Springs, CO

Figure 3.23   Richard Feldman

Figure 3.24   AP/Wide World Photos

Figure 3.25   Linda Essig

Figure 3.26   Special Collections, University of Bristol, UK

Figure 4.2   ROBERT VAN DE HILST/CORBIS

Figure 4.3   Robert Frew Ltd., London, UK

Figure 4.4   Steve Woods

Figure 4.5   Lighting Design and photo by Betsy Adams, Blue Hill Design, Inc.

Figure 4.6   Chris Parry/Axiom Lighting

Figure 4.7   Judy Gailen, Gailen Designs

Figure 4.8   Photo and Lighting by Stephen Quandt. Original color photo available online at www.quandt.com/srq.html

Figure 4.9   John Ambrosone

Figure 4.10   Anne Militello

Figure 4.11   Fine Arts Museum of San Francisco Achenbach Foundation for Graphic Arts, A101131

Figure 4.12   Carol Rosegg

Figure 4.15   Photo by Peter Cunningham, courtesy Allen Lee Hughes

Figure 4.16   Low sidelight sculpts the dancers' bodies in "Bad Blood" from the Alvin Ailey American Dance Theater Repertory. Photo by Gert Krautbauer. Lighting design by Al Crawford.

Figure 4.17   Robert Laberge/Getty Images

Figure 5.1   Linda Essig

Figure 5.2   Melanie Schuessler

Figure 5.3   Johan Elbers

Figure 5.4   Linda Essig

Figure 5.5   Martha Swope

Figure 5.6   Joan Marcus

Figure 5.7   Billy Rose Theatre Collection, The New York Public Library for the Performing Arts, Astor, Lenox, and Tilden Foundation

Figure 5.8   Mary Evans Picture Library

Figure 5.9   T. Charles Erickson

Figure 5.10   Linda Essig

Figure 6.1   The Metropolitan Opera, New York, NY

Figure 6.2   ©2001 George Mott/ Glimmerglass Opera

Figure 6.3   Mary Evans Picture Library

Figure 6.4   Linda Essig

Figure 7.1   Bob Barrett photo

Figure 7.2   James Seawright

Figure 7.3   Linda Essig

Figure 7.5   Linda Essig

Figure 7.6   Dan Gallagher

Figure 7.7   Linda Essig

Figure 7.8   Andrea Bilkey

Figure 7.9   Maggie Bailey

Figure 7.10   Research Funded by: The Nuckols Fund for Lighting Education. The Graduate School of the University of Florida. The College of Fine Arts and the Department of Theatre and Dance and the School of Architecture at the University of Florida. Principal Investigators: Stan Kaye, Associate Professor and Lighting Designer, and Martin Gold, Associate Professor and Architect.

Figure 7.15   Schomburg Center for Research in Black Culture, The New York Public Library/Art Resource, NY

Figure 7.16   Richard Sexton

Figure 8.7   Photo by Percy Paukschta, courtesy the Bertoldt Brecht Archiv, Stiftung Archiv der Akademie der Kunster, Berlin, Germany

Figure 9.1   The Guthrie Theater, Minneapolis, MN

Figure 9.3   Graham Steans/Camera Press/Retna, Ltd.

Figure 9.5   Linda Essig

Figure 9.6   Linda Essig

Figure 9.7   Linda Essig

Figure 9.8   Linda Essig

Figure 9.9   Richard Feldman

Figure 9.10   City Theatricals, Bronx, NY

Figure 10.1   Linda Essig

Figure 10.4   Rosco Laboratories

Figure 10.5   Linda Essig

Figure 10.6   Linda Essig

Figure 10.7   Linda Essig

Figure 10.8   ©2001 George Mott/Glimmerglass Opera

Figure 10.9   Altman Lighting

Figure 10.11   Linda Essig

Figure 10.12   ©CORBIS

Figure 10.13   Altman Lighting

Figure 10.14   Altman Lighting

Figure 10.16   Linda Essig

Figure 10.17   DHAlighting

Figure 11.3   Linda Essig

Figure 11.4   Linda Essig

Figure 11.5   Linda Essig

Figure 11.6   Electronic Theater Controls

Figure 11.7   Linda Essig

Figure 12.10   Linda Essig

Figure 12.12   Rendering furnished courtesy of Prelite Studios, LLC

Figure 13.4   Linda Essig

Figure 13.6   Linda Essig

Figure 13.7   Linda Essig

Figure 13.9   Linda Essig

Figure A.4   Union Connector, NY

Color Figure 1   Peter Aaron/Esto

Color Figure 2   Dan Gallagher

Color Figure 3   Dan Gallagher

Color Figure 4   Dan Gallagher

Color Figure 5   Darron Cummings/AP/Wide World Photos

Color Figure 6   Erich Lessing/ Louvre, Paris/Art Resource NY

Color Figure 7   Restricted gift of Mr. and Mrs. Marshall Field, Jack and Sandra Guthman, Ben W. Heineman, Ruth Horwich, Lewis and Susan Manilow, Beatrice C. Mayer, Charles A. Meyer, John D. Nichols, Mr. and Mrs. E. B. Smith, Jr., James W. Alsdorf Memorial Fund, Goodman Endowment, 1992.89/Photograph ©1999. Art Institute of Chicago

Color Figure 8   Melanie Schuessler

Color Figure 9   Linda Essig

Color Figure 10   Chart courtesy of General Electric Company

Color Figure 11   Roger Antrobus/CORBIS

Color Figure 12   Chart courtesy of General Electric Company

Color Figure 13   Compliments of Konica Minolta Photo Imaging U.S.A., Inc., Mahwah, NJ

Color Figure 14   Linda Essig

Color Figure 15   Anne Militello

Color Figure 16   Linda Essig

INDEX